COMMENTARY

on

GALATIANS

By

Cornelius R. Stam

Founder of the *Berean Bible Society*
and
Author of over Thirty Bible Study Books,
Including the Classic Work: *Things That Differ*

BEREAN BIBLE SOCIETY
N112 W17761 Mequon Road
PO Box 756
Germantown, WI 53022
(Metro Milwaukee)

BEREAN BIBLE SOCIETY
N112 W17761 Mequon Road
PO Box 756
Germantown, WI 53022

Second Printing 2006

ISBN: 0-9644541-7-3

Printed in the United States of America

SHERIDAN BOOKS, INC.
CHELSEA, MICHIGAN

Dedication

Pastor and Mrs. Stam dedicate this volume to the furtherance of the gospel of the grace of God!

IN GRATEFUL ACKNOWLEDGMENT

Heartfelt thanks are due the many friends who helped in the preparation of this volume.

To RoseAnn Kees who transcribed the audio tapes of Pastor Stam's messages on Galatians which originally aired over the radio. Needless to say, this required the patience of Job.

To Eileen League who edited the numerous repetitions from the original manuscript. This was a slow tedious process and mere words fail to convey our gratitude for her labor of love.

To Russ Miller for his methodical review of the manuscript, which included the timely placement of Pastor Stam's notes and writings into the text. This took the skill of a surgeon. In fact, one would be hard pressed to find where these insertions were made.

To Kevin Sadler who typeset the entire volume. Normally, this goes fairly smooth, but this particular work proved to be somewhat more challenging due to the numerous editings and corrections.

To Christine Mulholland for her graphic design of the cover which graces the front of the book.

To David Havard for proofreading the entire rough draft and offered a number of insightful suggestions. David also meticulously put together the Scripture Index which appears at the end of this volume.

To Fred Wisniewski who did the final proof on the manuscript. Fred's constructive criticism and thoughtful suggestions were deeply appreciated.

Most of all we owe heartfelt thanks to God who upheld us and aided us through the entire project. Surely, for this, all glory must go to Him for His grace and faithfulness.

CONTENTS

PREFACE

The commentary you are holding in your hand is perhaps the most complex project we have attempted in recent memory. We began with a rough transcription of Pastor Stam's messages on Galatians that were delivered over the radio some years ago. Of course, the first order of business was to eliminate the numerous repetitions found in the text. It is a common practice when delivering a verse by verse exposition over the radio to repeat large portions from the previous message to keep new listeners as current as possible. This trimmed the original manuscript from approximately 325 pages down to 200 pages.

Since the volume was somewhat lean, we decided to integrate some of Pastor Stam's notes and writings on Galatians into the text. This was comparable to the surgeon who has been called upon to perform a *delicate* surgery. Great care had to be taken with the insertion of these additions, not to impede the flow or continuity of the manuscript. Sometimes transition sentences were necessary when a new section was introduced to avoid the appearance of it merely being placed into the text without any explanation. Add to this two rounds of mirror editing to smooth out the text, five major proofreadings with corrections, and you have a dedicated staff who is inquiring about vacation destinations.

Pastor Stam has dedicated his entire life to the defense and confirmation of Paul's gospel. Thus, this work brings before you over 60 years of personal study, research, and experience. May the wealth of spiritual truth tucked away in the chapters which follow be used of the Lord to bring the reader into a fuller understanding of the Word, rightly divided.

Paul M. Sadler
President

Milwaukee, Wisconsin
December 15, 1997

INTRODUCTION

THE CHURCHES OF GALATIA

As the Apostle Paul penned his introduction to the *Book of Galatians,* it is interesting to note that he wasn't merely addressing one assembly, but rather a group of churches in the region of Galatia. Apparently, the infectious disease of *legalism* had spread throughout this northern tier of churches. Consequently, the apostle prescribes the spiritual antidote for this insidious teaching.

In this epistle, Paul uses some of the strongest language found in his writings to *vindicate* the gospel of the grace of God. "O foolish Galatians, who hath bewitched you, that you should not obey the truth...." He marveled that they were "so soon removed from Him that called you [them] into the grace of Christ unto another gospel." These Galatian believers had begun well. They had been saved by grace through faith and were rejoicing therein, that is, until the Judaizers arrived on the scene. They taught the Galatians, "Except you be circumcised after the manner of Moses, you cannot be saved." Thus the battle lines were drawn as confusion quickly swept through these assemblies.

For the sake of the gospel, the apostle rolls out the cannons of grace and fires one volley after another seeking to destroy the false notion that they could be justified by the works of the law. Hence, he boldly declares: "whosoever of you are justified by the law; you are fallen from grace." But what does it mean to "fall from grace?" This volume tackles this question and a host of others that most commentators avoid. For example: What is meant by the phrases, "If any man preach any other gospel unto you than that you have received, let him be accursed"; "And if you be Christ's, then are you Abraham's seed"; "But Jerusalem which is above is free, which is the mother of us all"; "We are not the children of the bondwoman, but of the free"?

Pastor Stam effectively shows how legalism had sapped the spiritual vitality of the Galatians and the various courses of action the apostle took to deal with the matter. This work is a *fresh* new look at a number of age-old problems! In a nutshell, it is a comprehensive study on the *unique* character of Paul's apostleship and message.

In regard to the subject matter of the *Appendix,* Brother Stam and I have never seen eye to eye. Although we are usually in agreement 85 percent of the time, there are a few areas we have "agreed to disagree," all of which center around *secondary issues*. Personally, I do not believe that the twelve apostles and the kingdom saints who were living at the beginning of this dispensation became members of the Body of Christ. I do concur that they acknowledged Paul's apostleship and message, and were even influenced by it, especially in regard to the Cross, but this is a far cry from saying that the twelve became members of Christ's Body, and eventually proclaimed Paul's gospel.

Nevertheless, Pastor Stam is the "master" and I am merely the understudy, therefore the reader would do well to prayerfully consider his conclusions in light of the Word, rightly divided.

On behalf of Pastor Stam who sends his love and greetings, may this volume be to the praise of His glory in Christ Jesus.

Paul M. Sadler
President

"Law is Law and Grace
is Grace and n'er the
twain shall meet again."

—C. O. Griggs

Chapter 1 — Galatians 1:1-5

THE DISTINCTIVE CHARACTER OF PAUL'S APOSTLESHIP AND MESSAGE

GRACE AND PEACE

"Paul, an apostle, (not of men, neither by man, but by Jesus Christ, and God the Father, who raised Him from the dead;)

"And all the brethren which are with me, unto the churches of Galatia:

"Grace be to you and peace from God the Father, and from our Lord Jesus Christ,

"Who gave Himself for our sins, that He might deliver us from this present evil world, according to the will of God and our Father:

"To whom be glory for ever and ever. Amen."

—Gal. 1:1-5

PAUL IN CONTRAST TO THE TWELVE

Paul's apostleship was "not of men, neither by man, but by Jesus Christ, and God the Father" (Gal. 1:1). As in the case of Matthias, Paul was appointed directly by God Himself. Paul never preached with the Twelve. Did you ever think of that? They preached at home in Judea and Samaria, hoping that their own kinfolks would accept Jesus Christ as the Messiah and King; afterward, they planned to go further into all the world. But when God's chosen nation rejected Christ and His Kingdom, God raised up Paul, the chief of sinners, saved him by *grace*, and sent him to all nations with an offer of *grace* and *peace*. That is why Paul opened each of his epistles with these wonderful words: "Grace be unto you and peace."

Some have thought that all of the twelve apostles died outside of Palestine. That sounds interesting, but it is not true. In the first two verses of Acts 12 we read that Herod, the king of Israel, killed the apostle James with the sword in Judea. Also, some say that Peter became the bishop of the Gentile church at Rome, but you will not find that recorded in the Scriptures. In Galatians 2:9, we are told that he shook hands with Paul publicly, and officially acknowledged that Paul had become God's apostle to the nations. Peter agreed to henceforth confine his own ministry to the nation Israel. If you do not believe me, check your Bible!

"For He that wrought effectually in Peter to the apostleship of the circumcision [the Hebrew nation], the same was mighty in me toward the Gentiles;

"And when James, Cephas [Peter], and John, who seemed to be pillars, perceived the grace that was given unto me, they gave to me and Barnabas the right hands of fellowship; that we should go unto the heathen [Gentiles] and they unto the circumcision [the Hebrew nation]" (Gal. 2:8-9).

God wrought effectually in Peter in working with his own nation and his own people; but that same God wrought mightily in Paul in his ministry to the *Gentiles*.

Thus, if Peter became bishop of Rome, he broke his solemn vow. But this he *did not* do, for years later we find him writing, not to Gentiles, but to the *Jewish* believers of the dispersion (*Diaspora*).

History can say so many things, and tradition so many more that are not true. All you have to do is read British and American histories of the Revolutionary War to see how much you can depend upon history. The Lord said so often that the traditions of men make void the Word of God." He warned us of that, so let us go only by the Holy, infallible, unchangeable Word of God, the Bible.

THE BIBLE A JEWISH BOOK

Paul's introduction here to the Galatian epistle is one of the most misunderstood passages of Scripture, and the results of this misunderstanding are beyond measure. Seldom, if ever, has a mistake of meaning been so far reaching in its effect.

Before we consider the passage in detail we would ask the reader to examine it carefully and prayerfully, noting exactly *what it says* and reading nothing into it. Before we deal with our text more fully, I want to press the point of Paul's distinct apostleship a bit further. Has it ever occurred to you that the whole Bible is Jewish, except for Paul's epistles to the Gentiles? After only eleven chapters in Genesis (You have hardly begun to read the Bible!), God set aside the Gentiles, and chose one man, Abraham, the father of the Hebrew nation. From there, right down to the end, the Bible is Jewish, except for the epistles which Paul wrote to the Gentiles.

I realize that technically the Hebrew race originated with Abram the son of Terah, and the Israelites originated with Jacob, who was later called Israel. The name "Jew" did not come into use until Judah, but we are using the term "Jewish" because it is the most familiar to us. All Jews today are physically the offspring of Abraham.

From Abraham in Genesis 12, through Pentecost in Acts 2, God had no message for the Gentiles. The Scriptures plainly state that the events of Pentecost concerned the Jews. In Acts 2, Peter, in his Pentecostal message, addressed his hearers as "ye men of Judea" (ver. 14), "ye men of Israel" (ver. 22), and "let all the house of Israel know" (ver. 36). So we see that from Genesis 12 through Pentecost, God had no message for the Gentiles apart from Israel. Romans 1:28 tells us that "Even as they [Gentiles] did not like to retain God in their knowledge, God gave them over to a reprobate mind...."

It is only when we come to Paul that God began dealing with the Gentiles again.

"For I speak unto you Gentiles, inasmuch as I am the apostle of the Gentiles, I magnify mine office" (Rom. 11:13).

He did not say this out of pride or self-will—it was written by divine inspiration. It is not only Paul writing to the Romans; it is God writing to us also and emphasizing Paul's apostleship to us Gentiles today. How sad to see so many people minimizing what God emphasizes in His Word.

So what does this apostle have to say to us Gentiles in the flesh? Gentiles, who "were without Christ, being aliens from the commonwealth of Israel, and strangers from the covenants of promise, having no hope, and without God in the world" (Eph. 2:12)? What does Paul write to such people?

"Grace be to you and peace from God the Father, and from our Lord Jesus Christ, Who gave Himself for our sins..." (Gal. 1:3-4).

How wonderful! "Grace" and "peace." This is the gist, the basis of Paul's whole wonderful message to Gentiles: "from God the Father, and the Lord Jesus Christ, Who gave Himself for our sins."

"But," you may ask, "Was not the death of Christ, His crucifixion, preached before Paul?" Yes, Peter talked about Christ's death, but not in the same way as Paul. Peter's sermon, at Pentecost, *blamed his hearers* for the death of Christ: "You took Him, and with wicked hands you slew Him!" When convicted, his hearers asked, "Men and brethren, what shall we do?" Peter answered, "Repent, and be baptized every one of you in the name of Jesus Christ for the remission of sins" (Acts 2:38).

God does not blame us now for the death of Christ, although we could be blamed. Paul proclaimed grace and peace to us because Christ *gave Himself for our sins*. This is why Paul called his message, "the preaching of the cross" (I Cor. 1:18), and this is good news for the believer today because He offers us grace and peace, forgiveness, justification from sin, all spiritual blessings in the heavenlies, and a position in Christ at God's right hand—all of this is based upon the death of Christ for our sins. It all rests upon the fact that in love Christ paid the penalty for our sins so that we could be free. Oh, what a message!

THE CUP WHICH MY FATHER HATH GIVEN ME

In the garden Jesus prayed "with strong crying and tears," and bloody sweat:

> **"O my Father, if it be possible, let this cup pass from Me: nevertheless not as I will, but as Thou wilt" (Matt. 26:39).**

As He went through agony, His three closest disciples, "Peter and James and John" did not help

Him (Mark 14:33). Back and forth to them He went, *three times*, and each time in an agony of prayer, but they were sleeping (Matt. 26:36-46). No wonder this event is prefaced with:

"Now is My soul troubled; and what shall I say? Father, save Me from this hour: but for this cause came I unto this hour" (John 12:27).

"My soul is exceeding sorrowful, even unto death: tarry ye here, and watch with Me" (Matt. 26:38).

He would have died then and there, had not the Father sent an angel to strengthen Him (Luke 22:43), but His disciples slept on. How touching were His words as He found them sleeping, yet He went back alone into the garden and prayed more earnestly. Finally, after having gone through much agony and then torture, Jesus was crucified. He was forsaken by all, even by the Father (Matt. 27:46).

JESUS ASSUMED MAN'S CURSE

"For He [God] hath made Him to be sin for us, [He] who knew no sin; that we might be made the righteousness of God in Him" (II Cor. 5:21).

"Christ hath redeemed us from the curse of the law, being made a curse for us: for it is written, Cursed is every one that hangeth on a tree" (Gal. 3:13).

One of the Godhead was made a curse for us!

Some have asked, "How could He be a member of the Godhead if He called His Father 'God'? ('My God, My God, why hast Thou forsaken Me?' Matt. 27:46)." We also note that the Father called *Him* God:

"But unto the Son He saith, Thy throne, *O God*, is for ever and ever: a scepter of righteousness is the scepter of Thy kingdom" (Heb. 1:8).

Think of it! On Calvary God the Son gave Himself in agony and disgrace to pay the penalty for our sins. *The Son of God became the Son of man that the sons of men might become the sons of God!* This is the basis for all the "good news" that we find in the epistles of St. Paul.

Remember, and never forget, that Christ poured out his life on Calvary's cross for our sins that we might be "seated with Him in the heavenlies" (Eph. 2:6).

"In whom we have redemption through His blood, the forgiveness of sins, according to the riches of His grace" (Eph. 1:7).

"And hath raised us up together, and made us sit together in heavenly places in Christ Jesus: That in the ages to come He might show the exceeding riches of His grace in His kindness toward us through Christ Jesus" (Eph. 2:6,7).

"[This is] the gospel which I preached unto you, which also ye have received, and wherein ye stand; By which also ye are saved...*how that Christ died for our sins according to the Scriptures*" (I Cor. 15:1-3).

Here we see that Paul was very different from the twelve. He began with the death of Christ in his ministry—the death of Christ as the payment for sin and the basis of his whole message. His epistles have nothing to say about the birth and life of the Lord Jesus Christ, for Christ came into this world, not primarily for a life on earth, but basically to die—to die for our sins.

This is why salvation is all by *grace*, and this is why Paul says in Galatians 1:8:

"But though we, or an angel from heaven, preach any other gospel unto you than that which we have preached unto you, let him be accursed."

And to emphasize the point he was seeking to make, he said again:

"If any man preach any other gospel unto you than that ye have received [that is, from Paul], let him be accursed" (Ver. 9).

Be careful about touching that blessed message of grace and mixing it up with the works of the law, the Sermon on the Mount, or anything else. The whole Bible is *for us*, but it was not all written *to* us, and it is certainly not all *about* us. The professing church has already drawn the curse of confusion and division, and has brought many other pains and sorrows upon itself by departing from Paul's message.

"For I speak to you Gentiles, inasmuch as I am *the apostle of the Gentiles*, I magnify mine office" (Rom. 11:13).

It is sad to see Satan "blinding the minds of them which believe not" (II Cor. 4:4). He keeps them laughing and dancing and cheering at sports. He keeps them wrapped up in making money, or in spending money. He keeps them thinking about the future, and keeps them from considering their eternal destinies. Millions are thrilled about going to the moon with its barren wastes, but are not sure that they are going to heaven. That should be the first priority, should it not?

Don't you be so foolish. Believe the good news that the Lord Jesus Christ gave Himself for our sins so that we might be free and have peace with God.

How wonderful that we do not have to tell the lost, "Do this, or that, to be saved," but we can say, "Friend, your sins have already been paid for."

WE ARE NOT ALONE

Did you notice that in the address of Paul's letter to the Galatians, he said: "and all the brethren which are with me...." He was not alone in this; there were many others who had come to know Christ by grace through faith. In our day we are not alone either. Everywhere there are believers who are beginning to grasp what Paul calls "the full assurance of understanding" (Col. 2:2).

DELIVERANCE

"Who gave Himself for our sins, that He might deliver us from this present evil world, according to the will of God and our Father" (Gal. 1:4).

Paul teaches us in Galatians 1:4 that "[Christ] gave Himself for our sins." Do you believe that? If you do, if you accept Christ's death at Calvary as the payment for your sins, *you are saved!* God says so, and you need never worry again about your eternal destiny. You can rejoice in an accomplished redemption because the Lord Jesus Christ "gave Himself for our sins."

He makes it crystal clear that our sins were fully paid for by the death of Christ on Calvary and that we have been justified: "[Christ] was delivered for our offences, and was raised again for our justification" (Rom. 4:25).

"Therefore being justified by faith, we have peace with God through our Lord Jesus Christ" (Rom. 5:1).

What a wonderful thing to have peace with God—to be delivered from the fear of death and judgment, and from the fear of standing before God some day to give an account for sin!

THE FEAR OF DEATH

As some of you know, my first wife Henrietta before her death was gravely ill with cancer for some time. I spent many hours with her in the hospital, and it was spiritually profitable for both of us, because we both had many opportunities to witness for Christ in that place. I was especially touched by a poor old woman who would not communicate with anyone. The nurses said, "We have not heard one word out of her since she came here!"

They would wheel her out into the corridor so that she could at least see people passing by, and I would stop every day and ask her how she was. Absolutely no response—just a blank stare! I would pat her on the back and tell her that I would pray for her, and would leave her some simple gospel tracts.

One day I noticed that she was in her room all alone, so I went in and sat down beside her and said, "How are you today?" No response. I said, "Evidently you can't talk to me, but I want to talk to you. Please listen very carefully to what I am going to tell you. It is most important: In the Bible there are five words that you should know and cling to. They are found in I Corinthians 15:3:

"Christ died for our sins."

"If you just believe those five words, and cling to them, you will be perfectly safe. It will not matter whether you live or die."

When I uttered that word "die," she spoke for the first time. She interrupted me to say, "It is going to be just that!" The ice was broken. I saw what was occupying her mind. She was a woman in mortal fear of death. So then, I knew better how to deal with her, and did so.

Later on, one of the nurses said to me: "How in the world did you get her to talk?" Then I had another grand opportunity to witness, saying to her: "Tell me, friend, 'Are you afraid to die? You need not be if you believe God's Word!'"

Galatians 1:4 tells us that "[Christ] gave Himself for us," that is, to pay for our sins. He took all the penalty upon Himself; so if we simply accept His payment for our sins, and trust Him as our Savior, what do we have to fear?

Paul has a very forceful message for those who are bound by the fear of death: "Forasmuch then as the children [that is, the children of Adam—all of us] are partakers of flesh and blood, He also Himself likewise took part of the same [He became man]; that through death He might destroy him that had the power of death, that is, the Devil; And deliver them who through fear of death were all their lifetime subject to bondage" (Heb. 2:14-15).

Isn't it wonderful to know that Christ gave *Himself*, on Calvary, to die in shame and disgrace for our sins and to take away our fear of death?

FURTHER TRUTH IN GALATIANS 1:4

There is more, much more to our verse of Scripture. It goes on to say, "He gave Himself for our sins, *that He might deliver us....*"

Notice exactly what the verse says, but do not read anything more into it either: *"that he might deliver us from this present evil world [age]."* It does not say that He gave Himself to *deliver* us from our sins; that is true also, but this verse does not say that. It does not say that He gave Himself to deliver us from the *penalty* of our sins, although this is also true. The fact that He gave Himself for our sins implies these truths, but this is not what the verse says. Neither does the verse say that He died for our sins to deliver us from the *evil* of this age. Nor does it say that He died for our sins to deliver us from the judgment that is coming upon this world [evil age].[1]

The verse says that "[He] gave Himself for our sins, that He might deliver us *from this present evil world [age].*"

EMANCIPATION FROM SATAN'S WORLD SYSTEM

Christ died to deliver us from this "evil age" itself! Beloved, this *is* an evil age. It is the age of Christ's rejection; all the *godlessness* and *crime* and *sin* reflect that fact. This age is doomed to end in terrible judgment, but God wants us to be lifted *by faith* above the sin and sorrow and trouble and confusion. He also wants to lift us above the shallow frivolous pleasures of this age—*and* He wants to bless us with "all spiritual blessings in heavenly places in Christ!"

SEATED IN THE HEAVENLIES

"But God, who is rich in mercy, for His great love wherewith He loved us, Even when we were dead in sins, hath quickened us together with Christ, (by grace ye are saved;) And hath raised us up together, and made us sit together in *heavenly places* in Christ Jesus: That in the

1. This evil age is doomed to horrible judgment, but that is not the subject here.

***ages to come* He might shew the exceeding riches of His grace in His kindness toward us through Christ Jesus" (Eph. 2:4-7).**

Paul tells us, as in all of his early epistles, the great basic truths of that unprophesied mystery of grace which are beautifully unfolded, and more fully developed, in his letters to the Ephesians and Colossians. This is a very important truth: Christ gave Himself for our sins to deliver us from this present evil age—from Satan's world system, and God desires to bless us "with all spiritual blessings in heavenly places in Christ."

"Blessed be the God and Father of our Lord Jesus Christ, who hath blessed us with all spiritual blessings in heavenly places in Christ" (Eph. 1:3).

If God has given you, who "by nature [are] children of wrath" (Eph. 2:3), this *position*, my Christian friends, should you not occupy it and enjoy it by faith? If He has given you these spiritual blessings in heavenly places (literally, "in the heavenlies") should you not appropriate them and enjoy them?[2]

Some Bible students claim that in Paul's statement, "If ye then be risen with Christ..." (Col. 3:1), the "if" means "since." I believe the "if" is used as *a word of challenge*. To illustrate: A mother might say to her twenty-one-year-old son who has been acting like a child, "*If* you are twenty-one, act like it!" She knows that he is twenty-one; there is no

2. The believer is seated together with Christ in heavenly places—that is—seated there positionally, even while physically remaining on earth.

Our elected representatives in Washington D. C. are "seated" in the Halls of Congress even when they are physically absent from that place. Their "seats" speak of prestige, honor, and authority. It is a matter of position.

question about that. But he is not acting it. This is the same kind of challenge here:

> **"*If* ye then be risen with Christ, seek those things which are above, where Christ sitteth on the right hand of God. Set your affection on things above, not on things on earth. For ye are dead, and your life is hid with Christ in God" (Col. 3:1-3).**

How sad that Christians continually renew their interest in the tinsel of earthly things. They set their affections on things down here, and in the meanwhile the work of the Lord suffers.

My Christians friends, you do not belong to yourselves; you are not your own; "For ye are bought with a price: therefore glorify God in your body, and in your spirit, which are God's" (I Cor. 6:20). God has given you all spiritual blessings in the heavenlies *in Christ*, and you should live your life down here for Him—wholly for Him—as the hymn writer so beautifully puts it:

> "I want to live above the world,
> Tho' Satan's darts at me are hurled;
> For faith has caught the joyful sound,
> The song of saints on higher ground."

You see, God wants us to live experientially *above* this world. What better example is there of this than Paul himself? He was in a prison at Rome: hated, despised, his own friends afraid to come to see him, when he wrote: "But I would ye should understand, brethren, that the things which happened unto me have fallen out rather unto the furtherance of the gospel" (Phil. 1:12). He told those believers, "Friends, do not feel sorry for me. God is using these hardships for the making known of the *gospel."* And he was therefore glad to be "the prisoner of Jesus Christ," for *"the fellowship of His sufferings"* (Eph. 3:1; Col. 1:24) was *joy* to him because he was not living down here, but *"seated in the heavenlies,"* and occupied with this position experientially.

Remember what we just read in Paul's epistle to the Ephesians. He wrote of "being seated in heavenly places in Christ." In a cell in Rome? Ah, but that was only physically. He could rejoice in that cell because, spiritually, he was seated in heavenly places in Christ. He was living far above this poor world. And God wants you to experience this, my friend. He wants you to live *above* this present evil age. This is why Christ "gave Himself for our sins, that He might deliver us from this present evil age."

BE NOT CONFORMED TO THIS WORLD

This brings us to something important, very important in the day in which we live—a day in which the Church has become permissive. The godlessness of this world has affected not only the professing church, but also the true Church. Many true Christians are very permissive, and they are living for this time of their lives instead of living for eternity. They are living for the here and now instead of the "up-there!"

"I beseech you therefore, brethren, by the mercies of God, that ye present your bodies a living sacrifice, holy, [fully] acceptable unto God, which is your reasonable service. *And be not conformed to this world [age]:* but be ye transformed by the renewing of your mind, that ye may prove what is that good, and acceptable, and perfect, will of God" (Rom. 12:1-2).

Christian women may say, "We have to dress like other women. This is the way everyone dresses—it is the style." No, you do not have to conform to this age. You can look very trim and very neat and yet be modest. You do not have to join the immodesty of the age.

Christians in general may say, "Well, everyone does it," as though this makes it all right. Almost everyone joined together to crucify Christ; almost everyone was against Paul. As I have said, "Do not be *Everybody*." Remember that nearly everyone was lost in the great flood, and only Noah and his small family were preserved alive. Never be afraid to stand alone. "Be not conformed to this world [age]: but be ye transformed by the renewing of your mind."

DISPENSATIONAL DIFFERENCES

As far as living experientially in the heavenlies is concerned, how different Paul's teaching is from the message that the twelve apostles were sent to preach! At Pentecost Peter said to the Jewish nation that if they would repent, God would send Jesus back down here to *earth* (Read Acts 3:19-20). But Paul teaches the Grace Church that if we believe He will take *us* "up there." He will give us a place in *heaven* with the exalted Christ, the One rejected on earth but honored in heaven by the Father.

In Philippians we read how Christ gave up His glory in heaven.

"Let this mind be in you, which was also in Christ Jesus:

"Who, being in the form of God, thought it not robbery [something to be grasped after] to be equal with God [He *was* God!]:

"But made Himself of no reputation, and took upon Him the form of a servant, and was made in the likeness of men:

"And being in fashion as a man, He humbled Himself, and became obedient unto death, even the death of the cross.

"Wherefore God also hath highly exalted Him, and given Him a name which is above every name:

"That at the name of Jesus every knee should bow..." (Phil. 2:5-10).

We see that the Christ who is rejected *on earth*, whose name is blasphemed on every street corner, is highly exalted *in heaven*. In Psalm 110:1, we find the Father saying to the Son, "Sit Thou at my right hand, until I make Thine enemies Thy footstool."

This present evil age, and this world system, is doomed to judgment. It is very apparent that the world is racing toward that judgment day right now. But Christ gave Himself to deliver us from it. Believe that Christ died for you. Believe that He gave Himself for you. And God will give you a seat with Christ, a position in Christ, at His own right hand.

Years ago when I was in business, and had declined to enter into a shady transaction, someone said to me in ridicule, "Stam, you do not belong down here. You should be in heaven." "That's right," I replied. "There is a song that I like to sing: 'I don't belong down here, since to God my heart I've given.'"

It is true that we are strangers and pilgrims here. We do not belong in this world. We are here as witnesses to the unsaved. God says that "our citizenship is in heaven," but in infinite grace He has left us here with the responsibility of telling others that Christ gave Himself for our sins:

"Now then we are ambassadors for Christ, as though God did beseech you by us; we pray you in Christ's stead, be ye reconciled to God" (II Cor. 5:20).

The world did not want Him; now He sends us as ambassadors for Christ. We have been given a message of "reconciliation," with an offer of grace and peace, "we pray you in Christ's stead, *be ye reconciled to God.*" That was the theme of the message of Paul, and it is our message.

PEACE OR WAR

We have seen from Galatians 1:3 that there is "grace and peace." They are the exact opposites of judgment and war.

"And I saw heaven opened, and behold a white horse; and He that sat upon him was called Faithful and True, and in righteousness He doth *judge* and *make war*" (Rev. 19:11).

When Christ comes again to set up His Kingdom, He is going to make war (Rev. 19). In Acts 8:1, man declared war on God. God is going to make a counter-declaration (I Thess. 5, II Thess. 2, Psa. 2). We are living, as it were, in the intense moments *between* man's declaration of war on God and God's counter-declaration of war on man. Be sure that He will judge this world for its rejection of His Son.

We are living during "the dispensation of the grace of God," when God is offering to His enemies everywhere "reconciliation" by grace through faith in His rejected Son. Will you trust Him as your Savior, and ask Him to be your Lord? Do this, and you will be saved, at this very moment, from the penalty of your sins, and from this present evil age.

In evil long I took delight,
  Unaw'd by shame or fear,

Till a new object met my sight,
And stopp'd my wild career.
I saw One hanging on a tree
In agonies and blood,
Who fixed His languid eyes on me,
As near His Cross I stood.
Oh, never 'til my latest breath
Shall I forget that look
He seemed to charge me with His death
Though not a word He spoke.
My conscience felt, and owned my guilt,
And plung'd me in despair;
I saw my sins His blood had spilt,
And help'd to nail Him there.
A second look He gave,
Which said, "I freely all forgive;
This blood is for thy ransom paid;
I die, that thou may'st live."
Thus, while His death my sin displays
In all its blackest hue,
Such is the mystery of grace;
It seals my pardon, too.

(Adapted from John Newton's hymn,
"The Lamb Upon Calvary.")

A SERIOUS MISUNDERSTANDING

Three times in the first five verses of Galatians, Chapter 1, Paul mentions the Father and the Son together, while any mention of the Spirit is omitted. This is certainly not because the Spirit is not one with the Father and the Son, or is of less importance. It is because the Father and the Son have a relationship to the subject in question which differs from that of the Spirit. To understand the passage we must view the rejected Son as seated in heaven with His Father, while the Spirit works on earth.

We must remember, too, that because of the continued rejection of the Son, whom the Father had sent, the nations, including even *the* nation Israel, were to be visited by judgment. This is clearly set forth in many Old Testament passages, of which the following are representative:

> **"Why do the heathen [nations] rage, and the people [of Israel. See Acts 4:25-27] imagine a vain thing?**
>
> **"The kings of the earth set themselves, and the rulers take counsel together, *against the Lord, and against His Anointed,* saying,**
>
> **"Let us break their bands asunder, and cast away their cords from us.**
>
> ***"He that sitteth in the heavens shall laugh: the Lord shall have them in derision.***
>
> ***"Then shall He speak unto them in His wrath, and vex them in His sore displeasure.***
>
> ***"Yet have I set My King upon My holy hill of Zion.***
>
> ***"I will declare the decree: the Lord hath said unto Me, Thou art my Son; this day have I begotten Thee.***
>
> ***"Ask of Me, and I shall give Thee the heathen [nations] for Thine inheritance, and the uttermost parts of the earth for Thy possession.***
>
> ***"Thou shalt break them with a rod of iron; Thou shalt dash them in pieces like a potter's vessel."***
>
> **—Psa. 2:1-9**

This passage, written about one thousand years before the coming of Christ, clearly predicts that the nations, including Israel, would be *judged* for imagining that they could do without Christ, God's anointed, and for setting themselves against the Father and His beloved Son. The Father declared that He would laugh at their folly, hold them in derision, "speak unto them in His wrath and vex them in His sore displeasure," while the Son would "break them with a rod of iron" and "dash them in pieces like a potter's vessel."

Another clear prediction that God would answer the rejection of His Son with judgment is found in Psalm 110:1, one of the fullest verses of all Old Testament prophecy:

"The Lord said unto My Lord, Sit Thou at My right hand, until I make Thine enemies Thy footstool."

Here in one short verse we learn of our Lord's rejection by His enemies on earth, His ascension to the Father's right hand, His session there, the judgment upon His enemies, and His return after their subjugation.

This is the consistent testimony of Old Testament prophecy. Judgment is always God's answer to the rejection of His Son. It is true that the "until" of Psalm 110:1 has been prolonged by the dispensation of grace, but this was never once predicted in the Old Testament, the Gospels, or early Acts. It was a mystery "hid from ages and from generations" and revealed by God as a surprise of mercy and love through the Apostle Paul, when the world was ripe for judgment (Eph. 3:1-3; Col. 1:26). Even at Pentecost, Peter, by the Spirit, declared that the last days had come and that the judgment was imminent (Acts 2:16-21). This was true, but in mercy and love God intervened, raising up Paul and ushering in the dispensation of grace. It is from this standpoint that we must view the introduction to the Galatian Epistle.

AN OFFICIAL PROCLAMATION

For many years the writer, along with the Church as a whole, supposed that Verse 3 of our passage was simply a beautiful, spiritual salutation: *"Grace be to you and peace."* In the light of the above, however, it proves to be much more. It is an *official proclamation* from the rejected Father and His rejected Son. This is the second reference to the Father and Son here in the opening verses of Galatians.

It is not a mere coincidence that every single one of the epistles signed with Paul's name opens with the declaration: *"Grace be to you and peace from God the Father, and from our Lord Jesus Christ."* All his epistles[3] open with this declaration because it was the theme of the message which he, as a duly appointed ambassador, had been sent to proclaim.

To appreciate this fully, we must again bear in mind the fact that as far as prophetic revelation was concerned, the time had come for the outpouring of divine wrath upon a Christ-rejecting world. Peter had declared at Pentecost that the last days of Joel 2 had already begun. The signs had begun to appear which would usher in the return of Christ, and it is with regard to this event that we read:

"And in righteousness doth He *judge and make war*" (Rev. 19:11).

But here, instead of *judgment* and *war* we have the exact opposite: *grace* and *peace*. Does this not

3. See the author's "Hebrews—Who Wrote It and Why?"

indicate as clearly as the raising up of Paul himself that the prophetic program had been interrupted by the bringing in of a new dispensation?

Had the prophetic program continued uninterrupted after Israel's rejection of the risen, glorified Christ, judgment and war would surely have followed. But in infinite mercy and love the Father and the Son reached down to *save* their archenemy, the rebel-leader Saul,[4] and sent him forth to proclaim *grace* and *peace* through the cross.

How rich and meaningful, now, become some of those passages from Paul's epistles which we have read so carelessly:

> ***"But where sin abounded, grace did much more abound: That as sin hath reigned...even so might grace reign..."*** **(Rom. 5:20,21).**

> ***"...[we] were by nature the children of wrath, even as others. But God..."*** **(Eph. 2:3,4).**

It may be argued that the epistles of Paul are addressed particularly to saints. This is true, but from most, if not all of his epistles to the churches, it is evident that he realized that some of the unsaved would also be present in the gatherings where his epistles were read, so that words of salvation are addressed to them.

This is important, for the proclamation of grace and peace is to *all*. It expresses God's attitude toward *mankind* during the present administration. Even with regard to the *un*saved we read:

> **"...God was in Christ, reconciling the world unto Himself, *not imputing their trespasses unto them;* and hath committed unto us the word of reconciliation" (II Cor. 5:19).**

---

4. In regard to the apostle, Saul was his Hebrew name, while Paul was his Roman or Gentile name.

God's part in reconciliation has already been accomplished through Christ and, as it has been well said, it is no longer the sin question but the *Son* question. If men remain unreconciled to God it will be because of their rejection of Christ and His redemptive work. It will be *their* doing, not God's, for in view of Christ's death God does not even impute their trespasses unto them.

Thus the apostle proclaims to *all mankind* "grace and peace...from God the Father, and from our Lord Jesus Christ," offering reconciliation to the lost, not on the basis of *their* payment for their sins, but on the basis of the death of *God's* Son (Rom. 5:10). And this when the world was fully ripe for judgment and wrath! What grace! What a message to proclaim!

To emphasize the fact that his ministry among the Gentiles was distinct from that of the twelve and was not related to prophecy, Paul calls himself *"the prisoner of Jesus Christ for you Gentiles,"* adding:

"If ye have heard of the dispensation of the grace of God which is given me to you-ward:

"How that by revelation He made known unto me the mystery..." **(Eph. 3:1-3).**

And to this the apostle goes on to add still greater emphasis, calling his message: *"the mystery of Christ, which in other ages was not made known...the unsearchable riches of Christ...the mystery, which from the beginning of the world hath been hid in God..."* etc. (Eph. 3:4-11).

Since the dispensation of grace, given by Paul by the revelation of Jesus Christ, was a mystery not based upon Old Testament covenants or prophecy, but upon God's "eternal purpose, which He purposed in Christ Jesus our Lord" (Eph. 3:11), we have no assurance that it will continue another day.

"We then as workers together with Him, beseech you also that ye receive not the grace of God in vain....Behold, *now* is the accepted time; behold, *now* is the day of salvation" (II Cor. 6:1,2).

And to the saved:

"See then that ye walk circumspectly, not as fools, but as wise, *Redeeming [buying up] the time, because the days are evil"* (Eph. 5:15,16).

THE BELIEVER'S POSITION IN CHRIST

And now the Father and the Son are referred to for the third time, as the apostle points out that our Lord *"gave Himself for our sins, that He might deliver us from this present evil world [Lit. age], according to the will of God and our Father; to whom be glory for ever and ever. Amen"* (Gal. 1:4,5).

Here, as in this entire introduction and, indeed, in all his early epistles, we find the very foundation truths of the mystery. To appreciate it fully we must again compare it with what Peter and the eleven had preached at Pentecost.

There Peter had called upon the people of Israel to repent and be converted, that their sins might be blotted out and therefore the prophesied times of refreshing might come from the presence of the Lord and He might send the rejected Christ back to earth again (See Acts 3:19-21).

But whereas Peter had said: Repent, and God will send Jesus to earth, Paul now says: Believe, and God will take you to heaven. They do not want Christ on earth, but God is willing to take you to heaven and give you a place at His right hand in Christ, blessed with all spiritual blessings. Not merely at some future date, but *now*, by faith, because this position was purchased for you through the finished work of Christ (See Eph. 1:3,18-21; 2:4-6).

We may—and should—therefore, occupy by *faith* the position that God has given us in Christ and thus be delivered from "this present evil age" with all its heartaches, temptations and delusive pleasures. How the apostle challenges us:

"If ye then be risen with Christ, seek those things which are above, where Christ sitteth on the right hand of God.

"Set your affection on things above, not on things on the earth.

"For ye are dead, and your life is hid with Christ in God" **(Col. 3:1-3).**

The long-promised "times of refreshing" still await a future day, but our blessed Lord gave Himself for our sins that He might deliver us from this present evil age and that *now*, by faith, we might enjoy a position and blessings in the heavenlies. Moreover, it is the Father's will that this should be so.

Why, then, do we fail so often to enter into these things? Only because of unbelief! As unbelief kept the children of Israel, under Moses, from entering the land of Canaan (Heb. 3:19), so unbelief keeps the majority of God's people today from occupying their position and appropriating their blessings in the heavenlies. Most believers, though truly born again, still continue to set their affection on "things on the earth" rather than on "those things which are above," because they do not really believe that the latter are more precious and enduring than the former. He who blinds the minds of unbelievers (II Cor. 4:4), continually wrestles with believers who would occupy their God-given position "in the heavenlies" (Eph. 6:10-18).

"What shall we then say to these things? If God be for us, who can be against us? He that spared not His own Son, but delivered Him up for us all, how shall He not with Him also *freely* give us all things?" (Rom. 8:31,32).

Chapter 2 — Galatians 1:6-9

THE GOOD NEWS PROCLAIMED BY PAUL

SO SOON REMOVED!

"I marvel that ye are so soon removed from Him that called you into the grace of Christ unto another gospel:

"Which is not another; but there be some that trouble you, and would pervert the gospel of Christ" (Gal. 1:6-7).

The apostle wrote these words to the relatively new converts in the Galatian churches.

Perhaps you will recall that as soon as God began sending the message of salvation by grace to the Gentiles through Paul, some of the believers at Jerusalem and Judea became concerned. They had known Christ only as their Savior King, because He *was* the Jewish Messiah. They observed the law of Moses and the covenant of circumcision like Christ Himself had done on earth. They knew nothing else. They simply believed in Christ as their Messiah, their Savior King.

They visited Galatia and they asked, "How can these Gentiles be saved and the children of God without submitting to circumcision and the law of Moses?" They were so greatly agitated that groups of them went to the churches in Antioch, Corinth, and Galatia. They convinced many of the Gentile converts, using the Old Testament Scriptures, that it was necessary for them to keep the law of Moses with all of its rites and ceremonies. The Galatian believers, it seems, had embraced this line of reasoning, and Paul had to send them an urgent letter to get them reestablished in the grace of God:

"I marvel that ye are so soon removed from Him that called you into the grace of Christ unto another gospel" (Ver. 6).

I believe I had made it clear previously that the twelve apostles had been sent forth to proclaim the gospel of the Kingdom, which was sometimes called the gospel of the circumcision, since it was directed *to* the circumcision.[1]

In Galatians Chapter 2 we will be reading that Peter had been commissioned to preach the gospel of the circumcision. What was that message? We find it in Acts 3:25-26 where Peter said to his Jewish hearers:

"Ye are the children of the prophets, and of the covenant which God made with our fathers, saying unto Abraham, And in thy seed shall all the kindreds [nations] of the earth be blessed.

"Unto you first God, having raised up His Son Jesus, sent Him to bless you, in turning away every one of you from his iniquities."

When the favored nation rejected Christ as their Messiah, God interrupted the promised Jewish program which had been prophesied, and raised up Paul to preach salvation and all spiritual blessings by grace alone. Whereas the twelve preached Christ as King to the Jews, Paul preached the gospel of the grace of God to the Gentiles, and these Galatian Gentiles had rejoiced in it. In this Galatian epistle Paul writes of their former blessedness, and says regarding his severe eye-trouble:

"...I bear record,... ye would have plucked out your own eyes, and have given them to me" (4:15).

---

1. Circumcision, as you know, was the physical rite separating Abraham's offspring from the Gentiles around them. The gospel of the circumcision was a term used to delineate the message proclaimed to descendants of Abraham.

But suddenly all of this had changed, and Paul had to ask them,

"Where is then the blessedness ye spake of?"

In Galatians 5:15, it is evident that they had lost the "blessedness" and were fighting amongst themselves, "biting and devouring one another." How did this happen?

They had lost their "blessedness" by letting the legalizers from Judea persuade them that the grace of God, and the finished work of Christ, were not enough to save and bless them unless they added the keeping of the Mosaic law. So Paul exclaimed, "I marvel; I cannot understand it; I am baffled, that you are so soon removed from Him that called you into the grace of Christ unto another gospel."

"Ye observe days, and months, and times, and years.

"I am afraid of you, lest I have bestowed upon you labor in vain."

"I desire to be present with you now, and to change my voice [tone]; for I stand in doubt of you" (Gal. 4:10,11,20).

He wondered whether they had really come to know the grace of God. It has often been explained that the Gauls, the people who migrated to Galatia were a fickle, changeable people. Truthfully, could not most politicians and statesmen from history all over the world testify that their constituents were fickle, that the populace was fickle? Mankind in general is fickle; men change their minds all too quickly. Galatians 1:6-7 should not be used to teach that the Gauls alone were changeable and fickle. Paul's words to them is also God's words to us.

Looking through the corridors of history from Paul's day to ours, the apostle could surely say of today's church as a whole, "I marvel that ye are so soon removed from Him that called you into the grace of Christ unto another gospel!" Even in Paul's own day departure from his God-given message of grace had begun. Only a faithful few remained steadfast. The majority returned to the message and program of a former dispensation, adopting large parts of it. It was a program contained in the laws of Moses and the Sermon on the Mount and it appealed to them because of the ritualism.

TWO GOSPELS?

What did Paul mean by saying that they had been removed to "another gospel: which is not another; but there be some that trouble you, and would pervert the gospel of Christ." Galatians 1:6,7 has been a puzzle to some.

There are two different words for "another" used here. In verse 6, the word is *heteros* meaning "one of a *different* sort." You have been removed to another gospel. In verse 7, the Greek is *"allos"* which means "one of the *same* sort." Thus some commentators have said that Paul meant, "you have switched to a different gospel which is not the same gospel." And they suppose that these Gentiles had accepted a spurious gospel which was not a gospel at all. But if this were so, would not Paul have said, "...another gospel which is not really a gospel at all?" He did not say that this new thing which they had accepted was not really a gospel. He said, "another gospel which is not another."

The idea is that there was no contradiction between the gospel of the Kingdom[2] and the gospel of

2. Or of the circumcision.

the grace of God. The latter was simply a further development, a further revelation of God's truth from the one that went before. God gave the law to reveal what sin is and to show that man needed a Savior. Again and again the apostle made it clear that his message was not a contradiction of what the twelve had preached.

I have been accused of teaching that Paul contradicted Peter. Not at all! Their messages were not the same but they were not contradictory. What Peter preached at Pentecost was true: he offered that if the Jews would repent God would send Jesus back to earth. There is no contradiction. When the Jews failed under the law, and rejected Jesus as King, God raised up Paul, the chief of sinners—saved him by His grace—and sent him forth with a new and further revelation called *"the dispensation of the grace of God."* The dispensing of grace was chronologically the next number on the program of God, and there was no contradiction.

LAW OR GRACE

In Romans 3:31 Paul asks, "Do we then make void the law through faith?" By saying that salvation is by grace through faith alone, do we make the law void? Paul's immediate response is "***God forbid***: Yea, we establish the law." The law was not given to help us to be good, but to show us that we are *not* good and need a Savior.

Those who say that the Judaizers came to the Galatians with a spurious gospel are wrong. The trouble was not apostasy, which means rejection of truth formerly embraced, for these Judaizers knew and believed the Scripture and used it for their argument. Their problem was that they failed to recognize the further *revelation* committed to Paul by the glorified Lord. This was a dispensational error, for they sought to bring the Galatian believers who were saved under the dispensation of the grace of God back under the dispensation of the law. We see that we can go far astray from the Word "rightly divided" by failing to recognize dispensational changes. The Judaizers were not unscriptural; they were undispensational![3]

EACH AGE IN SCRIPTURE HAD ITS GOSPEL

A major problem of Biblical interpretation comes from the belief that the Bible contains only one gospel. It is true that there is only one gospel for today. The gospel of the grace of God is that which should be preached. "Gospel" simply means "good news" and there are numerous gospels all through the Bible.

In Galatians 3:8, we read that long before Paul was raised up to preach grace to the Gentiles, God "preached before the gospel [good news] unto Abraham, saying, In thee shall all nations be blessed." Now, was that not a gospel? If God told *you* that through you all nations would be blessed, would you not consider that good news?

3. In Volume Two of our four-volume set on *the Book of the Acts* I have a whole section dealing with this matter. I consider it a very interesting subject and a very important one. The study is called "Acts Dispensationally Considered." It has been used as a text all over the world; churches have used it when they were without a pastor. It has been used in Sunday School classes, and many hearts and lives have been changed, because these books recognize the distinctive character of the apostleship of Paul as compared to that of the twelve.

The Book of Acts is a thrilling story book. But it also explains the jump, if you please, from the four Gospel records which are all Jewish, to Paul's epistles to the Gentiles.

God's Word names various gospels: the gospel of the Kingdom, the gospel of the circumcision, the gospel of the uncircumcision, the gospel of the grace of God, and several more. Do you suppose God would have given these gospels different names if they were all the same? Why does the housewife label the items in the pantry as strawberry jam, grape jelly, stewed tomatoes, pickles, peas, and so on, if they are all the same? How do you suppose they would taste if we mixed them all together? This is what people try to do with the "gospels" of the Word of God; they mix them all together. Then their message is just as mixed up.

Those persons who suppose that the various gospels of Scripture are really all the same gospel should think this through: If they are the same, why does God give them different labels? I can see how by some *misinterpretations* one might say that the gospel of the Kingdom and the gospel of the grace of God are the same thing, but how could the gospel of the *circumcision* and the gospel of the *uncircumcision* be the same? They are both mentioned in Galatians 2. Remember that the word "gospel" simply means good news. Whenever you read the word, "gospel," in the Bible, study the context and determine which "good news" is being discussed.

In effect, in Galatians 1:6-7, Paul says that the Galatian believers had failed to ask this question. They had been lured from the wonderful gospel of the grace of God to *another gospel* which had also been true, but which belonged to a former dispensation. It was still valid among the people to whom it had first been preached—the Jewish nation—but some zealous Jews were now perverting the good news about Christ for the Gentiles.

We need to get into our hearts and minds the cause of God's and Paul's deep concern: the danger of confusing the blessed message of the grace of God with the messages and programs that belong to former ages.

BY GRACE ALONE

My unsaved friends, God wants you to know the riches of His grace. He wants you to be saved simply by grace—no rituals, no forms, no deeds, no works, no payments—by grace alone!

"For by grace are ye saved through faith; and that not of yourselves: it is the gift of God:

"Not of works, lest any man should boast" (Eph. 2:8-9).

God is not going to have you boasting in Heaven how you got yourself there!

"Being justified freely by His grace through the redemption that is in Christ Jesus" (Rom. 3:24).

"In whom we have redemption through His blood, the forgiveness of sins, according to the riches of His grace" (Eph. 1:7).

The forgiveness of sins according to the riches of His grace! What more do you want; what are you waiting for? Why do you not accept this gift?

"The wages of sin is death; but the gift of God is eternal life through Jesus Christ our Lord" (Rom. 6:23).

"That in the ages to come He might show the exceeding riches of His grace in His kindness toward us through Christ Jesus" (Eph. 2:7).

THE LIGHT DIMMED

But alas, how the light has since been dimmed! How lightly men have esteemed the infinite grace of God! Indeed, it was during the apostle's own ministry that he had to write to the Galatians:

***"I marvel that ye are so soon removed from Him that called you into the grace of Christ unto another gospel"* (Gal. 1:6).**

And this he would certainly have to say, historically, with respect to the Church as a whole, for how soon the Church departed from the great revelation of the glorified Christ through Paul! This declension *began*, as we say, during Paul's own lifetime. One church after another was affected by it.

From the writings of the early-century fathers it is evident that rather than recognizing the distinctive character of Paul's message, they had it all confused with the kingdom message proclaimed by John the Baptist, Christ, and the twelve—even to the point of requiring water baptism for the remission of sins.

This declension continued until the dark ages, when Rome held sway and a mixture of Christianity, Judaism, and heathen idolatry prevailed. Later the Church *began* to emerge from the darkness and superstition of Romanism as Luther, Zwingli, Calvin, and others were used to recover Pauline truth. And, thank God, still greater advances were made under such men as Darby and Scofield. But much, very much, still remains to be done. Those who are now laboring to carry out the commission of the glorified Lord *to us*, II Corinthians 5:14-21, who desire to recover and make known the blessed message of grace and glory, will have to pray and toil and sacrifice as never before to make any impression upon the indifferent masses—including carnal Christians. Those who know the truth but maintain a discreet silence because they fear men or "love the praise of men," yes, and those who fail to proclaim the *whole* truth for "diplomacy's sake"—all these will have to cast aside their selfish interests if the grace of God is to shine forth with any degree of brightness again.

OUR RESPONSIBILITY TO RELIGHT THE TORCH

We know, of course, that the millennium will be brought in *by the return of Christ*, not by the efforts of men. But we have not been discussing the millennium. We have been discussing God's revealed program for "this present evil age," the time of Christ's rejection and absence, and it is God's command that we make the message of His grace known to all men. The fact that "evil men and seducers shall wax worse and worse" does not relieve us of this responsibility. Although the darkness may deepen, we are to "shine as lights in the world; *holding forth the Word of life*" (Phil. 2:15,16).

At first, God's grace was made to shine forth to all mankind in spite of the most bitter and Satanic opposition. But then the torch began to flicker and the world was plunged into the dark ages and scarcely a spark remained of the once bright torch of grace. Then, after centuries, it was lit again and began to burn somewhat more brightly. But it still must be made to blaze afar.

In these critical times shall we not make it *our one passion* to *know* God's Word, rightly divided, and to *make it known* to others, until the grace of God shines forth again as a blazing torch? Shall we not, *must* we not, put aside *every* other consideration and say with Paul:

***"But as we were [are] allowed of God to be put in trust with the gospel, even so we speak; not as pleasing men, but God, which trieth our hearts"* (I Thes. 2:4).**

Soon enough our Lord will appear in glory and our work will be done. *Now* He would have His *grace* appear *through us.* Whatever the opposition of Satan, then, and however deceitful its character, let us say with the apostle of grace:

***"But none of these things move me, neither count I my life dear unto myself, so that I might finish my course with joy, and the ministry, which I have received of the Lord Jesus, to testify the gospel of the grace of God"* (Acts 20:24).**

If we do this we shall also be able to say with him, when we come to the end of the way:

"I have fought a good fight, I have finished my course, I have kept the faith:

***"Henceforth there is laid up for me a crown..."* (II Tim. 4:7,8).**

THE GOSPEL PERVERTED

"But though we, or an angel from heaven, preach any other gospel unto you than that which we have preached unto you, let him be accursed.

"As we said before, so say I now again, If any man preach any other gospel unto you than that ye have received, let him be accursed" (Gal. 1:8,9).

The professing church yet today prefers forms and ceremonies, rites and rituals, to the simple, wonderful message and program of grace. They still proclaim the Law and the Sermon on the Mount, rather than the great truths of the epistles of St. Paul to the churches. And when we try to recover these truths for the Church, and show the difference, we are often asked, "Do you mean that the

Church has been wrong for 1900 years and only you are right?"

It is not a matter of our being right. We are simply pointing out what the Word of God says. The Church *has* been *wrong* in many of its teachings or it would not be in such deep confusion and division as that which grips it today. The Church today is no better than Israel of old when the nation kept departing from the law of Moses as God had given it. The Church keeps departing today from God's message and program of grace as revealed through the Apostle Paul.[4]

The departure among the Corinthians from the message of grace began when they embraced moral permissiveness, a partisan spirit, and things of the flesh. The Colossians departed from the grace gospel through false doctrine brought in from without. Among the Galatians it was *legalism* that caused them to question Paul's apostleship and his message of grace. They returned to the law of Moses, with all its ceremonies and requirements.

The Church has been mostly wrong, and only partly right. There have been only a faithful few who have remained true to the unadulterated gospel of the grace of God as committed by the glorified Lord to and through the Apostle Paul.

In Acts 19:10, we are told that "all they which dwelt in Asia heard the Word of the Lord." A few verses farther on we find former pagans burning their books and idols and leaving their heathenism, *"so mightily grew the Word of God and prevailed"*

4. I have written a book entitled "Moses and Paul, the Dispensers of Law and Grace." It reveals how both of those men were commissioned with a gospel message for their respective ages.

as the Apostle Paul preached the message of grace. How greatly the apostle was used of God in this province in Asia Minor! Yet in his last letter, he wrote to Timothy at Ephesus, "This thou knowest, that all they which are in Asia be turned away from me..." (II Tim. 1:15).

What a sad statement! The departure from Paul and his message of grace started in his own lifetime, and the declaration of this message has declined since then in the Church. The Church has become more and more formalistic, and more and more legalistic, and has remembered less and less of the great message of grace. Yes, this decline has continued ever since Paul.

Read most Bible commentaries today and you will find many wonderful truths, but when it comes to God's message and program for our day, you will find almost nothing about the absolute distinctiveness of Paul's God-given message and program for *"the dispensation of the grace of God."* Most commentaries have the law of Moses and the Sermon on the Mount and the Great Commission given to the twelve all mixed up with the revelation given to Paul by the glorified Lord in heaven. They have the gospel of the kingdom confused with the gospel of the grace of God, and they have the Messianic reign of Christ mixed up with the Body of Christ and its heavenly position. The Church today is confused and divided, so go by that Book, *rightly divided.*

We have shown from Scripture how this confusion began. Paul, the chief of sinners, saved by grace, had been sent by God to tell the Gentiles that they could now be saved by grace alone because Christ died for their sins. Some of the Jewish believers in Judea who were still zealous of the law became concerned about this. They recognized this as something different than they had known. When Christ was on earth, He was under the law; He went to the synagogue every Sabbath Day; He was circumcised the eighth day, He kept the feast days. So those believers in Judea became concerned about the Gentiles becoming the children of God and not keeping the law. They did not see how anyone could be saved by grace through faith alone. They went to Galatia and sought to bring the Galatian believers back under the law.

But see what Paul said about this in our passage in Galatians 1, verses 6 and 7. "I marvel that ye are so soon removed...." There was no contradiction between law and grace, only a further development of truth, a further revelation of truth. "...but there be some that trouble you, and would pervert the gospel [good news] of Christ."

Paul called these legalizers intruders and troublemakers, and the leaders at Jerusalem agreed with him. You see, the Galatian letter was written after the great council at Jerusalem where Paul and Peter, John, James, and the rest met to thrash out the problem. As Acts 15 tells us, certain men had come from Judea to Antioch and told the Gentile believers that submission to circumcision was the law and that the law was necessary to salvation. The record tells us that Paul and Barnabas had "no small dissension" and "disputation" with them.

Paul and some of his co-workers went to Jerusalem to talk to the leaders there about this matter (Gal. 2:2), but they "added nothing to me [him]" (ver. 6).[5] Contrariwise he added something to them; he told them something that they had not known.

"Contrariwise, when they saw that *the gospel of the uncircumcision* was committed unto me, as the gospel of the circumcision was unto Peter..." (Ver. 7).

The gospel of the circumcision was the good news that through Israel all nations could be blessed if they would simply accept Messiah as King. But they did not receive Him. Consequently, God raised up the Apostle Paul and sent him forth with the gospel of the *uncircumcision*, that now, poor Gentile sinners who had no promises, no covenants, no God, no Christ, and no hope, could find salvation offered by grace through faith on the basis of the finished work of Christ at Calvary.

"When James, Cephas [Peter], and John, who seemed to be pillars, perceived the grace that was given unto me, they gave to me and Barnabas the right hands of fellowship; that we should go to the heathen [Gentiles], and they unto the circumcision" (Gal. 2:9).

Peter, James and John shook hands with Paul and Barnabas, in a solemn, public, official agreement that Paul now was to be recognized as God's *apostle to the Gentiles* to preach to them the message of grace. They, the leaders at Jerusalem who had at first been sent into all the world, were now to confine their ministry to their own nation.

Peter and Paul were not working in opposition as some have supposed that we teach; they were in perfect agreement. They saw that the gospel of uncircumcision was committed unto Paul as the

---

5. They could not tell Paul anything about the Scriptures that he did not already know. We remember that he was more zealous of the traditions of his father than all the others. He knew the Old Testament!

gospel of the circumcision was unto Peter. "For he that wrought effectually in Peter to the apostleship of the circumcision, the same was mighty in me toward the Gentiles" (Gal. 2:7-8).

LEGALISM CAUSES DIVISION IN THE CHURCH

Those men from Judea who had gone to Antioch, and then to Corinth, and to Galatia, to bring Gentile believers back under the law of Moses were called *troublemakers*, not only by Paul, but Peter also, and the great leaders in the Jerusalem council. They wrote letters to the churches:

> **"...The apostles and elders and brethren send greeting unto the brethren which are of the Gentiles in Antioch and Syria and Cilicia:**
>
> **"Forasmuch as we have heard, that certain which went out from us have *troubled* you with words, subverting your souls, saying, Ye must be circumcised, and keep the law; to whom we gave no such commandment" (Acts 15:23-24).**

Beloved, I did not say this, the Bible says it. Be a Berean. Turn to Acts 15 and see that this is exactly what it says. To both Peter and Paul these legalizers were troublemakers. Their motives may have been good but they ignored the further revelation committed unto Paul. This had caused nothing but trouble, and it is the same today. Those who mix law with grace, or the commission to the twelve with that later given to Paul, cause trouble and division. Those who teach the gospel of the Sermon on the Mount, which was in order for the Jews then, instead of the gospel of the grace of God, which we are to preach today, cause trouble and division.

BELIEVERS CURSED?

Beloved, it is because of the failure to recognize and acknowledge the distinctive character of Paul's apostleship and message, as the one whom God ordained to give us *the truth* for our day, that the gospel has been perverted and subverted. Thus, those who should be enjoying the peace and assurance of resting in the all-sufficient finished work of Christ instead lose this blessedness. They doubt God's Word which teaches that they are *"complete in Christ"* and *"made accepted in the Beloved One"* (Col. 2:10; Eph. 1:6).

This is why Paul pronounced a curse upon those who proclaim any other gospel than that which was committed by the glorified Lord to him (Gal. 1:8,9).

Never hesitate to accept and proclaim the message of salvation by grace alone through faith as found in the epistles of Paul. Do not mix that blessed message with formal worship, rituals, and works of the law that were once required for salvation.

In these verses the apostle uses some of the strongest language of the whole epistle.

"But though we, or an angel from Heaven, preach any other gospel unto you than that which we have preached unto you, let him be accursed" (Gal. 1:8).

Paul knew that this was serious talk, and he solemnly repeated it.

"As we said before, so say I now again, If any man preach any other gospel unto you than that ye have received, let him be accursed" (Gal. 1:9).

This is such strong language that it behooves us to make certain what it means.

PAUL'S SINGULAR MESSAGE

The first thing to consider is the distinctiveness of Paul's apostleship and message. Paul was not one of the twelve. The end of Acts 1 and the beginning of Acts 2 tell us how our Lord had twelve apostles who were all filled with the Holy Spirit. This included Matthias who had been ordained to take Judas' place. Since Paul was not even converted at that time, he was certainly not included. He was chosen separately, on the road to Damascus, far away from the twelve, far from Jerusalem and Palestine, and he never went preaching with the twelve.

He was given further revelation beyond what the twelve had been proclaiming, and he was used to usher in a new age, called, *"the dispensation of the grace of God"* (Eph. 3:1-3). The twelve had been proclaiming the Kingdom to the Jews. Paul proclaimed the gospel of the grace of God among the Gentiles.

When we point out these simple facts of the Scripture record some people conclude that we teach that the twelve and Paul worked at cross-purposes, that Paul contradicted the others. Far from it, beloved. They all believed in the same God and the same Christ. They all taught that Christ was the rightful King of Israel, and that some day He will reign here on earth sitting on the throne of David. Indeed, the twelve preached, "Repent, for the Kingdom of Heaven is at hand." It was within Israel's grasp, but when the nation rejected the King and the Kingdom, God temporarily interrupted the prophetic program, and raised up the apostle Paul to proclaim the good news of His grace to all nations.

The twelve agreed with Paul in this! We saw this in the passage in Acts 15. There was a divinely governed agreement between them.

It is really quite simple. Paul was not contradicting Peter and the others. He knew very well and testified that they had preached the truth, and he confirmed them in it. They had preached the truth when they had proclaimed and offered the Kingdom reign of Christ on earth. But when that Kingdom was rejected, God in infinite grace raised up Paul and gave him further revelation of His plan. The twelve had agreed that this was *now* God's message for the nations.

"...so say I now again, if any man preach any other gospel unto you than that which ye have received, let him be accursed" (Gal. 1:9)!

Beloved, this is serious language indeed, and it is the Word of God. It ought to make us tremble. I will never forget when these verses really came home to my understanding. To paraphrase the apostle's words, "...even if I myself should come and preach something different, or if an angel should come, let him be accursed" (Ver. 8).

We need to remember that according to II Corinthians 11:13-15, Satan and his angels are behind all the false teaching in the world. They have their own message of salvation, but it is not God's righteousness imputed to sinners. It is man making something of himself.

SOMETHING NEW

"According to the grace of God which is given unto me, as a wise masterbuilder, I have laid the foundation, and another buildeth thereon..." (I Cor. 3:10).

Does not this make it clear that something new began with Paul? *"I have laid the foundation."* Then he went on, "But let every man take heed how he buildeth thereupon."

We must not take Mosaic material or Petrine material and build with it on the Pauline foundation. The foundation is Christ and His finished all-sufficient work at Calvary. Abundant grace flows from that finished work. If we tamper with God's message for today, beloved, that blessed gospel of the grace of God, we shall *reap* a curse. These verses say so, with *double* emphasis.

What does it mean, that word *curse*? Does it mean that if you get Paul's message mixed up with that of Moses, or with the Sermon on the Mount, you will lose your salvation and be lost again? *NO!* But you will lose the blessing that goes with God's wonderful grace.

Always put blessing opposite cursing. They are opposite one another. Don't we have to admit that the present professing church has *lost* the blessing and *reaped* the cursing of confusion and division, by adding *to* grace? They have mixed grace with law, and with the program of the Kingdom, as we find it in the Sermon on the Mount. These two systems were in force in their dispensations but because man could not fulfill them, God raised up Paul to go forth with a new message of salvation.

FAILURE OF THE GALATIAN CHURCHES

The Galatian believers had lost the blessing of God. When Paul was first with them he was ill, very ill, with some painful disease, evidently something that affected his eyes.

"Ye know how through infirmity of the flesh I preached the gospel unto you at the first" (Gal. 4:13).

He was detained there because he was ill, and still he preached. *What a man of God!*

"And my temptation [testing] which was in my flesh ye despised not, nor rejected; but received me as an angel of God, even as Christ Jesus.

"Where is then the blessedness ye spake of? for I bear you record, that, if it had been possible, ye would have plucked out your own eyes, and have given them to me" (Gal. 4:14-15).

I can imagine the Galatian believers saying, "Poor man, how greatly he is used; what blessings he has brought to us. And what pain he has to suffer, headaches, serious troubles with his eyes. Ah, we wish he could have our eyes."

These Galatians had been so eager to hear Paul that they would have gladly given him their own eyes! But all that had changed. They were cursed with fighting and bickering until Paul had to say, "Take heed that ye be not [devoured] one of another" (5:15). Why this sad change? Had they denied the Scriptures? No, the legalists had come to them with Scriptures from the Old Testament. They had done what nine-tenths of the professing church is doing today. They took rites and ceremonies and forms and decrees from a former dispensation and added them *to*, and mixed them *with*, God's pure message of grace. Paul said by divine inspiration, "Beloved, do not tamper with grace or you will reap a curse."

God says through Paul, "Do not tamper with My grace. Do not change it in any way; do not confuse it with the law or the Sermon on the Mount, or with Peter's message at Pentecost. This is a further revelation; if you corrupt it you will bring a curse upon yourselves and upon those to whom you minister."

It is not according to how much we repent or try to do better, but by His grace.

"For by grace are ye saved through faith; and that not of yourselves: it is the gift of God:

"Not of works, lest any man should boast" (Eph. 2:8-9).

And we must not miss the verse about the riches of grace in II Corinthians 8:9: "For ye know the grace of our Lord Jesus Christ, that, though He was rich, yet for your sakes He became poor, that ye through His poverty might be rich." Also Ephesians 2:7: "That in the ages to come He might shew the exceeding riches of His grace in His kindness toward us through Christ Jesus."

"For what saith the Scripture? Abraham believed God, and it was counted unto him for righteousness" (Rom. 4:3).

God counted Abraham's faith for righteousness although Abraham was not personally righteous. The record shows again and again that he was a sinner. He was a sinner just like us. But he believed God, and God counted *his faith* for righteousness, because God was going to provide everything necessary for the payment of sin.

"Now to him that worketh is the reward not reckoned of grace..." (Rom. 4:4). A reward does not come of grace but by works. A reward is earned.

"But to him that worketh not, but believeth on him that justifieth the ungodly, his faith is counted for righteousness" (Rom. 4:5).

My friend, take hold of that truth. You say that you have been ungodly. God says that there is nothing for you to do for salvation, as Christ did it all at Calvary (Rom. 4:25-5:2).

Chapter 3 — Galatians 1:10-24

PAUL'S ORDINATION CERTIFICATE

THE SERVANT OF CHRIST

"For do I now persuade men, or God? or do I seek to please men? for if I yet pleased men, I should not be the servant of Christ" (Gal. 1:10).

Does The Preacher Please Men Or God?

With forceful sarcasm Paul asks in Galatians 1:10: "Am I trying to persuade God to fall in line with my program?" "No," he said, "I am trying to get *you* to fall into line with *His* program."

Beloved, especially you who are engaged in the work of the Lord, this is a stern rebuke to those who constantly have their fingers on the peoples' pulse; who constantly ask, "Do they like my message? Am I giving them what they want?" Such leaders have no liberty. They are the slaves of men. Remember that when we seek to please men we are not true servants of Christ. This is what verse 10 says.

How many preachers there are whose aim is to just keep the people coming, and the congregation growing, and having a nice, happy fellowship. They will not tolerate anyone who might rock their little boats by pointing to some important truth that should be recognized. There must be peace at any price! Whatever the cost, let us have peace! Speakers are often chosen on the basis of popularity, rather than on the content of their messages. Well, here we have it: such workers are not in that measure the servants of Christ.

Paul was once like that. He wrote that he "profited in the Jews' religion" (1:14). Why? Was it because he was more *zealous* of the truth of God's Word? No, but because he was "more exceedingly zealous of the traditions of my fathers." He was with the *"in"* group, you see.

Do you recall what the Lord Himself said about this? He said to the Pharisees (of whom Paul was one), "By your traditions you make void the Word of God." And so did Paul also while he was still a Pharisee.

I often asked my Bible classes, "Would you rather be orthodox or Scriptural?" Paul once wanted to be very orthodox; he wanted to be true to the teachings of the elders. But this made him the enemy of Christ, and the persecutor of Christians.

He had learned his lesson, and how beautifully he stated his feeling in I Thessalonians 2:4: "As we are allowed of God to be put in trust with the gospel, even so we speak; not as pleasing men, but God, who trieth our hearts."

"Therefore seeing we have this ministry, as we have received mercy, we faint not; But have renounced the hidden things of dishonesty, not walking in craftiness, nor handling the Word of God deceitfully; but by manifestation of the truth commending ourselves to every man's conscience in the sight of God" (II Cor. 4:1-2).

In Acts 20:24 we see Paul, on his last journey, facing bonds and imprisonment and affliction, but listen to what he said and you will see that he had not lost the blessedness:

"But none of these things move me, neither count I my life dear unto myself, so that I might finish my course with joy, and the ministry, which I have received of the Lord Jesus, to testify the gospel of the grace of God."

Oh, for more such men of God today, men with sincere passion to know only, and obey, and preach God's Word, *rightly divided*; His message for today, the undiluted, unadulterated, unconfused gospel of the grace of God!

"THAT OTHER APOSTLE!"

"But I certify you, brethren, that the gospel which was preached of me is not after man.

"For I neither received it of man, neither was I taught it, but by the revelation of Jesus Christ" (Gal. 1:11,12).

Paul threw down, as it were, the certificate of his apostleship. "Examine this; see whether you can find any flaw in it!" Chapters 1 and 2 of Galatians give proof after proof of his *divine* calling, so that there can be no question about it. This is important, for remember again that Paul's words to the Galatians is also God's Word to us. This epistle is divinely *inspired* and his irrefutable proofs to the Galatians also apply to those today who minimize Paul's apostleship.

"I certify you, brethren, that the gospel which was preached of me is not after man."

It seems to me that two facts stand out clearly in Galatians 1:11. First, his gospel was new and different from the gospel of the Kingdom which the twelve preached. Otherwise, why would he speak as he did so often of "the gospel which was preached of me" and "that gospel which I preach among the Gentiles," and three times, "my gospel" (Rom. 16:25; 2:16; II Tim. 2:8)? Second, that gospel was not "after man;" he did not get it from men as we get the gospel. We hear others preach it, or friends tell us about it, but Paul got it directly from the Lord Jesus Christ Himself and no one else.

In verse 12 there is an interesting comparison with verse 1. In verse 1 he introduced himself as "Paul, an apostle, not of men, neither by man." In verse 12 he says of his message, "I neither received it of man, neither was I taught it, but by the *revelation* of Jesus Christ." Thus it is evident that his message did not originate with man, but again, as verse 1 says, God did not use men to teach it to him. He received his message on his way to Damascus while he was "breathing out threatenings and slaughter against the disciples of the Lord." It was then that the Lord revealed Himself to Paul and committed to him this wonderful message of grace. Is it not important then that he put so much emphasis upon this?

Notice that phrase, "by the revelation of Jesus Christ." This is the second time we read that Paul did not merely have a revelation *from* Christ; Paul actually had Christ revealed *to* him. He *saw* the glorified Lord and he received one revelation after another about God's plan as Christ was revealed to him.

In Acts 26:16, Scripture says that Christ appeared to Paul and talked with him: "...for I have appeared unto thee for this purpose, to make thee a minister and a witness both of these things which thou hast seen, and of those things in the which I will appear unto thee."

Then in Acts 22:17,18, Jesus talked with him again: "when I was come again to Jerusalem, even while I prayed in the temple, I was in a trance; And saw Him saying unto me...."

In II Corinthians 12:2, he told how he also was "caught up" to the third heaven and heard things so glorious that he could not relate them, and this in connection with the previous verse where he spoke about Christ being revealed to him: "I will come to visions and revelations of the Lord."

This is why he emphasized so often, and so strongly, that he received his message *"by the revelation of Jesus Christ."* Mark well that he saw and talked with the *Lord Jesus Christ*; he did not talk with Jesus in His humiliation on earth as the twelve had done, but he talked with Christ in His glory in heaven.

Paul knew the ascended Christ, exalted "far above all principality, and power, and might, and dominion, and every name that is named, not only in this world, but also in that which is to come" (Eph. 1:21).

Let us turn again to Galatians 1:12 where the apostle "certifies" that he did not receive his message from men, neither had he been taught it by men. I would like to *clinch* this point by calling your attention to Galatians 1:15-17:

"But when it pleased God, who separated me from my mother's womb, and called me by His grace,

"To reveal His Son in me, that I might preach Him among the heathen; immediately I conferred not with flesh and blood:

"Neither went I up to Jerusalem to them which were apostles before me; but I went into Arabia, and returned again unto Damascus."

These verses are important, and very significant, for Paul did not go immediately and talk it over with human beings. When I was first saved I could not get enough fellowship with other believers, and I listened with rapt attention to those great men of God who were teaching the Scripture in those days. Would you not think that when Paul was converted to Christ he would have gone immediately to those who were apostles before him, since the Lord Jesus had appointed him an apostle? But he said that this was not what he did. "I did not confer with flesh and blood. I did not go to Jerusalem to those who were apostles before me."

He went into a desert place, doubtless to be alone with God. It may well be that there he received the basic revelations about God's secret eternal purpose of grace:

"Then after three years I went up to Jerusalem to see Peter, and I abode with him fifteen days.

"But other of the apostles saw I none, save James the Lord's brother" (Gal. 1:18,19).

Galatians 2:1 tells us that Paul went up again to Jerusalem fourteen years later. So in seventeen years he had conferred with only one apostle, and that was for only fifteen days! He surely did not get his apostleship and his message from the twelve apostles.

The record as given in the Acts of the Apostles might make us conclude that there is a contradiction with this account, so let us turn to the passage, Acts 9:26-28:

"And when Saul was come to Jerusalem, he assayed to join himself to the disciples: but they were all afraid of him, and believed not that he was a disciple."

We note that the word is not *apostles*, but *disciples*, meaning the general body of believers. They were afraid of him; many of them had been whipped and persecuted and scourged by him. They shrank with dread from the man who had so violently persecuted and killed relatives and friends. They doubted that he was a believer in Jesus. They thought that this might be a trick to ensnare them.

"But Barnabas [great loving, big-hearted Barnabas who was called the son of consolation] took him, and brought him to the apostles [right straight to headquarters!], and declared unto them how he had seen the Lord in the way, and that He [Christ] had spoken to him, and how he had preached boldly at Damascus in the name of Jesus. And he [Paul] was with them coming in and going out at Jerusalem" (Acts 9:27,28).

A CONTRADICTION?

This is a very touching story, but does it contradict Paul's account in the letter to the Galatians? There he said that he saw only one apostle, Peter, apart from James, the Lord's brother. In the Acts 9 account Luke writes that Barnabas brought him to the apostles, and that he was "with them coming in and going out."[1]

In Galatians 1:18 Paul said that he abode with Peter for fifteen days. It appears that Peter took him into his [own] home. Further, in the Galatians record, James, who was also called an apostle (in a secondary sense), was not one of the twelve. It does not say in Acts 9:27 that Barnabas took Paul to the company of apostles or that Paul went with them. It would be quite natural that the other apostles were out ministering in other parts of Palestine (Acts 9:31) while Peter remained at headquarters with James, the Lord's brother, who was head of the Jerusalem church. The difference here, in the Acts record, is that Luke generalized, while in the

1. A Hebraism, or colloquial saying, meaning "life-style." Paul joined their daily routine.

epistle to the Galatians, Paul defended his apostleship by carefully going into every detail.

In Acts 9:27, we see Barnabas proudly introducing Saul to the disciples at Jerusalem. He explained who Saul was, "how he had seen the Lord," and they accepted him to the extent that he joined in with the program of the various disciples ("with them coming in and going out").

The Galatians letter does not actually deny that Paul met any of the apostles. He talked instead about *"not conferring"* (ver. 16) with them concerning his own mission. His point was that he had not gone to the designated Kingdom authority, the men who had the keys of the Kingdom, for instruction. They did not commission him to carry out the Kingdom program. His unique commission was given directly from God. Three years later he did go to Jerusalem to confer with Peter for fifteen days. At that time only James was present (ver. 18).

"And when he had received meat, he was strengthened. Then was Saul was certain days with the disciples which were at Damascus.

"And straightway he preached Christ in the synagogues, that He is the Son of God.

"But all that heard were amazed, and said; Is not this he that destroyed them which called on this name in Jerusalem, and came hither for that intent, that he might bring them bound unto the chief priests?

"But Saul increased the more in strength, and confounded the Jews which dwelt at Damascus, proving that this is very Christ" (Acts 9:19-22).

"Immediately I conferred not with flesh and blood:

"Neither went I up to Jerusalem to them which were apostles before me; but I went into Arabia, and returned again unto Damascus" (Gal. 1:16,17).

"And after that many days were fulfilled, the Jews took council to kill him:

"But their laying await was known of Saul. And they watched the gates day and night to kill him.

"Then the disciples took him by night, and let him down by the wall in a basket" (Acts 9:23-25).

"In Damascus the governor under Aretas the king kept the city of the Damascenes with the garrison, desirous to apprehend me:

"And through a window in a basket was I let down by the wall, and escaped his hands" (II Cor. 11:32,33).

"And when Saul was come to Jerusalem, he assayed to join himself to the disciples: but they were all afraid of him, and believed not that he was a disciple.

"But Barnabas took him, and brought him to the apostles, and declared unto them how he had seen the Lord in the way, and that he had spoken to him, and how he had preached boldly at Damascus in the name of Jesus.

"And he was with them coming in and going out at Jerusalem.

"And he spake boldly in the name of the Lord Jesus, and disputed against the Grecians: but they went about to slay him.

"Which when the brethren knew, they brought him down to Caesarea, and sent him forth to Tarsus" (Acts 9:26-30).

Paul solemnly swore—"Now the things which I write unto you, behold, before God, I lie not" (Gal. 1:20).

Why all of this emphasis on the separateness of his apostleship and message from that of the twelve? Obviously, because it is of the most vital importance to us, and God the divine author of the Scriptures included it in this passage. When we confuse the message of the four Gospels with that of Paul's epistles and fail to rightly divide the Word of truth, we disobey and dishonor Him.

"Study to show thyself approved unto God, a workman that needeth not to be ashamed, rightly dividing the Word of truth" (II Tim. 2:15).

When we confuse Paul's message with that of the twelve, we do not stand approved of God and we ought to be ashamed. Go back again to Acts 20:24 and see what Paul's great theme was from start to finish:

"But none of these things moved me, neither count I my life dear unto myself, so that I might finish my course with joy, and the ministry, which I have received of the Lord Jesus, to testify the gospel of the grace of God."

Despite terrible affliction it was still his desire and determination to finish, with joy, the course which he had begun. And what was that course? "The ministry, which I have received of the Lord Jesus, to testify the gospel of the grace of God." Ah, what a message he was privileged to proclaim! His epistles are filled with it.

PROOFS OF PAUL'S APOSTLESHIP

PROOF ONE

"I Persecuted the Church"

"For ye have heard of my conversation in time past in the Jews' religion, how that beyond measure I persecuted the church of God, and wasted it:

"And profited in the Jews' religion above many my equals in mine own nation, being more exceedingly zealous of the traditions of my fathers" (Gal. 1:13,14).

In Galatians 1:13, Paul presented his first indisputable proof that his apostleship was not of men, neither by man, but that he was appointed directly by the Lord Jesus Christ from heaven. He said in verse 13, "Ye have heard of my conduct in time past in the Jews' religion, how that beyond measure I persecuted the church of God, and laid it waste."

It was widely known that Saul was the chief persecutor of the followers of Jesus. The fact that they all knew this is very important. We recall that just after Saul's conversion the Lord called a Jewish believer in Damascus to go talk to *"Saul of Tarsus."*

Now Ananias was in Damascus, Syria; not Palestine, or Judea, or Galilee, or Jerusalem, but in Damascus, and he was afraid, and said:

> **"Lord, I have heard by many of this man, how much evil he hath done to Thy saints at Jerusalem: And here [in Damascus] he hath authority from the chief priests to bind all that call on Thy name" (Acts 9:13-14).**

This is why, when Paul went to Jerusalem, the disciples did not trust him. "They believed not that he was a disciple." So well known, and notorious, was Saul of Tarsus.

> **"But the Lord said unto him [Ananias], Go thy way: for he is a chosen vessel unto Me, to bear My name before the Gentiles, and kings, and the children of Israel: For I will show him how great things he must suffer for My name's sake" (Acts 9:15,16).**

It is not strange, then, that at Damascus Saul's former Jewish friends went about to kill him. They said, "He is a turncoat. He came here to arrest the Christians, and now he has joined with them, preaching Christ."

The persecutor would become the persecuted! Far away in Damascus, Syria, Saul, the enemy of

Christ, was already known by many, and his conversion spread the news about him even farther. His name was on many tongues.

Paul's Account of Himself

"Though I might also have confidence in the flesh. If any other man thinketh that he hath whereof he might trust in the flesh, I more:

"Circumcised the eighth day, of the stock of Israel, of the tribe of Benjamin, an Hebrew of the Hebrews; as touching the law, a Pharisee;

"Concerning zeal, persecuting the church; touching the righteousness which is in the law, blameless" (Phil. 3:4-6).

Paul has told us a great deal about himself and his life, and Luke has told still more about him in the Acts of the Apostles.

Here Paul told us all about his background. Peter and the eleven gave us no such record of themselves. When and where were they all converted? We do not know. But the story of Saul's conversion is told, at length, *three* times in the Scripture. What churches, if any, did Peter found? And where? We do not know. But we have many details in the accounts of Paul's three great apostolic journeys. It is filled with the details of his ministry and the churches that he founded.

Did you know that in Paul's epistles he refers to himself by name some thirty times, and by the personal pronoun, several hundred times? There is an important reason for this. I have written about it in my book, *Moses and Paul, the Dispensers of Law and Grace*.

We see by what is written in Acts and what he wrote about himself in all of his epistles, that Paul belongs to the inspired Word of God. God put all this emphasis upon Paul so that there may be no question that he is indeed God's chosen apostle for this present dispensation of grace.

"For I speak to you Gentiles, inasmuch as I am the apostle of the Gentiles, I magnify mine office" (Rom. 11:13).

Paul opened the defense of his apostleship by reminding the Galatians of what they already knew about him. His argument was this: How could I have been appointed an apostle or received my message about Christ from men, even from the twelve? I was the most bitter enemy of Christ and of all who followed Him. I persecuted the church of God and laid it waste. How then could I have learned my message from the followers of Christ? They could not get near me. I was the one they feared.

Now let us consider this whole picture as it is given to us in the Book of Acts. There was at that time only one nation which God recognized as His own. And that nation, Israel, rebelled against Him. Who inspired and led that rebellion? Saul of Tarsus. And who was Saul of Tarsus? A wicked ruffian? No! He was one of the chosen race, and was highly respected by his nation. He was a scrupulous observer of the law, zealous of the traditions of his fathers. Was he so ignorant of Old Testament prophecy that he did not recognize Christ? No, he was a Pharisee, the son of a line of Pharisees, a Hebrew of the Hebrews, of the tribe of Benjamin, a spiritual leader in Israel with a profound knowledge of the law and the prophets. Yet this man led his nation in bitter persecution against the followers of Jesus, determined to stamp out the very name and the memory of Jesus Christ of Nazareth.

Luke tells us that when Stephen was stoned, Saul was consenting unto his death. He was saying, "That's right, kill him, kill him! He's an evil doer." And Luke informs us that the murder of Stephen touched off a great persecution in which Saul "made havoc of the church, entering into every house, and haling [dragging out] men and women committed them to prison." (Read it in Acts 8:1-3.)

This, of course, caused the flight of the Jerusalem believers to the regions of Judea and Samaria, and even farther away. Acts 11:19 states, "Now they which were scattered abroad upon the persecution that arose about Stephen travelled as far as Phenice, and Cyprus, and Antioch." In Acts 26:11 Saul says,

"And I punished them oft in every synagogue, and compelled them to blaspheme; and being exceedingly mad against them, I persecuted them even unto strange cities."

But what happened on the way to Damascus (Acts 9:1-2)?

"And Saul, yet breathing out threatenings and slaughter against the disciples of the Lord, went unto the high priest,

"And desired of him letters to Damascus to the synagogues, that if he found any of this way, whether they were men or women, he might bring them bound unto Jerusalem."

Armed with authority and a commission from the chief priests, Saul made it his purpose to arrest as many as he could and bring them bound to Jerusalem to be punished. Thank God, his purpose was never fulfilled in Damascus, for he himself was *arrested* by the glorified Lord and saved on the road to that city.

Paul's argument for his apostleship is a strong one. How could the twelve, or any of the other believers for that matter, have appointed him *an apostle of Jesus Christ?*

"Beyond measure I persecuted the church of God, and laid it waste" (Gal. 1:13).

What is Meant by "Church"

Some readers, when they see the word "church" in this passage, suppose that the church of today, the Body of Christ, began at Pentecost. It is true that we read about a church in Acts 2, but beloved, the church of today is a "joint body" made up of Jewish and Gentile believers, with a heavenly position and blessing. The church at Pentecost, and from Pentecost to Paul, was composed of Jews only (Acts 11:19). They had an earthly calling with Christ as their King to reign at Jerusalem according to the prophecies of the Old Testament.

The word "church" simply means *a called-out assembly*, and God has always had His "called-out" people, His church, in every age. In Acts 7:38, Israel, under Moses' leadership, is called "the church in the wilderness," and it *was* the church for that day. They were God's called-out people. But God's church of today, His called-out ones, are the believers in Christ from every nation, whose home, outlook, and prospect is *not* earthly, but heavenly. Paul speaks about our calling, position, and blessings in heaven, as well as our prospects when the Lord Jesus comes to "catch us" away to heaven.

But Peter at Pentecost, in Acts 3:19-20, said very clearly to the Jews, "If you will repent, God will send Jesus back *to earth.*" They had said, "Away with Him," but Peter promised that if they would repent, change their minds about Him, God would send Him back, and the times of refreshing, those wonderful times predicted through the Old Testament prophets, would come from the presence of the Lord. Since the offer was refused and Christ and His Kingdom were rejected, a new dispensation has been ushered in. It is called, in Ephesians 3:1-3, *"the dispensation of the grace of God."* This new dispensation, *this age of grace*, was ushered in by that *other* apostle, Paul. He does not say, "If you will repent, God will send Jesus back down *here*." He says, "If you will believe, He will take you up *there*." You will go to heaven! How much we find about this matter in the epistles of Paul!

PROOF TWO

"I Profited in the Jew's Religion"

"And [I] profited in the Jews' religion above many my equals in mine own nation..." (Gal. 1:14).

We have so often seen how hard it is to get people who are prospering in their present situations to enter some position that will cause financial loss, or persecution, or suffering, or death. Men by nature cling to what they enjoy most. What an enemy to the truth is temporal prosperity!

We recall the story of the maniac of Gadara in Mark 5 who was possessed by a legion of demons. The Lord cast them out and allowed them to enter into a herd of swine which all ran into the sea and drowned. But the former maniac—look at him! He was sitting, and clothed, and in his right mind. No more pacing with a madman's nervousness; no more nakedness and cutting himself with stones;

no longer deranged, but sitting clothed, and in his right mind.

But the swine were now all dead. Business in the area had been hurt. They went to Christ as a group and begged Him to please, please leave them. With them, as with many Christians today, material prosperity came first.

Christians often sing "All to Jesus I surrender...." Nonsense! Most of them do not surrender even ten percent of their gross income to the Lord as the people of Israel were obliged to do under the law. We ought to do more under grace than the Jews did under the law!

There was the case of the poor demon-possessed girl in Acts 16. "Her masters made much gain" from her soothsaying, that is, her divining and predicting (Verse 16). She was possessed of a demon and Paul, by the power of God, cast out the demon and restored her to sanity. Verse 19 tells us that when the owners saw that their source of gain was gone, they caught Paul and Silas, dragged them to the rulers of the city, and had them thrown in jail for disturbing the peace. Think of it! They did not care that the poor girl was now a normal person. The thing that mattered to them was that they had lost some money. Their business had been hurt. Believing Christians have this same nature in them as well.

Paul said to those who question that God had called him as an apostle of Christ, "I profited in the Jews' religion above many my equals in mine own nation." As a young man he was already a member of the Supreme Court of the nation Israel, and he was respected and honored by all. He said, "Why would I leave that to follow the rejected Christ if it is not that Christ Himself worked in my life and spoke to my heart?"

I think that the best example of the power of his argument, because it shows the power motive, is found in Acts 19:23-27:

"And the same time [this was in Ephesus] there arose no small stir about that way."[2]

"For a certain man named Demetrius, a silversmith, which made silver shrines for Diana, brought no small gain unto the craftsmen;

"Whom he called together with the workmen of like occupation, and said, Sirs, ye know that by this craft we have our wealth.

"Moreover ye see and hear, that not alone at Ephesus, but almost throughout all Asia, this Paul hath persuaded and turned away much people, saying that they be no gods, which are made with hands:

"So that not only this our craft is in danger to be set at naught; but also that the temple of the great goddess Diana should be despised, and her magnificence should be destroyed, whom all Asia and the world worshippeth."

This Demetrius, this silversmith, was of course the human instrument whom Satan used to touch off that great uproar at Ephesus. He appears to have been the head of a guild of silversmiths and others of like occupation who had been instrumental in bringing "no small gain" to themselves through the sale of silver shrines for the heathen goddess Diana.

The devotees of Diana would buy the miniature shrines to carry with them, display in their homes, or leave in the temple itself as an act of worship.

2. "That way" refers to the message Paul preached.

Moreover, Ephesus was one of the largest seaports on the Aegean Sea, and travelers from far and near would also purchase these silver shrines to take home as mementoes of the world-renowned Diana and her beautiful temple. Concerned because of the sharp decline in business since Paul's appearance in Asia, Demetrius called the guild members together to discuss the situation and with rude simplicity stated the purpose of the gathering, the real reason for his concern over Diana and her temple: "By this craft we have our wealth" (Ver. 25). This was the human cause behind the uproar. Paul was hurting their business by saying that they are not gods which are made with hands. Little matter whether Paul was right or wrong in his contention, he was causing them personal loss.

This passage teaches further that those who stood to gain by idolatry actually wanted the gullible masses to attach supernatural importance to this merchandise "made with hands." Otherwise, why would they object to Paul's contention that these were not gods? As we have pointed out, Satan is "the god of this world" (II Cor. 4:4). He was moving behind the scene, diverting men's worship away from God, and his efforts in this direction have continued to this day.

The spirit that prompted Demetrius to call a meeting of his guild still prevails, even among religious people. Vested interests play a prominent role in the stubborn resistance to spiritual advances and reforms. How transparent Demetrius' argument was: "Paul's teaching is endangering our business, and of course, the glory of our goddess, Diana." Why did he have to cover up his greed with a cloak of religion? It was the danger to their wealth that aroused Demetrius and his co-businessmen against Paul. God help us today. God keep us from putting personal gain first!

I Corinthians 12:13 says, "For by one Spirit are we all baptized into one body...." Not by water, but by one Spirit. Many would accept and proclaim this blessed doctrine of grace with its one body and its one baptism, but vested interests stand in the way. Paul was "profiting" in Judaism, which represented a career to him. No *man* could have persuaded him to leave that profitable position to take his place with the despised followers of a rejected Jesus. The fact that he forsook such a profitable career is proof that his apostleship was the result of God's work in his life.

PROOF THREE

"Being More Exceedingly Zealous"

"And [I] profited in the Jews' religion [in and] above many my equals in mine own nation, *being more exceedingly zealous of the traditions of my fathers*" (Gal. 1:14).

Now we come to argument number three. With Paul it was more than a matter of temporal gain. The very reason he received promotion after promotion in Judaism is found at the end of Galatians 1:14.

He was totally sincere.

How impossible then for the twelve, or any of the disciples, to reach Saul, a man "making havoc of the church" and "laying it waste"; a man profiting because he was so utterly sincere. But, note that he was not zealous of the Holy Scriptures. He said,

"I was exceedingly zealous of the *traditions of my fathers*" (Ver. 14). "I verily thought with myself, that I ought to do many things contrary to the name of Jesus of Nazareth" (Acts 26:9). Remember what the Lord said about this: He said to these same Pharisees, of whom Saul was one, "By your traditions you have made void the Word of God."

We have looked at the first three proofs that Paul was a special apostle, separate from the twelve, raised up to usher in the dispensation of the grace of God, and to proclaim the gospel of the grace of God. We ought to study his epistles, and learn more about this wonderful message of grace for poor lost sinners today.

PAUL'S COMMISSION WAS ALL OF GOD

The Revelation Of Jesus Christ In Glory And In Grace

"But when it pleased God, who separated me from my mother's womb, and called me by His grace,

"To reveal His Son in me, that I might preach Him among the heathen; immediately I conferred not with flesh and blood:

"Neither went I up to Jerusalem to them which were apostles before me; but I went into Arabia, and returned again unto Damascus.

"Then after three years I went up to Jerusalem to see Peter, and abode with him fifteen days.

"But other of the apostles saw I none, save James the Lord's brother.

"Now the things which I write unto you, behold, before God, I lie not" (Gal. 1:15-20).

The appointment of Paul as an apostle was no makeshift arrangement. It was not an after-thought on God's part; it was not as though God said to Himself, "Now, they have rejected my Son; they will NOT accept Him as King; they will not accept His Kingdom. What should I do? I know what I will do, I will postpone the Kingdom and I will choose another apostle to preach grace." No, no, no! Paul said that he was set apart for this from his very birth; every step of his life had led up to this, every step in his life had prepared him for the great ministry that God was to give him.

But what does Paul mean when he wrote, "It pleased God...to reveal His Son in me"?

HIS REVELATION IN GLORY

The true title of the last great book of the Bible is not "The Revelation of St. John the Divine," but *"The Revelation of Jesus Christ,"* as indicated in its opening phrase (Rev. 1:1).

It is not difficult to understand why God gave it this title, for our Lord's Second Coming to earth, His revelation in glory, is the very theme of the book. It shows Him coming to judge and make war, putting down the world's rebellion and taking the throne in majesty and power to reign as King over Israel and the world.

This is what Peter referred to when he told the believing Jews of his day: "Hope to the end for the grace that is to be brought unto you at THE REVELATION OF JESUS CHRIST" (I Pet. 1:13).

We must not forget that Peter had been sent forth with *the gospel of the kingdom*, that Christ had given him *the keys of the kingdom* and that he had been promised *a throne in the kingdom* (Matt. 10:7; 16:19; 19:28).

Peter was among those who asked the Lord after His resurrection: *"Lord, wilt thou at this time restore again the kingdom to Israel?"* (Acts 1:6). The Lord simply answered: "It is not for you to know the times and the seasons...," for the postponement of the kingdom was still a "mystery," or secret, later to be revealed to and through Paul (Rom. 11:25,26).

At Pentecost, Peter "filled with the Holy Ghost," pointed to the prophetic signs and declared that the "last days" had come, showing from Scripture that God had raised Christ from the dead to sit on David's throne (See Acts 2:16,17 and 2:29-36). In the next chapter (Acts 3:19-21) we read that he went so far as to tell the "men of Israel" that if they would repent God would send Jesus and the times of refreshing would come from the presence of the Lord.

As the Book of Acts shows, Israel did *not* repent. Nevertheless, for some considerable time after Pentecost God still continued to "stretch forth His hands unto a disobedient and gainsaying people" (Rom. 10:21). His mercy lingered long over the obstinate nation.

It is no wonder, then, that Peter continued to look for the return of Christ in glory and that he wrote to the believing Jews of his day:

"Wherefore gird up the loins of your mind, be sober, and *hope to the end* for the grace that is to be brought unto you at *the revelation of Jesus Christ*" (I Pet. 1:13).

HIS REVELATION IN GRACE

But St. Paul uses this significant phrase too. He says in Galatians 1:11,12:

"But I certify you, brethren, that the gospel which was preached of me is not after man, for I neither received it of man, neither was I taught it, but by *the revelation of Jesus Christ.*"

Surely this is not the *same* "revelation of Jesus Christ." This is not "the revelation of Jesus Christ" in glory and power, but "the revelation of Jesus Christ" in *grace*; not His revelation to the world *in person*, but His revelation to and *through* Paul, the chief of sinners, saved by grace.

We must always distinguish between grace in a dispensation and *the dispensation of grace*. The *principle* of law is eternal, but the *dispensation* of law was not. It was wrong for Cain to kill his brother, and he was judged for it, yet the law was only given some 2,500 years later, by Moses (John 1:17). Just so the *principle* of grace is eternal, but the *dispensation* of grace is not. It was only as Israel continued in her rejection of Christ that God reached down to save Saul of Tarsus, the leader of the rebellion, and usher in the dispensation of grace.

"Where sin abounded *grace did much more abound*, that as sin hath reigned, unto death, even so might *grace reign*" (Rom. 5:20,21).

It was on the road to Damascus that Saul first saw the glorified Lord and heard those tender words, *"Saul, Saul, why persecutest thou me?"* But not only did the Lord reveal Himself *to Saul* from heaven, He revealed Himself *to the world* through Paul. In Galatians 1:12, he says he got his message *"by the revelation of Jesus Christ,"* but in Verses 15 and 16 he says, "...it pleased God...TO REVEAL HIS SON IN ME." What a revelation to the world and to Israel when God saved Saul, His blaspheming enemy!

He did it to show that He wanted all to be reconciled, *"that He might have mercy upon all"* (Rom. 11:15,32; cf. I Tim. 2:3-7).

II Thes. 1:7,8: *"...the Lord Jesus shall be revealed from heaven with His mighty angels,*

"In flaming fire taking vengeance on them that know not God, and that obey not the gospel of our Lord Jesus Christ."

I Tim. 1:16: "Howbeit *for this cause* I obtained mercy, that *in me first* [or "chiefly"] Jesus Christ might show forth all long-suffering, *for a pattern* to them which should hereafter believe on Him to life everlasting."

Gal. 1:15,16: *"...it pleased God...to reveal His Son in me."*

What a contrast between "the revelation of Jesus Christ" in glory and His revelation in *grace!*

The Beloved Son had been rejected but God postponed the day of judgment and instead revealed Christ in matchless grace, through the conversion of the chief of sinners.

Now that Saul had seen Christ and tasted of the riches of His grace, he was a new man. Even before God he was a new man, for God did not behold him as the wicked blasphemer and murderer, but viewed him now *in Christ*, who had died in his place (II Cor. 5:17). And not only was Paul now *in Christ*, but *Christ was in Paul!* They had exchanged places. He says: "...it pleased God...TO REVEAL HIS SON IN ME."

Christ once died in Paul's stead. Now Paul stands in Christ's stead, pleading with sinners to be reconciled to God. It is as if he said: "Christ could not be here. You didn't want Him. But I am here in His place." See II Cor. 5:20: "...We pray you IN

CHRIST'S STEAD, be ye reconciled to God." This is doubtless what Paul had in mind when he said "[I] now rejoice in my sufferings for you, and FILL UP THAT WHICH IS BEHIND OF THE AFFLICTIONS OF CHRIST...." Christ's *vicarious* suffering was over, but He was still despised and rejected, and chose to remain so rather than to judge this wicked world. But looking down from His glory in heaven He said to the chief persecutor: *"Saul, Saul, why persecutest thou Me?"* And from then on Saul the persecutor became Saul the persecuted, and he bore it gladly to show forth the grace of the rejected Christ. He called it *"the fellowship of His suffering,"* and "filling up" that which remained of the afflictions of Christ.

According to I Timothy 1:13-16, Paul was God's "pattern" for believers in this dispensation of grace. The words "me first" might well be translated, "me as leader."

Paul, the new man in Christ, reminds us of the "one new man" God is now forming of reconciled Jews and Gentiles (Eph. 2:14-16). Paul is the pattern. Like Paul, we too stand before God *in Christ*, "complete in Him," because He died in our stead. And as we stand before God *in Christ*, so Christ stands before the world *in us*, as we pray men "in Christ's stead" to be reconciled to God. And so God still reveals His Son to the world through sinners saved by grace.

Our blessed Lord is still rejected, but we are glad for "the fellowship of His sufferings" and rejoice to fill up that which still remains of the afflictions of Christ because it shows forth the wonders of His grace.

These are dark days. Thousands of God's children are wondering how soon the Rapture of the Church may be (and the "Great Tribulation" and "the revelation of Jesus Christ in glory" to follow). These are questions we cannot answer. We can only praise God for "the revelation of Jesus Christ" in grace and seek earnestly to win the lost for Him while there is still time.

PAUL LEFT JERUSALEM

"Afterwards I came into the regions of Syria and Cilicia;

"And was unknown by face unto the churches of Judea which were in Christ:

"But they had heard only, That he which persecuted us in times past now preacheth the faith which once he destroyed.

"And they glorified God in me" (Gal. 1:21-24).

Why did Paul return to his native land, after seeing only Peter? That was of course where he had come from originally. Why did he go back there then? Why was he unknown by face to the churches of Judea? One would think that Peter would have taken this converted persecutor and showed him off, as it were, introduced him all over Judea to the believers there. But he did not do so. Why not?

"And he [Paul] spake boldly in the name of the Lord Jesus, and disputed against the Grecians:[3] but they went about to slay him. Which when the brethren knew, they brought him down to Caesarea, and sent him forth [back] to Tarsus" (Acts 9:29-30).

The fact is that Paul's visit with Peter was cut short by both God and man.

---

3. These were Greek-speaking Jews who had lived outside of Palestine.

His friends knew that this man was not safe at Jerusalem and sent him back home, but God had a hand in this too.

"And it came to pass, that, when I was come again to Jerusalem [his first visit after his conversion], even while I prayed in the temple, I was in a trance;[4]

"And saw Him saying unto me, Make haste, and get thee quickly out of Jerusalem: for they will not receive thy testimony concerning Me.

"And I said, Lord, they know that I imprisoned and beat in every synagogue them that believed on Thee:

"And when the blood of Thy martyr Stephen was shed, I also was standing by, and consenting unto his death, and kept the raiment of them that slew him.

"And He [Christ] said unto me, Depart: for I will send thee far hence unto the Gentiles" (Acts 22:17-21).

Paul had wanted to begin his ministry, like the twelve, at Jerusalem, but God said, "No Paul, I have concluded them in unbelief. I know that they will not listen to your testimony, so get out and go among the Gentiles."

So God, as well as man, sent Paul away from Jerusalem, away from the Pentecostal influence there, away from the influence of the Messianic church there. Why was this so important? God clearly showed that Paul's ministry was to be separate and distinct from that of the twelve. He was God's apostle of grace for the new dispensation of grace. God has a special message for us today found in the epistles of Paul, the chief of sinners, saved by grace! Beloved, remember this. All the Bible is for us but not all of it is written to us or about us.

4. The Greek word used here should be explained. It has nothing to do with some subjective vision; he actually saw Christ.

PAUL'S GOSPEL MESSAGE

"Now to him that is of power to stablish you according to my gospel, and the preaching of Jesus Christ, according to the revelation of the mystery, which was kept secret since the world began, But is now made manifest..." (Rom. 16:25-26).

Paul had his own particular message given to him by the Lord Jesus Christ Himself, and that is why he said in Romans 16:25—"Now to Him that is of power to stablish you according to *my* gospel." Some folk stumble over that. Three times Paul spoke of "*my* gospel" (Rom. 2:16; 16:25; II Tim. 2:8), and many times he said *"that gospel which I preach,"* and the *"gospel which was preached of me,"* and *"that gospel which you heard of me."* He frequently talked about his gospel. He could use this term because God had given him special revelation:

"For this cause I Paul, the prisoner of Jesus Christ for you Gentiles,

"If you have heard of the dispensation of the grace of God which is given me to you-ward:

"How that by revelation He made known unto me the mystery..." (Eph. 3:1-3).

Paul was dispensing grace, and so are we. "For by grace are you saved through faith; and that not of yourselves: it is the gift of God: Not of works, lest any man should boast" (Eph. 2:8,9).

WE ARE NOT SAVED BY KEEPING RULES

I once thought as do many others today, and as perhaps you do also, that one must keep the law of the Ten Commandments, and thereby please God, to be sure of heaven. I thought that the law was given as God's rule of life to help us to be good and to gain heaven at last; but the Word of God tells us that it was given for the opposite purpose.

"Now we know that what things soever the law saith, it saith to them who are under the law: that every mouth may be stopped, and all the world may become guilty before God" (Rom. 3:19).

It was given to show us that we are not good and that we need a savior. The law was given that every mouth might be stopped and all the world might be brought in guilty before God. That is a very important fact. "Moreover the law entered, that the offense might abound" (Rom. 5:20).

"Therefore by the deeds of the law there shall no flesh be justified in His sight: for by the law is the knowledge of sin" (Rom. 3:20).

Friends, if you want to be saved from the just penalty of sin, remember this: *There is one thing that God the judge of all expects from you: He wants you to stop saying things in your own defense!*

It is not sin that keeps men from heaven; it is attitude. God in His love has made provision for sin. He paid the penalty for sin; but He made *no provision* for a self-righteous attitude. Sometimes a defendant has to come to the place where his attorney says to him, "It will be to your advantage to plead guilty and throw yourself upon the mercy of the court." This is exactly our position. How can we talk about law-keeping when we are all guilty of *law-breaking?* Keep defending yourself and God will never save you, for He shall have no boasting in heaven. Confess your guilt! Throw yourself upon the mercy of God.

"Be it known unto you therefore, men and brethren, that through this Man [Jesus Christ] is preached unto you the forgiveness of sins:

"And by Him all that believe are justified from all things, from which ye could not be justified by the law of Moses" (Acts 13:38-39).

You and I find God's plan of salvation for today in the writings of God's apostle for today, the Apostle Paul. There are truths in other areas of Scripture, but the gospel of the grace of God is found only in the epistles of Paul, the apostle of grace.

PAUL'S GOSPEL WAS A NEW GOSPEL

Before we begin Chapter 2 of Paul's letter to the Galatians, there is one more detail to discuss about the last two verses of Chapter 1. It may seem insignificant at first, but I think that you will see the importance of it.

"But they had heard only, That he which persecuted us in times past now preacheth the faith which once he destroyed.

"And they glorified God in me" (Gal. 1:23-24).

It says in Verse 22 that Paul had been *unknown* to the churches of Judea, and that none of them had ever met him or seen him, but that they had heard of him—that he which persecuted them in times past "now preacheth the faith which once he destroyed."

Paul has given us proof after proof that his message was not the same as that which the twelve had been preaching. Yet the believers in Judea were saying, "...[he] now preacheth the faith which once he destroyed." Does this mean that Paul was, after all, preaching the same gospel which the twelve had been preaching? Some men have used this verse to seek to prove that this was the case. Paul used the greater part of Chapters One and Two to prove that his message was different, but this does not mean that what the twelve had been preaching was not true. They had preached Christ as the prophesied King, now risen from the dead. Paul had once denied this and had persecuted those who believed it.

Then one day Christ Himself had appeared to Saul, and he saw that He was alive, and Israel's rightful King. Thereafter, wherever he went, he sought to convince the Jews of that fact. After all, how could they trust Christ as Lord and Savior if they did not know that He was their true Messiah, risen from the dead? And how could they trust Him as the exalted dispenser of the grace that Paul presented, if He were an impostor whose dead body now lay in a Judean grave? Paul confirmed what Peter and the twelve had been preaching. In that sense, and to that degree, he preached the faith which once he had destroyed.

But even though he confirmed the message of the twelve, never once do we find him preaching the good news of the Kingdom—the good news that the Kingdom was about to be established. He never, like Peter, offered the Kingdom and the return of Jesus Christ if the Jews would repent.

The time for that was past. The establishment of the Messianic kingdom is, even yet in our own day, being held in abeyance until a future time; meanwhile, God offers reconciliation to his enemies by grace through faith. The King and His Kingdom had been rejected and the prophesied judgment was ready to fall, but in mercy and love God has said:

"But where sin abounded, grace did much more abound: That as sin hath reigned unto death, even so might grace reign through righteousness unto eternal life by Jesus Christ our Lord" (Rom. 5:20-21).

In this new program all things are of God. You have nothing to do. You cannot pay; you cannot pray; you cannot say anything; you cannot do things.

Paul was so intense about *his new gospel* that it seemed to some people that he was mad. One judge told him, "Much learning doth make thee mad" (Acts 26:24) to which he replied: "I am not mad, most noble Festus; but speak forth the words of truth and soberness" (ver. 25). But whether they believed that he was sober or mad, it was for their sake. He left it in God's hands:

"For whether we be beside ourselves, it is to God: or whether we be sober, it is for your cause.

"For the love of Christ constraineth us; because we thus judge, that if One died for all, then were all dead:

"And that He died for all, that they which live should not [now] henceforth live unto themselves, but unto Him which died for them, and rose again.

"Wherefore henceforth know we no man after the flesh: yea, though we have known Christ after the flesh, yet now henceforth know we Him no more.

"Therefore if any man be in Christ, he is a new creature: old things are passed away; behold, all things are become new" (II Cor. 5:13-17).

Chapter 4 — Galatians 2:1-21

PAUL'S UNIQUE APOSTLESHIP

FOURTEEN YEARS AFTER

"Then fourteen years after I went up again to Jerusalem with Barnabas, and took Titus with me also" (Gal. 2:1).

At this visit, fourteen years later,[1] we find another evidence of the distinctive character of Paul's ministry and message. Paul and Barnabas had been preaching God's grace to Gentiles at Antioch in Syria, far outside of Palestine, and a large church had been established there. This caused anxiety among the believers at Jerusalem who were trusting Jesus Christ of Nazareth as their Messiah.

This problem had come up earlier when Peter had gone to the household of Cornelius, the Roman centurion at Caesarea. Peter had *not* wanted to go there at first, but when messengers from Cornelius arrived, the Lord told Peter, "Go with them, doubting nothing: for I have sent them" (Acts 10:20). When Peter arrived, he said to Cornelius and his household: "Ye know how that it is an unlawful thing for a man that is a Jew to keep company, or come unto one of another nation; But God has showed me that I should not call any man common or unclean"[2] (ver. 28).

---

1. This fourteen years has to be added to the three years of Galatians 1:18, when Paul first went back to Jerusalem. His first visit was three years after his conversion, at which time he saw only one of the twelve apostles, and that for a few days only (Gal. 1:18). Meanwhile, he was *unknown* to the Judean church. In seventeen years he had conferred with only one of the twelve apostles.

2. The "uncleanness," here, was a ceremonial matter.

Cornelius, and his whole household of uncircumcised Gentiles, were wonderfully saved as Peter preached Christ (Messiah) to them, but the matter did not end there. When Peter got back to Jerusalem his Jewish brethren took him to task: "Thou wentest in to men uncircumcised; and didst eat with them" (Acts 11:3). All that Peter could do was tell them the facts of this single incident and say, "Forasmuch then as God gave them the like gift as He did unto us, who believed on the Lord Jesus Christ; what was I, that I could withstand God?" (Ver. 17).

We can imagine how the Judean believers felt when they heard that there was a whole church of uncircumcised Gentiles at Antioch. "How could this be genuine?" "How could these people be true believers and ignore God's law as to circumcision?" "And certain men which came down from Judea taught the brethren, and said, Except ye be circumcised after the manner of Moses, ye cannot be saved" (Acts 15:1). Everyone knew that circumcision was the basic requirement of the law that separated the Jewish nation from the licentious Gentiles around them.

These well-meaning Judeans did not settle anything. They unsettled matters, for Acts 15:2 goes on to say, "When therefore Paul and Barnabas had no small dissension and disputation with them, they [the church at Antioch] determined that Paul and Barnabas, and certain other of them, should go up to Jerusalem unto the apostles and elders about this question [problem]."

This explains why Paul went up to Jerusalem the second time, fourteen years after his first visit, and seventeen years after his conversion. Why all this dissension and disputation with the Judean believers? Why this extended trip by Paul to Jerusalem, if he were preaching the same thing among the Gentiles that Peter and the others were preaching in Judea? Here is strong *proof* of the distinctive character of Paul's apostleship and message.

"Even the mystery which hath been hid from ages and from generations, but now is made manifest to His saints" (Col. 1:26).

Through the centuries men of God have risen to recover and defend this great truth, but again and again their voices have been stilled as tradition and human opinion have made void the Word of God. The Church goes back to a commission never given to it, trying in vain to carry out the program in which there were signs and tongues and diverse miracles. Some in the Church are presently trying to imitate that program today. Many try to carry out a commission which commanded baptism for the remission of sins, and some even teach submission to the law of Moses. They go back again to a commission that says nothing of salvation by grace alone, nothing about salvation by faith without works, nothing about salvation through the shed blood of Christ, nothing about the joint body of Jewish and Gentile believers, and nothing about our heavenly position and blessings. They are following a commission that does not belong to the Body of Christ.

No wonder there is confusion and division in the Church! They ask, "Who is greater, Jesus or Paul?" and answer, "Jesus is greater," so they go back to the earthly ministry of Jesus, and the Sermon on the Mount, and the so-called Great Commission, which they certainly cannot obey. They take us back to Pentecost, forgetting that when Christ and His Kingdom were rejected, the glorified Lord from heaven commissioned *another* apostle, and all of us, to proclaim the glorious truth that "we have redemption through His blood, *the forgiveness of sins*, according to the riches of His grace" (Eph. 1:7). Salvation *through His blood* was unheard of before Paul and a *heresy* amongst the Jews (Acts 24:14).

"AND I TOOK TITUS WITH ME ALSO"

We recall that all of the 3,000 people who were baptized at Pentecost were Jews; they belonged to what the Bible calls the *circumcision*. Acts 11:19 says that until Peter went to that one Gentile household, the disciples had preached the Word *"to none but unto the Jews only."* When Peter, contrary to his own desires in the matter, was sent to the home of an *un*circumcised Gentile, he got into trouble with the Jews because of it.

In Galatians 2:1, we read Paul's words, *"and [I] took Titus with me also."* A Gentile taken to Jerusalem! This was evidently very important for Paul to take Titus, a Gentile believer, with him to Jerusalem. There were at least two reasons. One of them is found in verse 3:

"Neither Titus, who was with me, being a Greek, was compelled to be circumcised" (Gal. 2:3).

Titus was a test case. Paul wanted the Jewish believers to see for themselves an *uncircumcised Gentile* who had been genuinely saved and regenerated, entirely apart from circumcision or the law of Moses. He was determined to have them acknowledge that Titus was indeed a child of God.

The word *compelled*, in verse three—"Neither [was] Titus *compelled* to be circumcised"—infers that some tried to compel Titus to be circumcised, and others tried to intimidate both him and Paul.

"And that because of false brethren unawares brought in, who came in privily to spy out our liberty which we have in Christ Jesus, that they might bring us into bondage:

"To whom we gave place by subjection, no, not for an hour; that the truth of the gospel might continue with you" (Gal. 2:4-5).

The new evangelicalism of our day talks of love so much that there are very few who obey Paul's injunction to be "a good soldier of Jesus Christ" and "fight the good fight of faith." They do not want to put on "the armor" of Ephesians six and get into the *fight* against Satan and his *lies*. It is strange, though, that when we show them from the Scriptures the fallacies of their teaching, the love does not exactly overflow to us.

We are glad that Paul was a *good soldier* of Jesus Christ. When the legalizers from Jerusalem tried to bring the Gentiles under the bondage of the law of Moses, Paul did not say, "Well, let us have one of them speak at one of our meetings to give their viewpoint." Ah, no indeed. He did not say, "Let us dialogue about it." No! His pulpit was not a forum for the discussion of various views; it was a *pulpit* where the truth was proclaimed. He and Barnabas *disputed* with the legalizers. And when they arrived in Jerusalem, and were told that Titus must be circumcised, Paul "gave place by subjection, *no, not for an hour;* that the truth of the gospel might continue with you [Gentiles]."

The Gentiles were "without God," "having no hope," and "strangers from the covenants of promise"

(Eph. 2:12). They did not belong to the chosen nation. Yet God was saving Gentiles by grace through faith in the Christ who died for sin.

The new evangelicals would have said, "We all believe in Christ; there is room for us all. Let's all work together, forget our minor differences, and win souls to Christ." Not so with the great Apostle Paul. God had commissioned him to preach what he called in Galatians 3:23, "the faith which should afterwards be revealed." Like "a good soldier of Jesus Christ" he fought to maintain the purity of his message. The result was that he went back to Antioch with letters from the great Jerusalem Council acknowledging that Gentile believers were not under Moses' law. What a great victory he won that day, getting the Jewish apostles and elders to acknowledge this publicly by the shaking of hands before everyone.

A SECOND REASON

There was another special reason why Paul selected Titus to accompany him to Jerusalem on that occasion. We can get a glimpse of the kind of person Titus was by comparing him with Timothy, who, like Titus, became one of Paul's most faithful co-workers. From the two letters written to Timothy it is evident that he was cultured, refined, and a student of the Scriptures from his youth. The apostle wrote to him about his childhood, about his mother, and grandmother, and about his tears. He prescribed for his oft physical infirmity. At times he seems to have been concerned lest Timothy withdraw from the battle, for he urged him not to be ashamed but to endure hardness, and to be a partaker of those persecutions that went with preaching this wonderful message.

Titus was by nature a different character. This is evident from Paul's letter to him in which he addressed him as a general in the army might address his lieutenant. He directed him to "set in order the things that are wanting;" to "exhort and convince the gainsayers;" to stop the mouths of "unruly and vain talkers;" to "rebuke sharply" those who lived in sin, and to reject willful "heretics." All of this I have quoted directly from Titus (1:5,9,10,11,13 and 3:10).

An interesting comparison between Timothy and Titus can be found in what Paul had to say with regard to the visits they both made to Corinth. Timothy was, of course, far above the careless Corinthian believers both morally and spiritually. Yet when Paul sent Timothy to Corinth he had to write a letter in advance, exhorting them, "Now if Timotheus come, see that he may be with you *without fear*: for he worketh the work of the Lord, as I also do. Let no man therefore despise him..." (I Cor. 16:10-11). Later when Titus had been to Corinth and had returned, Paul wrote to the church there something very different: "And his [Titus] inward affection is more abundant toward you, whilst he remembereth the obedience of you all, how with *fear* and *trembling* ye received him" (II Cor. 7:15). Quite a difference!

The Corinthians were living very loosely, much as the Church today, and there was great permissiveness. Timothy was sent there to teach them, and Paul had to write ahead: "Do not make him feel shy or afraid; do not despise him. He is working the work of the Lord." But he did not have to write a letter ahead for Titus. When they knew that he was coming they began to tremble! He was a man of great character and authority. He was clearly the more robust character of the two men.

Paul needed a deputy like Titus. The apostle's anxiety and mental depression at Troas and in Macedonia was partly due to his apprehensions about the church at Corinth, but it was also due to his disappointment in not finding Titus whom he expected to be there. He failed to find him whose brilliant faith had so often refreshed and encouraged him, and he left Troas and did not enter the door that he says the Lord had opened to him "because I found not Titus my brother" (II Cor. 2:12-13).

Titus was clearly the man for Paul to take to Jerusalem as a test case for Gentile liberty from the law of Moses. Titus was outgoing, brilliant, warm-hearted, and truly devoted to the Lord; at the same time he was bold where the truth was concerned. Paul felt certain that he would not waver, and his confidence was justified.

Why take Titus, a Gentile, to Jerusalem and make the Jewish believers acknowledge that he was truly saved? Why make an issue of it? Obviously because the truth of the gospel of the grace of God was at stake here and it was precious to Paul. He knew how much it meant to Gentile believers not to let it become adulterated. How sad today to see how this precious message has become so adulterated and diluted that Christians are confused and do not know what to believe. It is in the epistles of Paul that we find God's message to us today.

"Not by works of righteousness which we have done, but according to His mercy He saved us, by the washing of regeneration, and renewing of the Holy Ghost" (Titus 3:5).

A PRIVATE CONFERENCE

"And I went up by revelation, and communicated unto them that gospel which I preach among the Gentiles, but privately to them which were of reputation, lest by any means I should run, or had run, in vain" (Gal. 2:2).

In Acts 15 we read that the church at Antioch sent Paul to Jerusalem. This was true, but there is more to this than that, of which Luke does not inform us. Paul declares that Christ sent him *by special revelation.*

However he was not sent to check with the twelve or to make sure that he was preaching the same message as they. Rather, the Lord sent him to Jerusalem to communicate to the leaders "that gospel which I [Paul] preach among the Gentiles." Why did he need to tell them what he had been preaching to the Gentiles, and why this phraseology if his gospel was exactly the same as their gospel? This is not the only place where he used such wording regarding the message which he preached. Three times he called his good news "my gospel" (Rom. 2:16; 16:25; II Tim. 2:8). Frequently he said, "Our gospel," or "that gospel which I preach unto you" or "that gospel which ye have received of me," or "the gospel which was preached of me." His epistles are filled with such phraseology. Why should he put such emphasis on the distinctiveness of his message if it were not distinct and separate from that which the twelve had been preaching?

In Galatians 2:2 it is quite natural to read, "I went up by revelation, and communicated unto them that gospel which I preach among the Gentiles." But he gave us further proof as he continued: "I went...privately to them which were of reputation, lest by any means I should run, or had run, in vain." Does this not prove that it was necessary for him to persuade the leaders at Jerusalem that this new message, "the gospel of the grace of God," was indeed God's message? It is also evident from the dissension and disputation that arose between Paul and the Judaizers, who had come to Antioch, that Paul's gospel was distinct from that of the twelve.

This is proof that *the gospel of the grace of God* committed to him was new and different from *the gospel of the Kingdom* which had been committed to the twelve. And it is proof that the commission given to him, and to us, is different from the Great Commission given earlier to the twelve.

Galatians, Chapter 2, shows the basic differences in their messages. The twelve had preached Christ as Israel's King and, at that point, had not yet learned that through His death the Mosaic law was to be set aside. Paul's whole message to the Gentiles was based on the setting aside of the law, and the unfolding of the dispensation of the grace of God and the all-sufficient finished work of Jesus Christ at Calvary.

A QUESTION OF AUTHORITY

"But of these who seemed to be somewhat, (whatsoever they were, it maketh no matter to me: God accepteth no man's person:) for they who seemed to be somewhat in conference added nothing to me" (Gal. 2:6).

The Lord chose twelve apostles, and when one of them betrayed Him, He instructed the eleven how to choose another. When Matthias was chosen, he was numbered with the eleven "and they were all filled with the Holy Ghost" (Acts 2:4). So we see that Christ had his twelve apostles again. What about this other apostle, Paul? God later raised him up as *another* apostle, and he had to prove the validity of his apostleship to the leaders in the Jewish church at Jerusalem. He also had to prove the validity of his God-given message, the gospel of the grace of God, with its good news of salvation apart from the religious rites or ceremonies of the Mosaic law. He was presenting salvation by grace through faith in the finished, all-sufficient, work of the Lord Jesus Christ at Calvary.

In Galatians 2:6, Paul made a strong statement about the leaders of the church at Jerusalem: "But of these who seemed to be somewhat, (whatsoever they were, it maketh no matter to me: God accepteth no man's person:) for they who seemed to be somewhat in conference added nothing to me." Is it not strange that Paul should describe the leaders, James, Peter, and John as those "who seemed to be somewhat"?

There was good reason for it. The James referred to here is not the same James of the four Gospels, "Peter, James, and John." The apostle James had already been killed by wicked King Herod (Acts 12:2). The James referred to here in Galatians 2 is James "the Lord's brother" (Gal. 1:19) and for that reason he had attained superiority over the twelve apostles and the church at Jerusalem. This was not right for several reasons. His physical relationship to Christ did not make him (or any man) any more spiritual, or any greater, than another. It did not qualify him in any way to preside over the church at Jerusalem. This is brought out in the four Gospels, and nowhere more clearly than in Matthew 12:47-50:

"...Behold, Thy mother and Thy brethren stand without, desiring to speak with Thee.

"But He answered and said unto him that told Him, Who is My mother? and who are My brethren?

"And He stretched forth His hand toward His disciples, and said, Behold My mother and My brethren!

"For whosoever shall do the will of My Father which is in heaven, the same is My brother, and sister, and mother."

He was not belittling His beloved family, but He was showing His uniqueness: He was the Son of God as well as the Son of man. No human being—not His mother, nor His brothers, were any closer to Him, nor had any more influence over Him, than anyone else.

Secondly, the Lord had made *Peter*, not James, the head of the apostles and of the Pentecostal church at Jerusalem. We find this in the Gospel records: "And I will give unto *thee* the keys of the kingdom of heaven: and whatsoever *thou* shalt bind on earth shall be bound in heaven: and whatsoever *thou* shalt loose on earth shall be loosed in heaven" (Matt. 16:19); and in early Acts: "Peter stood up in the midst of the disciples, and said..." (1:15). "Peter, standing up with the eleven" (2:14), "Peter and the other apostles..." (Acts 5:29). Peter was always at the head because Christ made him the head of the twelve and of the Messianic or Pentecostal church. James, the Lord's brother, was *not* one of the twelve. "For neither did His brethren believe in Him" (John 7:5). What was he doing as the chairman of the council? Why had Peter relinquished his God-given position, and why had the other apostles permitted it?

James was not even a believer in our Lord (Psa. 69:8; John 7:5) until after His resurrection:

"After that, He [Christ] was seen of Cephas, then of the twelve:....After that, He was seen of James; then of all the apostles. And last of all He was seen of me also, as of one born out of due time" (I Cor. 15:5,7-8).

Thus Paul calls the twelve, "them of reputation" (Gal. 2:2), "those who seemed to be somewhat" (Gal. 2:6), and "those who seemed to be pillars" (Gal. 2:9). He also said "in conference [they] added nothing to me" (Gal. 2:6). What could those former fishermen and tax collectors tell him about God's Old Testament prophecies and their program? What could they tell him about Messiah and the promised Kingdom? He was "a Hebrew of the Hebrews" (Phil. 3:5), "a Pharisee, the son of a Pharisee" (Acts 23:6), brought up in the Scriptures under the teaching of Gamaliel (Acts 22:3). He was the greatest Pharisee of his time (Phil. 3:5; Acts 23:6). Paul knew the Old Testament Scriptures far better than they. He knew, by the revelation of Jesus Christ, how those Scriptures had been fulfilled in Christ for he had now seen Him glorified in heaven.

The twelve added nothing to Paul (Gal. 2:6,7), but he added something to them. This agrees with Galatians 2:2 because if the gospels were the same, why did Paul go up by revelation, *and communicate unto them* that gospel which he preached among the Gentiles?

THAT HISTORIC HANDSHAKE

"But contrariwise, when they saw that the gospel of the uncircumcision was committed unto me, as the gospel of circumcision was unto Peter;

"(For he that wrought effectually in Peter to the apostleship of the circumcision, the same was mighty in me toward the Gentiles;)

"And when James, Cephas [Peter], and John, who seemed to be pillars, perceived the grace that was given unto me, they gave to me and Barnabas the right hands of fellowship; that we should go unto the heathen, and they unto the circumcision" (Gal. 2:7-9).

Verse 7 says that they saw the validity of his argument and of his apostleship and message. Verse 9 says that they perceived "the grace that was given unto me."

Many people have asked what is meant by the terms "the uncircumcision" and "the circumcision." Paul said that the good news of the circumcision was given to Peter. He did not say, "to James." He specifically said "Peter" because he did not recognize James as the leader of the council. He recognized the council as a whole but he said that this message was given to Peter, and that God wrought effectively in him (Peter) to the gospel of the circumcision. What is that gospel of the circumcision?

Abraham was given the rite of circumcision to separate himself and his circumcised seed from the licentious Gentiles all about him. It was in connection with this great covenant, that through Abraham's seed the nations would be blessed, that Peter preached "good news" to Israel. They were the seed of Abraham, the physical offspring. They were called the circumcision. Peter told the Jews: "Ye are the children of the prophets, and of the covenant which God made with our fathers, saying unto Abraham, And in thy seed shall all the kindreds of the earth be blessed. Unto you first God, having raised up His Son Jesus, sent Him to bless you, in turning away every one of you from his iniquities" (Acts 3:25,26).

They had rejected the King and His Kingdom. Peter therefore called upon them to acknowledge Jesus Christ as their true Messiah so that He might come back and the wonderful covenant might be fulfilled (Acts 3:19-21). It was through them, the circumcision, the offspring of Abraham, that all the nations of the earth were to be blessed. This was the good news, the gospel of the circumcision, that was committed to Peter.

Paul, however, declares that "the gospel of the *uncircumcision* was committed to me" (Gal. 2:7), and that Christ "was mighty in me toward the Gentiles" (Ver. 8).

We must remember that before Abraham was ever circumcised, as a Gentile to whom God had made no previous promises, he was justified by faith alone:

"What shall we say then that Abraham our father, as pertaining to the flesh, hath found? For if Abraham were justified by works, he hath whereof to glory; but not before God. For what saith the Scripture? Abraham believed God, and it was counted unto him for righteousness" (Rom. 4:1-3).

God revealed Himself to Abraham. Abraham believed God and his faith was counted to him for righteousness. But the question arises: "How was it then reckoned [to Abraham]? when he was in circumcision, or in uncircumcision?" And the answer: "Not in circumcision, but in uncircumcision" (Rom. 4:10). It is on *this* basis that Paul proclaimed the wonderful gospel of the UNcircumcision":

"Now to him that worketh is the reward not reckoned of grace, but of debt. But to him that worketh not, but believeth on him that justifieth the ungodly, his faith is counted for righteousness" (Rom. 4:4,5).

This is the message Paul defended at the Jerusalem council. This is why he took that wonderfully converted Gentile, Titus, to Jerusalem. He wanted to show a true man of God, a Gentile, who had not gone through any rites, but who had simply trusted Jesus Christ as his Lord and Savior.

"When James, Cephas, and John...perceived the grace that was given unto me, they gave to me and Barnabas the right hands of fellowship" (Gal. 2:9).

This is yet another strong proof of Paul's unique apostleship and message. Both Peter and John confirmed this statement in their letters later, for their epistles are filled with what theologians call "Paulinisms." In fact, Peter closed his last letter with the words:

"And account that the longsuffering of our Lord is salvation; even as our beloved brother Paul also according to the wisdom given unto him hath written unto you...But grow in grace, and in the knowledge of our Lord and Savior Jesus Christ. To Him be glory both now and forever. Amen" (II Pet. 3:15,18).

FINANCIAL HELP FOR THE JERUSALEM CHURCH

How many proofs we have already found of the distinctive character of Paul's apostleship and of the change in dispensation that came with him! What a blunder the Church in general has made in contending that Paul was simply another apostle and that he preached the same message and practiced the same program as the twelve. They had originally been sent "into all the world to preach the gospel to every creature" (Mark 16:15), "and teach all nations" (Matt. 28:19), which of course included the Gentiles. But our Lord also told these same twelve, "Whatsoever ye shall bind on earth shall be bound in heaven: and whatsoever ye shall loose on earth shall be loosed in heaven" (Matt. 18:18).

In Galatians we are considering an occasion on which both *"loosing"* and *"binding"* took place. The twelve, and the leaders of the church at Jerusalem, under the guidance of the Holy Spirit, *loosed* themselves from the so-called Great Commission, and agreed to *bind* Paul as *"the apostle of the Gentiles"* (Rom. 11:13) and to confine their ministry to the nation Israel.

"Only they would that we should remember the poor; the same which I also was forward to do" (Gal. 2:10).

The kingdom program, with its "all things common...possessions and goods [sold], and parted them to all men" (Acts 2:44,45) was *failing*. This is further proof of Paul's apostleship and message. After carefully reading Galatians, Chapter 2, how can men of God in the pulpit today say that the commission given to the twelve is our commission today!? This is very important because, under the prophetic Kingdom program which was in force while our Lord Jesus Christ was on earth, and until after Pentecost, the Jews were told not to lay up store for the future.

In my booklet entitled, "The Ant and the Raven," I deal with a seeming contradiction in the Bible. Solomon pointed to the ant, and said, "Go to the ant, thou sluggard [you lazy man]; consider her ways, and be wise" (Prov. 6:6). She lays up store in the summer for the time when the rain and the winter comes, so that she will be able to survive. The person who does not do this is lazy or a fool.

"Consider the ravens: for they neither sow nor reap; which neither have storehouse nor barn; and God feedeth them: how much more are ye better than the fowls?" (Luke 12:24). The raven does not have storehouses or barns, does not put away anything for the winter, yet the Lord cares for the ravens. "Therefore, I say unto you, Take no thought for your life..." (Ver. 22). In other words, Do *not* lay up anything for the morrow, but trust the Lord to take care of you. This was because under the Kingdom they were not to lay up store for the future, but were to have all things in common.

We may try to explain this away, but our Lord stated clearly to the rich young ruler, "...sell whatsoever thou hast, and give to the poor..." (Mark 10:21). Jesus said to the twelve as He sent them out, "Provide neither gold, nor silver, nor brass in your purses" (Matt. 10:9-10). In Luke 12:32-33, He said to all of His disciples, "Fear not, little flock; for it is your Father's good pleasure to give you the Kingdom. Sell that ye have, and give alms."

Many people quote Luke 12:32 but they do not practice verse 33, and it is seldom quoted. The apostles, however, were not only instructed to pray "Thy Kingdom come," but were also to add, "Give us this day our daily bread" (Matt. 6:10,11) in anticipation of the Kingdom of Heaven.

At Pentecost, when they were "all filled with the Holy Spirit," they actually began the practice of this program.

"And all that believed were together, and had all things common; And [they] sold their possessions and goods, and parted them to all men, as every man had need" (Acts 2:44-45).

Have you ever seen a multitude of even five Christians fully of one heart and one soul? Here there were 5,000, and nowhere is it stated more emphatically that they were all filled with Spirit:

> **"And the multitude of them that believed were of one heart and of one soul: neither said any of them that ought of the things which he possessed was his own; but they had all things common....Neither was there any among them that lacked: for as many as were possessors of lands or houses sold them, and brought the prices of the things that were sold, And laid them down at the apostles' feet: and distribution was made unto every man according as he had need" (Acts 4:32,34-35).**

Later, after the Kingdom had again been rejected, after Stephen had been stoned, and after Paul had been raised up, the eleventh chapter of Acts records that a delegation was sent from Jerusalem to the Antioch church. In that delegation was a prophet "named Agabus, [who] signified by the Spirit that there should be great dearth throughout all the world" (Acts 11:28). Now this Jerusalem church, as the Lord had commanded them, *had nothing in store*, anticipating the Millennial kingdom. At Antioch, however, the record states that *they were not having everything in common*, and that they sent financial aid to the church at Jerusalem.

Clearly, the Kingdom program at Jerusalem had broken down. "Then the disciples, every man according to his ability, determined to send relief unto the brethren which dwelt in Judea: Which also they did, and sent it to the elders by the hands of Barnabas and Saul" (Acts 11:29,30).

Paul later wrote about "the poor saints which are at Jerusalem" (Rom. 15:26), and he had much to say about *the collections* from all the Gentile churches to the church at Jerusalem. But in writing to Timothy, do you see how the program had changed:

"But if any provide not for his own, and specially for those of his own house, he hath denied the faith, and is worse than an infidel" (I Tim. 5:8).

A STERN REBUKE FROM A DEAR BROTHER

"But when Peter was come to Antioch, I withstood him to the face, because he was to be blamed.

"For before that certain came from James, he did eat with the Gentiles: but when they were come, he withdrew and separated himself, fearing them which were of the circumcision.

"And the other Jews dissembled likewise with him; insomuch that Barnabas also was carried away with their dissimulation.

"But when I saw that they walked not uprightly according to the truth of the gospel, I said unto Peter before them all, If thou, being a Jew, livest after the manner of Gentiles, and not as do the Jews, why compellest thou the Gentiles to live as do the Jews?" (Gal. 2:11-14).

It must not be supposed that the communication from the church at Jerusalem, even though confirmed by credited witnesses, had brought complete and lasting peace to Antioch from the trouble which the legalizers had stirred there. The influence of those Judaizers was to be felt for a long time to come; in fact, we are still feeling this legalistic tendency in professing churches today. It was undoubtedly at this point in the history of the Acts of the Apostles that we must place Peter's visit to Antioch and his stern *rebuke* by Paul. It took place after the council at Jerusalem and before the separation between Paul and Barnabas.

The record of this incident is given to us here in Paul's letter to the Galatians. This is the second time that Peter got into trouble over the Gentile question, and there is a significant connection between this incident at Antioch and the previous one at Jerusalem. Jerusalem was the headquarters of the *Jewish* church; Antioch was the headquarters of the *Gentile* church. When Peter returned to Jerusalem after ministering to Cornelius, they that were of the circumcision contended with him (Acts 11:2). At Jerusalem he was called to account for eating with the Gentiles (Ver. 3). At Antioch he was rebuked because he stopped eating with the Gentiles (Gal. 2:12).

At Jerusalem he had rightly defended his action; he had done right by eating with the Gentiles. At Antioch he had *no defense* to offer for he was wrong; he should have continued to eat with, and have fellowship with the Gentiles.

There was naturally a keen interest at Jerusalem concerning the developments among the Gentiles. It was soon after the council at Jerusalem that Peter traveled to Antioch to visit the church there himself. It must have seemed like a further fulfillment of the sheet vision that God had given him when he sat to eat with those Gentiles and enjoyed the fellowship. But then something happened. A report came that certain people from James' party had arrived at Antioch. As soon as the announcement was made, a separation took place among those who had been thus enjoying each other's fellowship. First Peter withdrew and separated himself, fearing them of the circumcision.[3]

3. What an influence James and his party had over these men to be able to intimidate even the chief of the apostles in that way! But James had ascended to the supremacy contrary to our Lord's specific instructions; he was the one who presided over the council and said, "Wherefore my sentence is..." (Acts 15:19).

Peter's separating himself from the Gentiles was, of course, cowardly. Not only cowardly, it was hypocritical as well, for if Peter's fellowship with the Gentiles had been acceptable to God before, why was it wrong when people came from James? Then as a result of Peter's action the "other Jews dissembled likewise with him; insomuch that Barnabas also was carried away with their dissimulation" (Gal. 2:13). Think of it!

It must have been heart-breaking for Paul to see Barnabas deserting him. It was Barnabas who had first brought him to the apostles when they were afraid of him (Acts 9:27). It was Barnabas with whom he had accomplished so much among the Gentiles under God's guidance. Barnabas had stood with him against the intrusion of the Judaizers. And, at the Jerusalem council Barnabas had evidently stood with Paul without wavering, for Paul's words, "We gave place by subjection, no, not for an hour," follow the statement, "I went up to Jerusalem with Barnabas."

As to the results of the council: "They gave to me and Barnabas the right hands of fellowship; that we should go unto the heathen, and they unto the circumcision" (Gal. 2:9). But at Antioch, Barnabas followed Peter in his cowardly and hypocritical separation from the Gentiles. As a result, Paul *"withstood Peter to the face"* and rebuked him before them all.

The question may well be asked here whether Paul was not making more trouble in the assembly than Peter and the others were making by withdrawing. Surely feelings must have been running high, and relations must have been strained as Paul openly and publicly rebuked the great apostle from Jerusalem. Was Paul forgetting the dignity of Peter's position—that Peter had been appointed the chief of the twelve apostles by the Lord Himself, and that he had been used to lead thousands to Messiah even before Paul was saved? Was Paul practicing what he preached and later wrote to believers, that they should walk, "with all lowliness and meekness, with longsuffering, forbearing one another in love; endeavoring to keep the unity of the Spirit in the bond of peace" (Eph. 4:2,3)?

Was Paul the troublemaker in Antioch? Not at all, for the trouble was more subtle than appears on the surface. God had been breaking down the middle wall of partition between Jew and Gentile (Eph. 2:14), and, of the apostles at Jerusalem, no one knew this better than Peter. He had been shown in a vision that God wanted him to eat and have fellowship with the Gentiles in Cornelius' home, and he had helped Paul's cause in the dispute at the Jerusalem council by reminding the Judaizers of that incident. He had declared that "God, which knoweth the hearts, bear them witness, giving them the Holy Ghost, even as He did unto us; And put no difference between us and them, purifying their hearts by faith" (Acts 15:8-9).

Peter had known and testified to the oneness of Jewish and Gentiles believers in Christ, but at Antioch he *"withdrew"* himself from the Gentiles. He had done it hypocritically for fear of those of James' party. He may have done it with the most kindly attitude, with many apologies and explanations to the Gentiles, but the fact remained that he was causing a division among believers. Nor was this merely a local matter. It was a repudiation of the decision of the council with which he previously had so much to do, and it was a *repudiation* of God's revealed will.

What if Paul had kept silent? Had he not spoken up boldly, a division might well have started in Antioch which would have opened an irreparable breach between the Jewish and Gentile believers. The truth that all believers are one Body in Christ could have been negated. Silence in such a case would not have helped to keep the unity of the Spirit, but would have helped to break it. Peter may have excused himself most apologetically, and, though Paul's open rebuke may have seemed harsh and unkind, it was *Peter* who was causing the division; it was Paul who was endeavoring to restore unity.

What should our attitude be in such cases? If we speak out against error, some will remind us that we should "endeavor to keep the unity of the Spirit." But let us fix it well in our minds that silence in the face of the present confusion would be as wrong as the divisions themselves. If we truly believe that we should be one, then we should know the remedy for the division, our seven-fold oneness in Christ:

"There is one Body, and one Spirit, even as ye are called in one hope of your calling; One Lord, one faith, one baptism, One God and Father of all, who is above all, and through all, and in you all" (Eph. 4:4-6).

In the incident at Antioch it was Peter, rather than Paul, who "was to be blamed." We have the inspired Word of God to prove that. He had been guilty of dissimulation; he had not walked uprightly. He had made himself a transgressor in his attempt to build again the barrier which he himself had helped to break down—the middle wall of partition between Jew and Gentile. While Paul's rebuke may have rankled in his bosom for some time, he would have realized that had not Paul leaped to support him as he stumbled, he might have dragged many down with him in his fall. Thus not only did Peter recover from the rebuke, but the last person he mentioned in his writings was *"our beloved brother Paul"* (II Peter 3:15).

ONE BODY

That the day of the dispensation of grace was dawning brighter and brighter is shown by Paul's ascendency over Peter, the chief apostle to the Jews, in their three recorded meetings thus far. At the first meeting Paul acquainted Peter with his call and commission (Gal. 1:18), at the second he received public recognition from him (Gal. 2:9), and at the third he rebuked him as his superior (Gal. 2:14).

What a lesson on the oneness of believers in Christ! How serious it is to depart from the faith and "the truth of the gospel" and so to break "the unity of the Spirit." Consider these passages of Scripture about this joint-body of believing Jews and Gentiles and our oneness in Christ:[4]

"So we, being many, are one body in Christ, and every one members one of another" (Rom. 12:5).

"For by one Spirit are we all baptized into one Body, whether we be Jews or Gentiles..." (I Cor. 12:13).

"For ye are all the children of God by faith in Christ Jesus. For as many of you as have been baptized into

4. Some people think that the Body of Christ did not begin until after Acts 28. This cannot be true because we read about it in Paul's early epistles. See the author's booklet, *The Early Ministry of Paul*.

Christ have put on Christ. There is neither Jew nor Greek,...for ye are all one in Christ Jesus" (Gal. 3:26-28).

Do you see that this baptism into Christ could only be wrought by the Holy Spirit who makes us *one* with Christ? Compare all of these Scriptures with what we find in Ephesians 2, written after the close of Acts:

> **"For He is our peace, who hath made both one, and hath broken down the middle wall of partition between us;...That he might reconcile both unto God in one body by the cross, having slain the enmity thereby" (Eph. 2:14,16).**

Is it not plain that Paul's ministry in the Book of Acts tells the story of the breaking down of the middle wall of partition? Is it not plain that the oneness of Jewish and Gentile believers in Christ was already being shown *before* Acts 28, during Paul's early ministry while God was in the process of setting the Kingdom program aside?

A study of Acts 15 will show that Peter had no small part in swaying the council at Jerusalem toward the recognition of Gentile believers by the Jewish church. He had shown how God had "put *no difference* between us and them, purifying their hearts by faith" (Acts 15:9). As the leaders of the twelve had extended "the right hands of fellowship" to Paul and Barnabas, it had become evident that the Jewish believers could *now* fellowship with Gentile believers. Peter had seen this very clearly and had gone to Antioch to enjoy it.

Picture the scene before the legalizers arrived. Believing Jews and Gentiles were all around one table rejoicing and sharing in Christ. But when the Jerusalem Jews appeared, Peter withdrew and separated himself, fearing those of the circumcision. This was the real trouble at Antioch, not Paul's rebuke, nor his protest. It is easy to see what would have happened if Paul had not spoken out. It was not a question of "endeavoring to keep the unity of the Spirit." That unity had already been broken and needed to be restored. It was no lack of humility on Paul's part when he "withstood Peter to the face" and rebuked him before them all. It was the only right and honest thing to do, and it was necessary since the whole assembly was being affected by Peter's action. Though Paul's rebuke may not have had immediate results, it was nevertheless a lesson to the church. It was a lesson to Peter. It is a lesson to us today as to the importance of the unity of the Body of Christ. How wonderful that we can each be a member of that Body and we need not care about names like Baptists, Presbyterians, Methodists, Lutherans, Catholics, and so on. We can each be a member of the true Church, the Body of Christ, by believing in the Lord Jesus Christ, trusting Him as Lord and Savior.

"Believe on the Lord Jesus Christ, and thou shalt be saved." The moment you are saved you have joined that Church, and you can never be "dismembered" from it because you are part of the Body of Christ.

THE FAITH OF CHRIST

A Precious Blessing Too Few Believers Appreciate

It is amazing that so few of God's people understand the simple significance of one of the most precious phrases in the Pauline epistles: *"the faith of Christ."*

The apostle uses this phrase no less than seven times in his letters to the saints, yet the vast majority of believers today utterly fail to understand, yea, even *mis*understand its wonderful meaning.

As the emphasis in evangelism today is placed upon man rather than upon God, so has the truth about faith *in* Christ been given the precedence over the truth about "the faith *of* Christ," until it has all but crowded it out.

Two Aspects of Faith

The Scriptures speak of faith in two ways: *objectively* and *subjectively. Objectively,* faith is simple *trust in another,* or in what another has said or done; it moves toward an object—it is the *character* which constitutes one *worthy of trust. Objectively,* faith is associated with what one *does;* he *believes* in *another. Subjectively,* it is a *quality* one *possesses*: fidelity, dependability, *worthiness to be believed in.* Thus, if I have faith in you, you had better keep faith with me or I can no longer trust you. Any complete English dictionary will give these two definitions of the word "faith," and the same is true of its Greek equivalent, *pistis.*

The Scriptures also speak of "*the* faith" as that which is to be believed (I Cor. 16:13, etc.), but for the present, we confine our discussion to *faith* in its two-fold significance as shown above.

The adjective "faithful," in both English and Greek, is also used in these two ways.

Abraham is called "faithful" because he *believed*

God implicitly (Gal. 3:6,9). He was *faith-full,* abounding in faith toward God.

But on the other hand, *God* is called faithful, not because He believes in others, but *because He is true to His Word.* Thus we may believe what He says, because "He is faithful that promised" (Heb. 10:23). Abraham is called "faithful" in the *objective* sense; God is called *faithful* in the *subjective* sense. Abraham was *"faith-full"* toward God and God proved *"faithful"* to him.

Objective Faith

The Scriptures have much to say about objective faith. For example, in Romans 4 we read that:

"...ABRAHAM BELIEVED GOD, and it was counted unto him for righteousness" (Ver. 3).

And thus:

"...TO HIM THAT WORKETH NOT, BUT BELIEVETH ON HIM THAT JUSTIFIETH THE UNGODLY, HIS FAITH IS COUNTED FOR RIGHTEOUSNESS" (Ver. 5).

This is the *objective* aspect of faith; trust in another or in what another has said or done.

Subjective Faith

But the Scriptures, especially Paul's epistles, also have much to say about *subjective* faith. For example, we read in Romans 3:3:

"What if some did not believe? shall their unbelief make THE FAITH OF GOD without effect?"

Here "the faith of God" is clearly His *fidelity.* His *worthiness to be believed.* The apostle says, in effect: "What if some refused to trust Him, does that affect His perfect trustworthiness?" This same truth is stated in II Timothy 2:13, though in somewhat different phraseology: "If we *believe* not, yet He abideth *faithful*"; i.e., though we fail to trust Him, yet He remains infinitely worthy of our trust.

A good example of subjective faith, or the lack of it, is found in II Thessalonians 3:2, where Paul asks for prayer,

"...that we may be DELIVERED from UNREASONABLE and WICKED MEN; for ALL MEN HAVE NOT FAITH."

The apostle surely does not refer here to those who did not *believe in Christ,* but to those who themselves *were not to be trusted;* "unreasonable" and "wicked" men, from whom he needed to be "delivered."

The Faith of Christ

As we have pointed out, the "faith of Christ" is referred to seven times in the Pauline epistles. Let us now examine these passages and see how *our* (objective) "faith" is always based upon *His* (subjective) "faith." It would be foolish of us to "exercise faith" in one who did not "keep faith"; to be "faith-full" toward one who was not "faithful." Conversely, we believe that were the "faith of Christ" given greater emphasis in our preaching, more people would exercise "faith in Christ," both for salvation and spiritual blessing.

"The Promise"

"But the Scripture hath concluded all under sin, that the promise, by FAITH OF JESUS CHRIST, might be given to them that believe" (Gal. 3:22).

It should be carefully noted that this passage does not refer to the historical act of God in concluding all in unbelief, as does Romans 11:32, but rather to the fact that the *Scriptures* had long ago concluded all under sin (e.g., Psa. 53:2,3). Thus also, the "promise," in Galatians 3:22, evidently refers to the central promise of redemption, for as the mysteries of Paul's epistles revolve around a central "mystery," so the promises of the Old Testament Scriptures revolve around a central promise: that of redemption.

The point here is that since man could not accomplish his own redemption, the Scriptures concluded all under sin so that the thing promised might be given to believers by the *"faith of Christ,"* i.e., *His* perfect fidelity.

That this phrase does not refer to man's faith in Christ is evident from the fact that man's faith in Him is referred to in a separate phrase at the end of the verse: *"them that believe."* Those who "believe" receive redemption by, or on the basis of, *His "faith,"* or *fidelity*.

While "His promise," in Ephesians 3:6, may refer to the promise God made to Himself with regard to believers before the world began (Titus 1:2), this passage also teaches that Gentile believers are made "joint heirs" with Jewish believers, in a "joint body," and "partakers of His promise IN CHRIST by the gospel." This is another way of saying that our salvation is based on what Christ has done and what He is.

Thus our faith in Christ, necessary as it is to salvation, must always be secondary to "the faith of Christ." We can place our trust in Him only because He is so infinitely trustworthy.

Righteousness

With regard to the righteousness which believers possess in the sight of God, Paul places great emphasis on the fact that this is conferred upon us because of the fidelity of *Christ*, not because *we* proved true to God.

After demonstrating the impotence of the law to save the sinner, the apostle goes on to say, in Romans 3:21,22:

"But now the righteousness of God without the law is manifested...even the righteousness of God WHICH IS BY FAITH OF JESUS CHRIST...."

And to emphasize the fact that he does *not* here refer to faith *in* Christ, but to Christ's *fidelity*, he *then* adds: "unto all and *upon all them that believe*." Thus Christ's "faith" (fidelity) and man's faith are complementary. Those who "believe" are

"...JUSTIFIED FREELY BY HIS GRACE THROUGH THE REDEMPTION THAT IS IN CHRIST JESUS" (Ver. 24).

So too the apostle himself counted all his "gain" as "loss," that he might win Christ,

"And be found in Him, not having mine own righteousness, which is of the law, but THAT WHICH IS THROUGH THE FAITH OF CHRIST..." (Phil. 3:9).

And once again he *then* adds: "the righteousness which is of God by faith," i.e., by *believing Him*.

Here indeed man's failure and Christ's faithfulness are set in vivid and striking contrast. Who could have been more zealous of the law than Paul? Who could have lived more blamelessly in its sight? Yet it probed beneath the surface and condemned him to death as a vile sinner. He saw that he could not stand before God in his own false righteousness, but only in that true righteousness offered to the sinner by the faith, the fidelity, *of Christ* and appropriated by faith *in Christ.*

In Galatians 2:15,16 the Holy Spirit emphasizes these truths in the strongest way in the record of Paul's rebuke of Peter at Antioch, where Peter had shown anything but fidelity to his Lord. Says Paul to Peter:

"We who are Jews by nature, and not sinners of the Gentiles,

"Knowing that a man is not justified by the works of the law, but by THE FAITH OF JESUS CHRIST, even we have believed in Jesus Christ, that we might be justified by THE FAITH OF CHRIST, and not by the works of the law: for by the works of the law shall no flesh be justified."

In this intense, though controlled, outburst the Apostle Paul emphasizes and re-emphasizes not only the fact that man cannot be justified by the law, but that even his faith is but the response and complement to "the faith of Christ," who made the sinner's justification possible.

Access

Access to God logically follows justification. It is *sin* that separates from God, and there is no reason why those who are justified should be barred from His presence.

Some who see in the great Pauline revelation little besides a heavenly position and spiritual blessings, question whether believers today actually do have *access* into the presence of God. These argue that according to the Ephesian epistle we *already have* a position in the heavenlies at God's right hand and *have already* been blessed with "all spiritual blessings" there. Why, then, need they—indeed, how *can* they—*enter* God's presence?

The fact is, however, that this is positional truth which, in this life, is *experienced* only by faith. We *occupy* our heavenly position only by faith. We *appropriate* our spiritual blessings only by faith. If this were not so the apostle would not need to exhort us to "seek" and "set our affection" on "those things which are above, where Christ sitteth on the right hand of God" (Col. 3:1,2).

In the light of all this we would now ask the reader: How have you done lately? Have you been living in the heavenlies *experientially?* Have you been *experiencing* and *enjoying all* the spiritual blessings which are yours in Christ? How far we all come short here! How often we need to seek again those things which are above by fellowship with God at the throne of grace and in His Word, which is forever settled in heaven!

Thus it is that *this same Ephesian epistle*, which tells us of our high position and our great blessings in Christ, *also* tells us that we have *access* to God. And how is it that free access can still be offered to those who have failed so grossly to appreciate and appropriate their heavenly position and blessings? The answer is: *the faith of Christ.* It is only because of *His* fidelity, because *He* is so true to *His* pledge at Calvary that we are bidden to enter unashamed before His holy presence.

The passage in Ephesians which tells us this is Chapter 3 and Verse 12:

"In whom we have boldness and access with confidence BY THE FAITH OF HIM."

As we say, we may enter into His presence because He is true to the pledge made at Calvary. We have "boldness to enter into the holiest *by the blood of Jesus*" (Heb. 10:19). But His "faith" extends even further than this. Comparing our Lord with the calloused high priests of Old Testament times, the apostle says, in Hebrews 4:15,16:

"For we have not an high priest which cannot be touched with the feeling of our infirmities....

"Let us therefore come boldly unto the throne of grace, that we may obtain mercy, and find grace to help in time of need."

The feeble faith with which we enter the presence of God is but a response to "the faith of Christ." It is *"by Him"* that "we have access by faith into this *grace* wherein we stand" (Rom. 5:2).

THE CHRISTIAN LIFE

Finally, in Galatians 2:20 the apostle declares:

"...the life which I now live in the flesh I live by THE FAITH OF THE SON OF GOD, who loved me, and gave Himself for me."

How believers need to learn this blessed truth! We are kept, while in the flesh, not by "our faith" but by *His faithfulness*. Our God-given faith is but the channel through which we *appreciate* and *enjoy* His never-failing faithfulness.

Our "faith" would be vain were it not for "the faith [fidelity] of the Son of God." The best of us would utterly fail were it not that "he ever liveth to make intercession for [us]" (Heb. 7:25) and "now appears in the presence of God *for us*" (Heb. 9:24).

"For if, when we were enemies, we were reconciled to God by the death of His Son, MUCH MORE, BEING

RECONCILED, WE SHALL BE SAVED BY HIS LIFE" (Rom. 5:10).

BUILDING AGAIN THE THINGS WHICH I DESTROYED

"But if, while we seek to be justified by Christ, we ourselves also are found sinners, is therefore Christ the minister of sin? God forbid.

"For if I build again the things which I destroyed, I make myself a transgressor.

"For I through the law am dead to the law, that I might live unto God.

"I am crucified with Christ: nevertheless I live; yet not I, but Christ liveth in me: and the life which I now live in the flesh I live by the faith of the Son of God, who loved me, and gave Himself for me.

"I do not frustrate the grace of God: for if righteousness come by the law, then Christ is dead in vain" (Gal. 2:17-21).

Peter, in separating from the Gentile believers, was building again something that he had helped to destroy, something which God Himself had destroyed—*"the middle wall of partition"* between believing Jews and Gentiles (Eph. 2:14). The Jewish believers at Jerusalem, including Peter, had recognized that the Gentile believers were brethren in Christ, but then Peter had actually rebuilt this wall again and separated himself.

"For I through the law am dead to the law, that I might live unto God" (Verse 19).

Let me illustrate. There is a man who has robbed and killed another man, and the police are looking for him. While they are cruising about, stopping at homes to ask questions, a call comes through to them about a serious accident elsewhere. There at the crash scene they find their criminal. He is dead, killed in the crash. Now what can the law do? Arrest him? Take him to jail? Try him in court? No. It is over. He is dead. The whole thing has been taken out of their hands.

Paul gives us this concept as just one of the reasons we are under grace and not under the law of Moses. Through grace they should do better than if they were under the law; but they are not under the law. The law has no more jurisdiction because they are dead to it.

"Know ye not, that so many of us as were baptized into Jesus Christ were baptized into His death?" (Rom. 6:3).

That is why the apostle goes on in Galatians 2:20:

"I am crucified with Christ: nevertheless I live; yet not I, but Christ liveth in me: and the life which I now live in the flesh I live by the *faith of* the Son of God, who loved me, and gave Himself for me."

Paul believed *Him* because *He* is trustworthy. How marvelous! "Who gave Himself for me." Does not that fully pay my debt of sin—that agony and blood at Calvary when the Creator died for me the creature? Does not that fully justify me before God? Does not that explain Ephesians 1:6 where Paul said that we have been "accepted in the beloved [One]"? Does not that explain Colossians 2:10 where he pronounced us "complete in Christ"? Does not that explain Romans 6:14 where he said that "sin shall not have dominion over us"? Why? Because we are "crucified," we are dead. We have died to sin and the law. We are not under law, but under grace.

This does not mean that we never sin. It is the "old man" whom God considers dead. The new man does not sin.

We are complete in Christ. We have liberty from the bondage of the law which no one could keep. This is what Paul fought for at Antioch and Jerusalem. Are you not glad that he fought this battle for you? Therefore, we do not stand in the way of grace, but let it have free course and say with Paul:

"I do not frustrate the grace of God: for if righteousness come by the law, then Christ is dead in vain" (Gal. 2:21).

Chapter 5 — Galatians 3:1-9

PAUL'S GOSPEL EXPLAINED

QUESTIONS FROM THE APOSTLE OF GRACE

"O foolish Galatians, who hath bewitched you, that ye should not obey the truth, before whose eyes Jesus Christ hath been evidently set forth, crucified among you?

"This only would I learn of you, Received ye the Spirit by the works of the law, or by the hearing of faith?

"Are ye so foolish? having begun in the Spirit, are ye now made perfect by the flesh?

"Have ye suffered so many things in vain? if it be yet in vain.

"He therefore that ministereth to you the Spirit, and worketh miracles among you, doeth he it by the works of the law, or by the hearing of faith?" (Gal. 3:1-5).

We have examined at length the certificate of Paul's apostleship as we find it in Chapters 1 and 2. We come now to Chapter 3, where he began his appeal to the Galatian believers. Turning from his controversy with Peter to his controversy with them, He said:

"O foolish Galatians, who hath bewitched you, that ye should not obey the truth, before whose eyes Jesus Christ hath been evidently set forth, crucified among you?" (Gal. 3:1).

Here indeed we find both the concern and the bluntness of love. He was so concerned over the critical spiritual condition of those Galatian believers that he had to use strong language to awaken them.

THEY WERE ADDING TO GRACE

Christ had died for them to justify them fully. Now they wanted to add to that, and Paul called them foolish. They wanted to add law to grace—the dispensation of the law of Moses to the dispensation of the unadulterated grace of God. That is why their situation was so serious; it was deceptive.

You have heard people say, "Yes, salvation is by grace, but we must do our part." What is our part? We have sinned every day of our lives. We have sinned in *thought* and *word* and *deed*. Do you suppose that by doing a few good deeds (which we ought to do anyway) we would add something to the mighty redemptive work of the Lord Jesus Christ in paying for our sins? Good is what we ought to do; do we expect credit for it?

"Beware lest any man spoil you through philosophy and vain deceit, after the tradition of men, after the rudiments of the world, and not after Christ. For in Him dwelleth all the fulness of the Godhead bodily. And ye are complete in Him..." (Col. 2:8-10).

TO OBEY THE LAW IS TO DISOBEY THE GOSPEL OF GRACE

"Foolish Galatians, who has charmed you?" asked Paul. "At one time you rejoiced that Christ died for you, that you were saved *freely* by the grace of God. You could joyously do the will of God, not because the law said you should, but out of sheer gratitude and love. Now these legalizers have persuaded you that you must add your little two-cent's worth to Christ's finished work, and you have lost the charm of knowing Him. Who has *bewitched* you, that you should not obey the truth?"

He pronounced them not merely foolish, but disobedient. Twice in Galatians 2, the Apostle Paul showed that "the truth of the gospel," his gospel of the grace of God, was the issue between God and Satan, and between God and unbelievers. If the message of the grace of God is true, if it is God-sent, *and it is*, then the Galatians were *disobedient* in turning from it.

"Now to him that is of power to stablish you according to my gospel, and the preaching of Jesus Christ, according to the revelation of the mystery, which was kept secret since the world began, But now is made manifest, and by the Scriptures of the prophets, according to the commandment of the everlasting God, made known to all nations for the obedience of faith" (Rom. 16:25-26).

Did you ever think that through? If it is true, you are obligated to accept it; otherwise you are dishonest with yourself, and sinful, and hypocritical. So you see, by submitting to the Mosaic law you *disobey* the truth. That is why Paul wrote in II Timothy 2:15 about "rightly dividing the Word of truth."

Circumcision, a big issue in Paul's day, had once been required for salvation in the Word of God, and so had water baptism. Both were historically done away as Paul was raised up to proclaim the finished work of Christ and salvation by grace through faith in His death for sin. That is why he asked the Galatians who had beguiled them into turning from the truth he had so plainly set forth.

Christ crucified was the great theme of Paul's gospel. He said:

"God forbid that I should glory [boast], save in the cross of our Lord Jesus Christ, by Whom the world is crucified unto me, and I unto the world" (Gal. 6:14).

In I Corinthians 1:17-18 he said:

"Christ sent me not to baptize, but to preach the gospel: not with wisdom of words, lest the cross of Christ should be made of none effect. For the preaching of the cross is to them that perish foolishness; but unto us which are saved it is the power of God."

Wherever Paul went he proclaimed Christ crucified. Everything he preached was based upon that. Our glorious position in the heavenlies is based upon His shame and agony at Calvary. Paul preached Christ crucified; he proclaimed it as all that we need in order to be saved.

We recall those wonderful words at the close of his first recorded sermon in the 13th Chapter of the Book of the Acts. He was speaking in what was evidently a large synagogue in Antioch of Pisidia. He began, of course, with Jesus of Nazareth, and went through Old Testament history because that was what would interest the Jewish listeners. Listen to the climax of his message:

"Be it known unto you therefore, men and brethren, that through this Man is preached unto you the forgiveness of sins: And by Him all that believe are justified from all things, from which ye could not be justified by the law of Moses" (Acts 13:38-39).

A FINISHED SALVATION

Beloved, salvation is clearly a question of "do" or "done." A large majority of religious clergymen say that you must do, do, do, do, to be saved. But God's Word says that "it" is already *done*, and let God be true and every man a liar. Hebrews Chapter 10 has a good deal to say about this truth:

"And every priest [the Old Testament priests] standeth daily ministering and offering oftentimes the same sacrifices, which can never take away sins:

"But this Man, after He had offered one sacrifice for sins for ever, sat down on the right hand of God;

"From henceforth expecting till His enemies be made His footstool.

"For by one offering He hath perfected for ever them that are sanctified" (Heb. 10:11-14).

The tabernacle and the temple had pieces of furniture—a table of shewbread, a golden altar, a golden candlestick, and the Ark of the Covenant. There was no chair for the priest to rest upon. "Every priest *standeth daily* ministering and offering, oftentimes the same sacrifices, which can never take away sin." Why? Because his work was never done.

My beloved friend, you can be as religious as you please every day of your life, and you can work as hard as you please, but you will never, never finish your task of saving yourself. It was Christ *alone*, who finished the work of salvation for man. It was the Creator, who died for the creature's sin. As He yielded up His spirit to His Father, He cried out that great word "FINISHED." It is done! (John 19:30).

"Every priest standeth daily....*But this Man*, after He had offered one sacrifice for sins forever, *sat down* on the right hand of God....For by one offering He hath perfected forever them that are sanctified" (Heb. 10:11-14).

IN CHRIST

Have you ever thought of that wonderful verse in Ephesians 1:6?

"To the praise of the glory of His grace, wherein He hath made us accepted in the Beloved."

We know that we could never be accepted in ourselves. But thank God, we stand before God *in*

Christ. Christ took our place, at Calvary, and died there not only for us but *AS* us! Paul explained that as "many of us as have been baptized into Jesus Christ were baptized into His death." When we take His death, and accept that His death is our death, then we are saved; then we are baptized into Christ. How wonderful!

My unsaved friend, you know that the old hymn writer was right when he said,

> "No resolution now I make,
> My best resolves I only break
> So save me for Thine own name's sake,
> And take me as I am."

That is the way God wants to save you.

Paul said to the Galatians, "I made it plain to you. Now what has happened to you? Who has charmed you? Is my message true? Why do you not obey it? Why do you not believe it any longer? Why do you not practice the obedience of faith?"

My friend, if you keep trying to be saved, you will never be saved. You will go out from this life "without hope," "without God," and "without Christ." He has told you that salvation is the gift of God. "The wages of sin is death; but the gift of God is eternal life through Jesus Christ our Lord" (Rom. 6:23).

ANOTHER QUESTION

The apostle asked a second question of the Galatians.

"This only would I learn of you, Received ye the Spirit by the works of the law, or by the hearing of faith?" (Gal. 3:2).

Paul had taught them salvation through faith, but they were appropriating Peter's Kingdom teaching.

In Acts 2:37-39, it is recorded that the convicted Jews came forward to Peter and the other apostles and said, "What shall we do; we acknowledge that we have sinned."

What was Peter's answer to them? He did not say, "Believe on the Lord Jesus Christ." Rather he obeyed the instruction of the Great Commission: "*Repent*, and be *baptized* every one of you in the name of Jesus Christ for the remission of sins, and ye shall receive the gift of the Holy Ghost" (Acts 2:38).

Then after the raising up of Paul (Acts 9) God did something startling with Peter. In Acts 10 we read how He sent Peter, against his own will, to a Gentile household in order to teach him about the change in dispensations—a change in God's dealings with mankind. As he spoke to those Gentiles about Christ, the Holy Spirit did something that terminated his message. He said, speaking of Christ, "To Him give all the prophets witness, that through His name whosoever believeth in Him shall receive remission of sins" (10:43).

But in Paul's message of grace, that revelation given by God to the world after the Jews rejected the King and the Kingdom, is *"believe" alone*. Nothing else! When Peter said to the Gentiles in Cornelius' house that through His name, "whosoever believes in Him will find remission of sins," God stopped him right there.

"While Peter yet spake these words, the Holy Ghost fell on all them which heard the word. And they of the circumcision which believed were astonished..." (Acts 10:44-47).

Of course they were astonished! This was something different to those Jews who had come with

Peter—"...because that on the Gentiles also was poured out the gift of the Holy Ghost. For they heard them speak with tongues, and magnify God. Then answered Peter, Can any man forbid water, that these should not be baptized, which have received the Holy Ghost as well as we?"

The careful student of the Scriptures will notice that, at Pentecost, something was required for the remission of sins: "Repent, and be baptized every one of you...for the remission of sins, and ye shall receive the gift of the Holy Ghost" (Acts 2:38). But in the later incident in Cornelius' house God stopped Peter while he was still speaking. The Gentile believers there were given "the gift of the Holy Spirit" and the sign of "tongues," *before* they were baptized.

God was not yet through with Israel. He had not officially set his favored nation aside, so baptism and the sign gifts continued until the end of the Acts period, even though they were no longer required for salvation.

Some people want to make baptism and sign gifts essential for salvation in our day. They do not require circumcision or sacrifices, but they do require baptism.

Some say that baptism is not necessary for salvation, but that we should be baptized anyway. I ask, "Why?"

"Oh, well...the Great Commission." But if you are going to obey the Great Commission then you have to practice the sign gifts also. And that would put you under the law again, would it not? That would make baptism essential for salvation.

My answer to all of this is that it was because God was not yet finished with Israel that He gave

Gentiles such signs to help the Jews see the truth. We have a picture of this in the conversion of Cornelius in Acts 10. Those of the circumcision were astonished. They saw that this was a real work of God.

Paul asks the Galatians, "Did you receive the Holy Ghost by the works of the law or by the hearing of faith?'" The answer was clear. They had heard him preach the unadulterated gospel of the grace of God and they had believed it. That was the hearing of faith. They had listened with attentive and receptive hearts. They believed and were saved. And that is how people are saved today in a dispensation where Jewish law is no longer required.

Do you wonder why God allowed the legalizers to charm the Galatians? I believe that it was so that we might have the Book of Galatians and learn these wonderful truths.

THE FOOLISH GALATIANS

The Galatians were not guilty of any outward wrongdoing. They wanted to do good things, but God had already accomplished the good.

God says that you are a hopeless sinner, and that He has paid for your sins. If you fail to accept this, but instead try to help Him save you, that is an insult to Him. It casts reflections upon His Word, upon His integrity, and upon the all-sufficiency of Christ's finished work of redemption. It robs Him of His glory.

Paul exclaimed to the great audience in the city of Antioch,

"Be it known unto you therefore, men and brethren, that through this man [Jesus Christ] is preached unto you the forgiveness of sins: And by Him all that believe are justified from all things, from which ye could not be justified by the law of Moses" (Acts 13:38-39).

Some people try to save themselves. They substitute their own "good" works, and go about to establish their own righteousness.

How very clever Satan is! He has no pleasure in drunkards or dope-addicts or harlots. They are not good advertisements for him. He is more interested in making people self-righteous. He wants to rob Christ of His glory. This is why Paul spoke of "the wiles of the devil" in Ephesians 6:11, and referred to him as the one that "beguiled Eve through his subtlety" (II Cor. 11:3).

"And no marvel; for Satan himself is transformed into an angel of light.

"Therefore it is no great thing if his ministers also be transformed as ministers of righteousness..." (II Cor. 11:13-15).

"For such," the apostle says, "are false apostles, deceitful workers, transforming themselves into the apostles of Christ" (Ver. 13).

DISPENSATIONAL CHANGE

Because such do-gooders can be very charming and very deceiving, Paul used strong language to bring the hypnotized Galatian believers to their senses. You see, it was largely a dispensational problem at Antioch—a problem of failing to rightly divide the Word.

Let me ask you, my dear Christian friends, can you find in the Bible where anybody before Paul ever proclaimed the wonderful message of grace? "But now the righteousness of God without the law is manifest..." (Rom. 3:21).

"Are you so foolish? Having begun in the Spirit, are ye now made perfect by the flesh?" (Gal. 3:3).

It is true that the Bible says that you must be circumcised and keep the law of Moses. Yes, the Bible says that! But the Galatians were not recognizing that a *further* revelation had been given to Paul, the apostle of grace. This is also the trouble today. All the cults can give you Scripture passages to confirm their teachings, but they do not use the Word *"rightly divided."*

The religious rite of circumcision had a 1500-year background in Paul's day. It was hard for some believers to accept that the finished work of Christ had abolished the need for the rite. We have a similar problem today. Water baptism has a 1900-year-old background, and though it too has been done away by Christ's redemptive work, there are many who want to add it to His finished work.

When it was in order, baptism was for the remission of sins: John the Baptist preached baptism for the remission of sins; Christ sent His apostles out to preach, "He that believeth and is baptized shall be saved." But then Paul entered the picture. He has taught us that the full dispensation of grace was ushered in through his ministry. When he said, "Know ye not, that so many of us as were baptized into Jesus Christ were baptized into His death?" (Rom. 6:3), he was not talking about a baptism of water. He spoke of baptism as a *oneness* with Christ: "I am crucified with Christ" (Gal. 2:20), and "By one Spirit are we all baptized into one Body" (I Cor. 12:13).

We wonder what believers think that water baptism can possibly do for them that Christ has not already done? Colossians 2:6 says:

"As ye have therefore received Christ Jesus the Lord, so walk ye in Him."

How did we receive Christ Jesus the Lord? We reached the end of ourselves and acknowledged that we needed help. We trusted Him and accepted Him by grace through faith. Paul taught that we should keep on walking by faith. That is where the Galatians had failed.

Oh, that Paul could thunder this verse again today,

"Are ye so foolish? having begun in the Spirit, are ye now made perfect by the flesh? Have ye suffered so many things in vain? if it be yet in vain" (Gal. 3:3-4).

They had rested in the finished work of Christ, and it had cost them persecution. They were not popular! They were suffering, as Paul did also, "the offense of the cross."

ABRAHAM THE FATHER OF BELIEVERS

"Even as Abraham *believed* God, and it was accounted to him for righteousness.

"Know ye therefore that they which are of *faith*, the same are the children of Abraham.

"And the Scripture, foreseeing that God would justify the heathen through *faith*, preached before the gospel unto Abraham, saying, In thee shall all nations be blessed.

"So then, they which be of *faith* are blessed with *faithful* Abraham" (Gal. 3:6-9).

a. A Puzzling Question

This passage from the pen of Paul has baffled many a diligent Bible student, since his quotation from Genesis 12:3 does not, it seems to them, prove the point he is making in the context, or even in the verse itself.

The argument of the passage as a whole—that God justifies *believers*—seems clear enough.

Verse 6: "Even as *Abraham believed God*, and it was accounted to him for righteousness."

Verse 7: "Know ye therefore that *they which are of faith*, the same are the children of Abraham."

Verse 9: "So then, *they which be of faith* are blessed with faithful [faith-full, believing] Abraham."

This is the argument of the passage as a whole, but how does God's promise to bless all nations through Abraham prove that the Gentiles were to be justified *by faith?*

b. What the Passage Does *Not* Say

To simplify matters let us first note clearly what Galatians 3:8 does *not* say.

1. It does *not* say that the Scriptures *foretold* that God would justify the Gentiles through faith. The word is *"foreseeing,"* not "foretelling."

2. It does *not* say that God *told Abraham* that He would justify the Gentiles through faith.

3. It does *not* say that the Scriptures foresaw that God would justify the Gentiles *through Christ.* This would have been true, but it is not the point here.

4. It does *not* say that God preached to Abraham the good news that *he* was justified by faith. It was not until about five centuries later that God moved Moses to write, *"And he* [Abraham] *believed*

in the Lord, and He counted it to him for righteousness" (Gen. 15:6).

It is sometimes taught from Galatians 3:8 that the gospel of the grace of God was preached to Abraham. This is certainly not what this passage teaches, for we are told explicitly that the gospel, or good news, which God preached to Abraham was that *"in thee shall all nations be blessed,"* and that would be good news to anyone.

5. It does *not* say that God would bless the nations through *Abraham's seed*, though we do find this promise elsewhere.

6. Finally, this passage does *not* say, "*like* thee shall all nations be blessed." If it did there would be no problem to solve, but we should then miss one of the most blessed truths which the Word of God has for us.

How then can we harmonize Paul's quotation from Genesis: *"In thee shall all nations be blessed,"* with his argument in the whole context, that God would justify the Gentiles *through faith?*

Rather than conclude that Paul, much less the Holy Spirit, made a poor choice of a text to prove his point, let us ask ourselves the basic question involved: *Just how* was Abraham to prove a blessing to all nations?

c. The Blessing of the Nations Through Abraham

It is true that all nations were to be blessed through Israel, Abraham's *multiplied* seed (Gen. 22:17,18). It is also true that all nations were to be blessed through Christ, Abraham's *single* Seed (Gal. 3:16). But the very *first* promise made to Abraham was that God would bless all nations through *him*, and the apostle quotes this promise in an argument that God justifies Gentiles *through faith*.

d. Abraham the Great Example of Faith

The original promise made to Abraham, then, holds out blessing to the world through Abraham *himself*.

How has Abraham himself proved a blessing to all nations? There is only one answer: *as God's great example of FAITH*. If there is anything that stands out in the record of Abraham's life it is the fact that he *believed God*. Even the *Encyclopedia Britannica* calls special attention to the fact that the outstanding characteristic of his life was implicit and childlike *faith in God*.

In Scripture Abraham is constantly held up as the great example of faith. This is especially true in the Pauline epistles. To the Jew, who goes about to establish his own righteousness by religious works, and boasts of circumcision, Paul exclaims, "Why, your own father, Abraham, was justified by faith *without works*. He received the sign of circumcision as a seal of the *righteousness which he already had!*" (Rom. 4:11). And he uses the same argument to persuade the Gentile that salvation is *by grace through faith*.

It was because God had chosen Abraham as the great example of faith that He said, *"In thee shall all nations be blessed."*

Now let us read again Galatians 3:6-9 and see how simple and consistent it is—and how appropriate is Paul's quotation from Genesis.

"...Abraham believed God, and it was accounted to him for righteousness.

"Know ye therefore that they which are of faith, the same are the children of Abraham.

"And the Scripture, foreseeing that God would justify the heathen through faith, preached before the gospel unto Abraham [the man of faith], saying, In thee shall all nations be blessed.

"So then, they which be of faith are blessed with faithful Abraham."

Now, it is most remarkable that God should have chosen *Abraham* to be the great example of faith, for if you should ask who is the most honored, most esteemed, most revered man of all history, there could be but one answer—*Abraham*. In this respect Moses and David and Solomon cannot stand in his shadow. As to our Lord, He *should* be most honored, but, alas, His name is still blasphemed on every streetcorner.

Without question Abraham is and has always been looked up to by greater numbers of people than any person in history. More than fourteen million Israelites, scattered all over the world, speak with reverence of their "father Abraham." Then there are more than one billion professing Christians, whether truly saved or not, who also look up to Abraham as the father of believers. Besides these, there are some 528 million Mohammedans who also claim Abraham as their father.

How appropriate, then, that God should point to *him* as the great example of justification by faith!

It is further significant that *Abraham*, God's great example of *faith*, was raised up so long before *Paul*, God's great example of *grace*.

Some centuries after Abraham, God was to give Israel the Mosaic law. If they obeyed it they would be God's peculiar treasure. But even then, God would show them that obedience to the law *in itself* could not procure His favor. It was only as they took the law seriously to be *God's Word* and obeyed it *because it was God's Word* that they could gain acceptance with Him. In other words, only as an expression of their faith in God could the works of the Law save them. It was *"the obedience of faith"* that God desired, and every Jew could look back to his father Abraham to learn this lesson, for Abraham had been justified by faith apart from works, so that his works were only an expression of his faith.[1]

But while all this could be understood by every Jew, the dispensation of the grace of God could not be ushered in until sin had abounded to such a degree that Israel had joined the Gentiles in rebellion against God and His Christ. It was then that Saul, the flaming leader of the world's rebellion against God (See Acts 8:3, Gal. 1:13, etc.), was saved and sent forth as Paul, the great example of *God's grace* (See I Tim. 1:12-16).

But now that God's grace has been manifested so freely, there is all the more reason to accept it by faith. Hence Paul, the great example of *grace*, points to Abraham, the great example of *faith*, urging all men everywhere to follow in his steps. Hear him plead:

"What shall we say then that Abraham our father, as pertaining to the flesh, hath found?

"For if Abraham were justified by works, he hath whereof to glory; but not before God.

---

1. Here see the author's *"Things That Differ,"* Chapter 1.

"For what saith the Scripture? *Abraham believed God, and it was counted unto him for righteousness.*

"Now to him that worketh is the reward not reckoned of grace, but of debt.

"*But to him that worketh not, but believeth on him that justifieth the ungodly, his faith is counted for righteousness*" (Rom. 4:1-5).

"...we say that faith was reckoned to Abraham for righteousness.

"How was it then reckoned? when he was in circumcision, or in uncircumcision? Not in circumcision, but in uncircumcision" (Rom. 4:9,10).

"Therefore it is of faith, that it might be by grace; to the end the promise might be sure to all the seed; not to that only which is of the law, but to that also which is of the faith of Abraham; who is the father of us all!" (Rom. 4:16).

"Now it was not written for his sake alone, that it was imputed to him;

"But for us also, to whom it shall be imputed, if we believe on Him that raised up Jesus our Lord from the dead;

"Who was delivered for our offences, and was raised again for our justification.

"*Therefore, being justified by faith, we have peace with God through our Lord Jesus Christ*" (Rom. 4:23—5:1).

"*So then, they which be of faith are blessed with faithful Abraham*" (Gal. 3:9).

Has this message, perhaps, fallen into the hands of a stranger to God's wonderful grace? If so, we beg you, whether Jew or Gentile, to look at Abraham and learn from him. He *believed God* and it was counted to him for righteousness. If *you* believe God, trusting in His Son as your Savior, it will be counted to *you* for righteousness. You will be *"accepted in the Beloved One"* (Eph. 1:6). God will look upon you as *"complete in Him"* (Col. 2:10), and will enrich you with *"all spiritual blessings in heavenly places in Christ"* (Eph. 1:3).

As long as you continue *trying* you will continue to fail. So begin *trusting. Believe God* when He says He loves you and gave Christ to die for your sins. *Believe God* when He offers salvation to you as the gift of His grace.

Will you do it? Will you do it *now?*

Chapter 6 — Galatians 3:10-18

THE ALL-SUFFICIENCY OF CHRIST

THE ONLY ALTERNATIVE

We have come in this study to a very important part of Paul's letter to the Galatians.

"For as many as are of the works of the law are under the curse: for it is written [Deut. 27:26], Cursed is everyone that continueth not in all things which are written in the book of the law to do them.

"But that no man is justified by the law in the sight of God, it is evident: for, The just shall live by faith.

"And the law is not of faith: but, the man that doeth them shall live in them.

"Christ hath redeemed us from the curse of the law, being made a curse for us: for it is written, Cursed is everyone that hangeth on a tree.

"That the blessing of Abraham might come on the Gentiles through Jesus Christ; that we might receive the promise of the Spirit through faith" (Gal. 3:10-14).

It is the function of the law to condemn, not to justify. Obviously, if everyone did what was right, we would not need law. This is why the Apostle Paul wrote by inspiration:

"...the law is not made for a righteous man, but for the lawless and disobedient" (I Tim. 1:9).

The function of law is to put the finger on sin and condemn it. Remember that you do not have to break the whole law to be a law-breaker.

"For whosoever shall keep the whole law and yet offend in one point, he is guilty of all" (James 2:10).

That makes sense. How many links must you break in a chain to break the chain? Just one. How many murders do you have to commit to be a murderer? Just one. How many sins do you have to commit to be a sinner? Just one. And we have all committed one, and keep on committing one or more every day.

Just one sin ruined this earth, beloved. Do not think for a moment that God will let you into heaven with one sin on your soul.

Do you remember the story of Mount Ebal and Mount Gerizim? To enter into Canaan the Israelites had to go between two mountains, Mount Ebal and Mount Gerizim. To teach them an important lesson about law and grace, God had two companies of Levites take up their stands on the two mountains. On Mount Gerizim the Levites were to bless the people, but on Mount Ebal God had them place two large stones with the law written in large letters upon them. The Levites on this mount were to pronounce curses upon those who disobeyed the law. In Deuteronomy 27 where the story is told, there is a long list of the curses—the Levites warning the people: "Cursed is everyone that doeth so and so, cursed is everyone that does not do this or that, cursed...cursed...cursed. Cursed if you do what is wrong or do not do what is right."

This is why Paul quoted from the same chapter of Deuteronomy, verse 26, in Galatians 3:10:

> **"For as many as are of the works of the law are under the curse: for it is written, Cursed is everyone that continueth not in all [the] things which are written in the book of the law to do them."**

When a lawyer came to Christ and said, "Master, what shall I do to inherit eternal life?" our Lord replied:

"What is written in the law? How readest thou? And he answering said, Thou shalt love the Lord thy God with all thy heart, and with all thy soul, and with all thy strength, and with all thy mind; and thy neighbour as thyself. And He said unto him, Thou hast answered right: this do, and thou shalt live" (Luke 10:25-28).

Man always wants to *do* something. Obviously none of us has perfectly kept the law of God, so the apostle said that if you are trying to be saved by keeping the law, you are under a curse:

"That no man is justified by the law in the sight of God, it is evident: for, The just shall live by faith" (Gal. 3:11).

The verse from Habakkuk which Paul quoted was very well known to them. In fact, he used this quotation several times in his epistles. This was the great verse that shook Martin Luther's theology to its foundation. It had such a profound effect on his life that he had it woven into the napkins at his table, and into the pillows about his house. He had it inscribed on the dishes and silverware; he even had it woven into the cuffs of his sleeves so that when he sat down to read or write he would see those words, *"The just shall live by faith."*

So if eternal life is to be had *by faith*, clearly it is not to be earned by good works, the works of the law, because "the law is *not* of faith."

"Now to him that worketh is the reward not reckoned of grace, but of debt" (Rom. 4:4).

When the working man gets his salary at the end of the week, he does not feel that the boss has given him some special gift. Of course not! He earned his wages! So do not forget, if you want to be saved by doing good and keeping the law, you are not saved by grace. However, *grace* is the *only way* by which you can be saved today.

"To him that *worketh not*, but believeth on Him that justifieth the ungodly, his faith is counted for righteousness. Even as David also describeth the blessedness of the man, unto whom God imputeth righteousness *without works*" (Rom. 4:5,6).

"But that no man is justified by the law in the sight of God, it is evident: for, The just shall live by faith. And the law is not of faith: but, The man that doeth them shall live in them" (Gal. 3:11,12).

The latter, here, is a quotation from Leviticus 18:5. Clearly, we must make a choice. If we want to be saved by the law we must keep it all perfectly and continue to do so. If we break it once, all hope is gone. Since we cannot keep it there is only one alternative for salvation. You must trust Christ who "died for your sins," the only One who ever kept the law perfectly and then died as a law-breaker.

"Who His own self bare our sins in His own body on the tree..." (I Pet. 2:24).

"For Christ also hath once suffered for sins, the just for the unjust, that He might bring us to God..." (I Pet. 3:18).

May I call your attention to an important fact? Peter did not preach these truths at Pentecost. He was then still preaching the gospel of the Kingdom, and when they asked, "What shall we do?" he replied, "Repent and be baptized every one of you in the name of Jesus Christ for the remission of sins."

But when as an old man he wrote the Epistles of Peter, he had long since learned the gospel of grace from Paul.

Paul put it beautifully in Colossians 2:14, where, speaking of the finished work of the Lord Jesus he declared: "Blotting out the handwriting of ordinances [decrees, laws] that was against us, which was contrary to us, and took it out of the way, nailing it to His cross." Beautiful! The Lord Jesus stripped the law of every claim it had against us when He paid for our sins.

"Christ hath redeemed us from the curse of the law, being made a curse for us: for it is written, Cursed is everyone that hangeth on a tree" (Gal. 3:13).

We are told that the first invention of man was the wheel. Actually, man's first invention was a garment of fig leaves that Adam and Eve devised to hide their nakedness. The fig leaves are a picture today of the poor paltry works that men weave to hide what is naked and open to the eyes of God.

"But now the righteousness of God without the law is manifested...."

"Being justified freely by His grace through the redemption that is in Christ Jesus."

"To declare, I say, at this time His righteousness..." (Rom. 3:21,24,26).

It was not always declared, *but now* the finished work of Christ could be revealed and declared. God's *"righteousness"* reckoned to the believer's account.

This is not the so-called Great Commission given to the eleven (Mk. 16:15). Oh, no! Romans 3:26-28 says that God is just, and at the same time the justifier of him that believeth in Jesus. Why? Because Jesus paid for our sins. "Where is boasting then?"

Wonderful answer: "it is excluded." "Therefore we conclude that a man is justified by faith, without the deeds of the law." To the poor Gentile jailer Paul said, "Believe on the Lord Jesus Christ, and thou shalt be saved."

THE BLESSING OF ABRAHAM

"Christ hath redeemed us from the curse of the law, being made a curse for us: for it is written, Cursed is every one that hangeth on a tree: That the blessing of Abraham might come on the Gentiles[1] through Jesus Christ; that we might receive the promise of the Spirit through faith" (Gal. 3:13-14).

The statement in Galatians 3:10 is that those who do not *keep* the law are cursed. But thank God, Christ has redeemed us from the curse of the law. The worst of the law-breakers in the Old Testament era were stoned to death, and then hanged on a tree. We thank God for that wonderful truth in Galatians 3:13—"Christ hath redeemed us from the curse of the law, being made a curse for us." In Deuteronomy 21:23 it is written, "Cursed is every one that hangeth on a tree."

"That the blessing of Abraham might come on the Gentiles through Jesus Christ; that we might receive the promise of the Spirit through faith" (Gal. 3:14).

What did Paul mean by this assertion? Why did he not say that Christ has redeemed us from the curse of the law that the blessing of *Israel* might come on the Gentiles? Simply because Israel also was condemned by the law.

Before the law Abraham was not only the physical father of the nation Israel but also the spiritual

1. A Gentile in Old Testament times could only be saved by becoming a Jew and keeping the law.

father of all believers. "Know ye therefore that they which are of faith, the same are the children of Abraham" (Gal. 3:7).

What is meant by the phrase, "the blessing of Abraham" (Gal. 3:14)? When Abraham believed God, and God counted it to him for righteousness, that was a very great blessing. Can you think of a greater blessing than to know that God has not merely pardoned us, but has justified us because our sins have been paid for, and the record is now clear?

It is now more than 70 years ago that I came to know the Lord Jesus Christ as my Savior, and the blessed truth really dawned upon me that Christ died for *my* sins. Think of it! I have never doubted my salvation. I have enjoyed peace with God. I have known that even when I failed Him, He still loved me. I am His, and He is mine. As the song says,

"Heaven above is a softer blue,
  Earth around is a sweeter green!
Something lives in every hue
  Christless eyes had never seen:
Birds with gladder songs o'erflow,
  Flowers with deeper beauty shine,
Since I know, as now I am known,
  I am His, and He is mine."

From "I Am His And He Is Mine"
—George W. Robinson

Let us look at the opening verses of Romans 4. Now we have not strayed from the subject because this passage confirms what Paul says in Galatians 3.

"What shall we say then that Abraham our father, as pertaining to the flesh, hath found? For if Abraham were

justified by works, he hath whereof to glory; but not before God" (Rom. 4:1,2).

God can see right through all our boasting, and if Abraham should boast, ah, he would not have dared to boast before God. He was aware that God knew about *his wife* (Gen. 12:13; 20:2) and how he called her his "sister" in order to save his own skin. God knew some of the other great failures in Abraham's life, but Abraham was justified by faith (Rom. 4:3).

"Even as David also describeth the blessedness of the man, unto whom God imputeth righteousness without works" (Rom. 4:6).

Do you see what Paul means when he says that "Christ hath *redeemed* us from the curse of the law...That the blessing of Abraham might come on the *Gentiles* through Jesus Christ" (Gal. 3:13-14). This blessing always comes through Christ. What a blessing Abraham had!

"Being justified freely by His grace through the redemption that is in Christ Jesus" (Rom. 3:24).

"In whom we have redemption *through His blood,* the forgiveness of sins, according to the riches of His grace" (Eph. 1:7).

Before A. C. Dickson died, he had a very unique experience. He did not think that there was any significance in dreams, but shortly before his death he had a dream that was strangely very true. He called his son, and said, "Son, you know that I place no confidence in dreams, but I had a dream, and it was so sweet that I want to tell you about it. I dreamed that God was opening the books in heaven, and the Book of Life. He said to me, 'You may come now, you may come.' And I said, 'O Lord, I cannot come into your presence and into heaven. I am such a sinner.' God turned to the book, and He looked into it and He said, 'Yes, you may come.' I said, 'Lord, you know that I am not good enough for heaven.' He said to me, 'There is nothing against you here.' He looked into the book again, and said, 'Yes, you come, you come, there is nothing against you in the record.'"

That is exactly true about every believer. Christ *paid* for our sins; He *died* for them. It was not an accident; He did not die an untimely death as a martyr. He came to give His life a ransom for many, to be testified in due time through the Apostle Paul.

Many of my friends remember when my first wife, Henrietta, went to be with Christ. Although she suffered dreadful pain, her good cheer continued to shine through as long as she was able to express herself. Some people said, "It was good that she could have that attitude." One man said, "It is wonderful how she conditioned her mind to meet that test." To everyone I said, "No, you have it wrong. She experienced that peace and joy because she simply believed God's Word and trusted Christ as her Savior. She knew that she would soon be with Him."

Paul, who lived after the covenant of the law had been abolished, pointed back to Abraham who lived before law was instituted, and said, "He believed God, and it was counted to him for righteousness." Now, let us all do the same as Abraham.

The Promise of the Spirit through Faith

Another question here—What did Paul mean when he said, "That we might receive the promise of the Spirit through faith" (Gal. 3:14)? Did he mean that we shall receive the promise of miraculous gifts, like at Pentecost? No. We read in I Corinthians 2:9-10:

"Eye hath not seen, nor ear heard, neither have entered into the heart of man, the things which God hath prepared for them that love Him, But God hath revealed them unto us by His Spirit...."

Some people think that verse 9 refers to heaven, but it refers to this present dispensation of grace in which we now live. God reveals precious truth to us by His Spirit.

THE PROMISE CONFIRMED

"Brethren, I speak after the manner of men; Though it be but a man's covenant, yet if it be confirmed, no man disannulleth, or addeth thereto.

"Now to Abraham and his seed were the promises made. He saith not, And to seeds, as of many; but as of one, And to thy seed, which is Christ.

"And this I say, that the covenant, that was confirmed before of God in Christ, the law, which was four hundred and thirty years after, cannot disannul, that it should make the promise of none effect.

"For if the inheritance be of the law, it is no more of promise: but God gave it to Abraham by promise" (Gal. 3:15-18).

We have learned that the Scripture foresaw that God would justify the Gentiles through faith, and that God preached (announced) that gospel, the good news, to Abraham. Remember that he was a Gentile, saved by the grace of God through faith, and God shared with him the good news that all nations would be blessed through him.

We know that the chief characteristic of Abraham's life from then on was his implicit faith in

God. Whatever God said, he believed. God had promised that in Isaac all his seed would be called, but God also told him, "I want you to offer Isaac up in sacrifice" (Gen. 22:1-14). Imagine the questions that would naturally arise in Abraham! "Does God want me to offer human sacrifice like the pagans do? Is it possible that He would have me kill the very son through whom this great nation is to arise?"

According to the record he obeyed, not wavering. He was strong in faith. He reckoned that God was able to raise Isaac from the dead. And so he passed the great test of faith. His faith pleased God, and God honored him for it. In effect God said, "This man trusts Me; he has placed all his confidence in Me. How can I fail him?" We should learn this lesson, beloved, that God is honored when we believe what He says.

Many people want to earn their way to heaven. They want to gain God's favor by keeping the Ten Commandments and doing what is right. Is it not true that the law was given as a binding covenant?

"Now therefore, if ye will obey My voice indeed, and keep My covenant, then ye shall be a peculiar treasure unto Me above all people..." (Ex. 19:5).

God brought in the added covenant of the law to teach that no one could be saved by keeping the law. First, because no man can keep it perfectly; no one has ever done so. Second, God planned that His Son would take upon Himself the curse of the broken law.

"Christ hath redeemed us from the curse of the law."

The law could only condemn and curse us. The law could only pronounce that we have sinned. God thus made provision for sin; He made a provision for the broken law.

A SIGNED CONTRACT

"I speak after the manner of men; Though it be but a man's covenant, yet if it be confirmed, no man disannulleth, or addeth thereto" (Gal. 3:15).

When a contract is signed, no one can take from it, or add to it. The Abrahamic covenant said, "I will bless you and make you a blessing. I will be your God and your seed shall be my people." Four hundred thirty years later God added the law. But the question that Paul now asks is:

"Wherefore then serveth the law? It was added because of transgressions..." (Gal. 3:19).

After saying that a man could not add to or take away from a signed contract, God said that the law was added. Added to what? It was added to the Abrahamic covenant. Nineteen hundred years before Christ, God said, "I will be their God." Four-hundred-thirty years after that He said, "If ye obey my voice indeed, and keep my covenant [the law], then you shall be a peculiar treasure unto me."

That is a very big *IF*. But before we consider the explanation of that *IF*, let us notice the focal point of Paul's argument. He has been saying that the only way that we can receive blessing and salvation is by faith. Abraham believed God and it was counted to him for righteousness, and those who also believe, like Abraham, are blessed along with him. But God has said that if you are under the law, you are under the curse. The law was added to the Abrahamic contract.

Galatians 3:15 states the focal point:

"Brethren, I speak after the manner of men [I am talking just as a human being]; Though it be but a man's covenant, yet if it be confirmed, no man disannulleth, or addeth thereto."

This one basic fact must stand, the initial covenant cannot be made null and void.

"And this I say, that the covenant, that was confirmed before of God in Christ, the law, which was four hundred thirty years after, cannot disannul, that it should make the promise of none effect" (Gal. 3:17).

The writer of Psalm 130 understood this principle. "If thou, Lord, shouldest mark iniquities, O Lord, who shall stand?" (Psa. 130:3). He realized that whatever these commandments of the law meant, whatever they signified, whatever they entailed, they could not possibly make the promise to Abraham void.[2]

"Even as David also describeth the blessedness of the man, unto whom God imputeth righteousness without works [of the law]" (Rom. 4:6).

The Psalmist knew the truth of Galatians 3:10 that those who are under the law are under a curse, but he also knew that there was forgiveness with God.

When the law was given and God said, "*If* you obey this law and keep it perfectly, then you shall be my people," what should the people of Israel have answered? They should have said, "Lord, on this basis none of us can be saved, because we cannot keep that law perfectly. Have mercy upon us. Surely you will not break your promise."

---

2. Or the principle of justification by faith.

But in their pride and folly the people all exclaimed together, "All that the Lord has spoken we will do" (Ex. 19:8). "Yes, we will keep His covenant. We will keep the law."

Before Moses arrived down from the mountain with the two tablets of the Ten Commandments, the people of Israel were dancing like pagans around a golden calf, an Egyptian god. Moses reminded them that they were the only nation that ever heard the voice of God speaking to them. The mount of Sinai was engulfed in smoke, it quivered and shook, and the people backed away: "And God spake all these words, saying, I am the Lord Thy God...Thou shalt have no other gods before me!" (Ex. 20:1-3).

God enunciated those Ten Commandments, and the people said, "Everything He says we will do." But before Moses could return they had broken the first commandment. So soon did God have opportunity to show them the *impossibility* of justification by the law.

If God did not mean to enforce the law, why did He make this covenant with Israel? Galatians 3:19, begins to answer—"It was added because of transgression."

"By the law is the knowledge of sin" and it was given "that sin by the commandment might become exceeding sinful" (Rom. 3:20; 7:13). In Paul's Epistle to the Galatians, God is driving them back to the promise, *to faith*. This is what God had in mind all the while, as we saw in Galatians 3:13 concerning the futility of salvation by good works. God was not playing games. It was at infinite cost that He made provision for the payment of sin. When God gave the law, which was bound to break fellowship between Him and Israel, He immediately began to make arrangements for a Tabernacle where He could restore fellowship with Israel. Now there is a paradox! He said, "If you will obey my voice indeed, then you will be my special people," but they did not obey, so He made plans for a Tabernacle where He could meet with them in fellowship!

"And let them make me a sanctuary; that I may dwell among them" (Ex. 25:8). Why? We see an inkling in the fact that the first article of furniture for the Tabernacle was the Ark. The word "ark" is simply the word "coffin." It is translated "coffin" in the last verse of Genesis. So, when God commanded the building of a tabernacle, the first thing He said was "Make me a coffin." Why a coffin?

"And thou shalt put into the coffin the testimony [that is, the law] which I shall give thee" (Ex. 25:16).

God immediately put the law in a coffin. On top of the coffin was the blood-sprinkled mercy seat. There God said, "I will meet with my people."

The law in a coffin! God later nailed the law to the cross.

"Blotting out the handwriting of ordinances that was against us, which was contrary to us, and took it out of the way, nailing it to His cross" (Col. 2:14).

How beautiful! The "law put to *death*," "*abolished*," "put *away*," are some of the phrases used by Paul in his epistles.

The law is the *standard* of God's righteousness, of course. It will abide *forever*; it is the Word of God. But as a *covenant* it was put out of the way, buried in a coffin.

"For the grace of God that bringeth salvation hath appeared to all men, Teaching us that, denying ungodliness and worldly lusts, we should live soberly, righteously, and godly, in this present world; Looking for that blessed hope, and the glorious appearing of the great God and our Savior Jesus Christ; Who gave Himself for us, that He might redeem us from all iniquity, and purify unto Himself a peculiar people, zealous of good works" (Titus 2:11-14).

Note the similarity to the words in Exodus. God told the people to keep the law in Exodus 19, only to show them that they could not do so. He tells us how Christ has redeemed us from the curse of the law by dying and bearing the curse for us.

A SIMPLE SOLUTION TO A PUZZLING PROBLEM

Back to Galatians 3:16

"Now to Abraham and his seed were the promises made. He saith not, And to seeds, as of many; but as of one, And to thy seed, which is Christ."

Here the Apostle Paul appears to state unequivocally that all the promises made to Abraham regarding his "seed" referred, not to his multiplied seed, but to Christ alone.

How many theological battles have been fought over this passage, and with what negative results!

The basic problem is that the word "seed," in Hebrew and Greek (as in English), may refer to one seed or to many, i.e., to a single seed or to a bagfull. In the latter case the word is used as a collective noun, yet in *both* cases the singular form is used. If I had a barn filled with individual seeds, it would be correctly referred to as "a barn full of *seed*." The plural form would *never* be used in such a case, *unless* a variety of *kinds* of seed were referred to: e.g.,

"The store carries twenty-four different seeds." But even then it would be more customary to say: "The store carries twenty-four different *kinds* of *seed*."

It is evident that the Apostle Paul, in Galatians 3:16, is not referring to a *variety* of seeds, however, so the problem remains: Why does he argue that the Holy Spirit's use of the word "seed," in the promises made to Abraham and his progeny, proves that He was referring to only *one particular* seed: Christ?

Albert Barnes, meeting this problem head-on in his commentary on Galatians, rightly says:

"Now no one ever probably read this passage without feeling a difficulty, and without asking himself whether this argument is sound, and is worthy of a man of candor, and especially of an inspired man."

The difficulties increase as we go to the particular passages in which God made the promises referred to, for very clearly *not one* of them refers to one particular seed, but *all* very obviously refer to his *multiplied* seed!

This makes it appear all the more that Paul, in Galatians 3:16, was seeking to win a point by the use of sophistry; by taking illegitimate advantage of the Holy Spirit's use of a word.

When this writer was still a young pastor and had barely begun to take a stand for "the preaching of Jesus Christ according to the revelation of the mystery," he received a striking letter from the president of a popular Christian college.

Said the president in effect: "I am an anti-dispensationalist, and you are generally considered an ultra-dispensationalist, but this I firmly believe:

Either you are right or I am right, but the Bible teachers in between are certainly wrong." He referred to those who believed that the Body of Christ had its historical beginning with Peter and the eleven at Pentecost.

Very graciously he invited me and any of my friends to spend one or more evenings with him at the college to discuss the matter.

Several of us accepted his invitation, but our discussion centered almost exclusively around one verse: Galatians 3:16! We couldn't seem to get away from it.

This passage, he contended, was the Holy Spirit's own exegesis, or explanation, of the promises made to Abraham. He insisted that no matter how plainly the promises themselves seemed to refer to Abraham's multiplied seed, God Himself *says* in Galatians 3:16 that they referred to one particular Seed alone: Christ.

We, on the other hand, contended that if God made promises to Abraham which obviously referred to his *multiplied* seed, but actually meant them to apply to only *one particular* seed, He was not being honest with Abraham. This we both agreed could not be the case, but it shows how important it is that we understand Galatians 3:16 correctly because the trustworthiness of God Himself is involved.

Before examining the original promises referred to, may we make one important suggestion to our readers, and particularly to our younger pastors? When you are faced with what appears to be an insoluble problem in Scripture, some seeming contradiction, do *not* strain or force the meaning of any passage in order to arrive at some solution which may seem acceptable to you. Rather, just wait and pray for further light.

But must we then accept so apparent a contradiction as that outlined above? Is it possible that Galatians 3:16 is the divine exegesis, God's own interpretation, of the promises made to Abraham? Let us be Bereans and search the Scriptures to see whether this is so. Let us see whether these promises can be fairly interpreted to refer to one single Seed: Christ.

a. The Promises to Abraham and His Seed

The first promise made to Abraham (then still called Abram) is found in Genesis 12:1-3:

"Now the Lord had said unto Abram, Get thee out of thy country, and from thy kindred, and from thy father's house, unto a land that I will show thee:

"*And I will make of thee a great nation*, and I will bless thee, and make thy name great; and thou shalt be a blessing:

"And I will bless them that bless thee, and curse him that curseth thee: and in thee shall all the families of the earth be blessed."

This promise was confirmed and enlarged upon several times, as we learn from the Book of Genesis.

Gen. 13:14-16: "And the Lord said unto Abram, after that Lot was separated from him, Lift up now thine eyes, and look from the place where thou art, northward, and southward, and eastward, and westward.

"For all the land which thou seest, to thee will I give it, and to thy seed for ever.

"And I will make thy seed as the dust of the earth: so that if a man can number the dust of the earth, then shall thy seed also be numbered."

Gen. 15:5: "And He brought him forth abroad, and said, *Look now toward heaven, and tell [count] the stars, if thou be able to number them: and He said unto him, So shall thy seed be.*"

Gen. 17:6-8: "And I will make thee exceeding fruitful, and I will make nations of thee, and kings shall come out of thee.

"And I will establish My covenant between Me and thee and thy seed after thee in *their* generations for an everlasting covenant, to be a God unto thee, and to thy seed after thee.

"And I will give unto thee and to thy seed after thee, the land wherein thou art a stranger, all the land of Canaan, for an everlasting possession; and I will be *their* God."

Gen. 22:17,18: "That in blessing I will bless thee, and *in multiplying I will multiply thy seed as the stars of the heaven, and as the sand which is upon the sea shore*: and thy seed shall possess the gate of his enemies;

"And in thy seed shall all the nations of the earth be blessed; because thou hast obeyed My voice."

Who could read the passages above with unbiased mind and question that in all these promises God had the *multiplied* seed of Abraham in mind and that Abraham would surely understand them so?

Concerning the passage last cited above, Barnes remarks (in dealing with Gal. 3:16) that obviously it refers to Abraham's multiplied seed "without *any* particular reference to an individual," and adds: "Such would be the fair and natural interpretation should it be read by hundreds or thousands of persons who had never heard of the interpretation here put upon it by Paul."

But we are not yet through, for remember, the apostle says in Galatians 3:16: "*To* Abraham and his seed were the promises made." Not "of" or "concerning" (though this is also true), but *"to,"* and we do indeed see these promises already confirmed to Isaac and Jacob in the very first book of the Bible, and then later to the children of Israel as a nation. And again Abraham's *multiplied* seed is unmistakably in view.

Note first the confirmation made to Isaac:

Gen. 26:4: "*And I will make thy seed to multiply as the stars of heaven*, and will give unto thy seed all these countries; and in thy seed shall all the nations of the earth be blessed."

And the further confirmation to Jacob is no less emphatic in its reference, not to one seed, but to many:

Gen. 28:14: "*And thy seed shall be as the dust of the earth, and thou shalt spread abroad to the west, and to the east, and to the north, and to the south*: and in thee and in thy seed shall all the families of the earth be blessed."

Perhaps the reader has noticed that already these promises in Genesis have been made to Abraham and *more* than "one" of his seed: Isaac *and* Jacob, but certainly these promises were made indirectly to more than these: to Abraham's greatly-multiplied seed.

It should be noted here that nowhere does God state that *all* of Abraham's seed are intended. Indeed the implication is clearly otherwise, for these promises were confirmed, not to Ishmael, but to Isaac; not to Esau, but to Jacob. That is, the multiplied seed through whom the world would some day be blessed would come through Isaac and then Jacob, from whom the "children of Israel" sprang (and it was even a certain generation of these that God had in mind). All this is perfectly consistent with the promises cited above; however, it would scarcely be honest of God to make such promises if He did *not* plan to bless the world through Abraham's seeds, but only through His single Seed: Christ.

b. Moses and the Prophets

But there is still more to consider before we go to the solution of this problem.

It is clear that *Moses and the prophets* understood these promises to refer to Abraham's multiplied seed. Here we could quote many passages in confirmation, but a few will have to suffice.

As Moses stood before the children of Israel at Kadesh-Barnea, just across Jordan from the land of Canaan, he proclaimed the divine challenge:

> **"Behold, I have set the land before you: go in and possess the land *which the Lord sware unto your fathers, Abraham, Isaac, and Jacob, to give unto them and to their seed after them.*"**
>
> **"*The Lord your God hath multiplied you, and, behold, ye are this day as the stars of heaven for multitude.*"**
>
> **"Behold, the Lord thy God hath set the land before thee: go up and possess it..." (Deut. 1:8,10,21).**

Isaiah surely understood God's promises as referring to Abraham's multiplied seed when he predicted concerning redeemed Israel:

> **"Arise and shine, for thy light is come, and the glory of the Lord is risen upon thee.**
>
> **"For, behold, the darkness shall cover the earth, and gross darkness the people: but the Lord shall arise upon thee, and His glory shall be seen upon thee.**
>
> **"And the Gentiles shall come to thy light, and kings to the brightness of thy rising" (Isa. 60:1-3).**

Jeremiah surely understood it so when he declared:

"And I will gather the remnant of My flock out of all countries whither I have driven them, and will bring them again to their folds; *and they shall be fruitful and increase.*"

"Behold, the days come, saith the Lord, that I will raise unto David a righteous Branch, and a King shall reign and prosper, and shall execute judgment and justice in the earth.

"In His days *Judah shall be saved, and Israel shall dwell safely...*" (Jer. 23:3,5,6).

To be sure, these blessings will come to Israel and Judah in the days of Messiah's reign, but it is still the *multiplied* seed to whom these blessings are promised.

Most certainly the prophet *Zechariah* also understood all these promises in the same way:

"And it shall come to pass, that as ye were a curse among the nations, O house of Judah, and house of Israel; so will I save you and ye shall be a blessing...."

***"Thus saith the Lord of hosts: In those days it shall come to pass, that ten men shall take hold out of all languages of the nations, even shall take hold of the skirt of him that is a Jew, saying, We will go with you: for we have heard that God is with you"* (Zech. 8:13,23).**

Surely this must refer to the multiplied seed of Abraham. It *could not* refer to Christ. Was Christ "a curse among the nations"? Did Christ have to be "saved" to become a blessing to them? These two verses from Zechariah 8 establish beyond the shadow of a doubt that it was God's plan—and it still is—to bless the nations through the *multiplied* seed of Abraham.

Does this all change when we come to the so-called "New Testament"? In no wise, for our Lord and His disciples went to none but *"unto the lost sheep of the house of Israel"* (Matt. 10:5,6; 15:24) simply *because* according to all covenants and prophecy Israel had to be saved before she could become a blessing to the Gentiles.

Did the crucifixion and resurrection of Christ, then, bring about a change in this plan? No, for *after* Pentecost we find Peter declaring to an audience of Israelites:

> **"Ye are the children of the prophets, *and of the covenant which God made with our fathers, saying unto Abraham, and in thy seed shall all the kindreds of the earth be blessed.***
>
> **"*Unto you first God, having raised up His Son Jesus, sent Him to bless you, in turning away every one of you from his iniquities*" (Acts 3:25,26; and cf. Vers. 19-21).**

Our Reformed and Presbyterian brethren have long held that God is through with Israel, that the Church is spiritual Israel, and that Christ, the King of the Church, is now sitting on David's "spiritual" throne in heaven. But this is arbitrarily altering the plain Word of God and, indeed, is contrary to reason.

Finally, Paul himself declares to the Roman believers:

> **"I would not, brethren, that ye should be ignorant of this mystery, lest ye should be wise in your own conceits: that blindness in part is happened to Israel, *until* the fulness of the Gentiles be come in.**
>
> **"And so *all Israel shall be saved, as it is written...*" (Rom. 11:25,26).**

With this present dispensation of the mystery and Gentile blessing through Israel's *fall* in view, the apostle says in the same chapter:

"For if the casting away of them be the reconciling of the world, what shall the receiving of them be, but life from the dead?" (Rom. 11:15).

Now it is evident that the latter "them" in this verse must be the same as the former "them." The latter cannot possibly refer to the Church, but to Israel, the nation which has been temporarily cast away. Verses 23 and 24 further confirm this.

What then is the explanation of Paul's words: *"He saith not, And to seeds, as of many, but as of one, And to thy Seed, which is Christ"?*

We can well see how our covenant brethren came to the conclusion that the promises to Abraham and his physical seed must be "spiritualized," for Paul clearly stated to the rejecting Jews of Pisidian Antioch:

"...It was necessary that the Word of God should first have been spoken to you, *but seeing ye put it from you and judge yourselves unworthy of everlasting life, lo, we turn to the Gentiles*" (Acts 13:46).

At first sight, and without the rest of Paul's epistles and the Word in general to guide us, it might well be gathered from this and similar passages that God was casting Israel aside forever. Indeed, in Romans 11:11 Paul himself declares that *now "through their fall salvation is come unto the Gentiles."*

But the so-called "spiritualization" of the Old Testament promises is really nothing less than an arbitrary altering of them by theologians so as to make them conform to their own systems of doctrine—*and we have no right to alter the written Word of God.* Moreover, Paul himself makes it crystal clear that the casting away of Israel is only temporary (see again Rom. 11:12,15,23-26).

c. The Glorious Solution

Why, then, does Paul say in Galatians 3:16:

"Now to Abraham and his seed were the promises made. He saith not, And to seeds, as of many; but as of one, And to thy seed, which is Christ."

In the light of the promises themselves and all their confirmations in the Book of Genesis, in the light of all the further confirmations in the law and the prophets, in the light of Peter's plain words in Acts 3:25,26, and in the light of Paul's own epistle to the Romans, is it not crystal clear that God planned—and plans—to bless the Gentile nations through *Israel*, Abraham's *multiplied* seed? Would it not be foolish and wrong to conclude from one passage, Galatians 3:16, that all these promises referred to one single Seed: Christ? To such a view the words of the puzzled little girl to her mother are rightly applied. She asked: "Mother, if God didn't mean what He said, why didn't He say what He meant?"!

God *did* mean exactly what He said and the wonderful, satisfying solution to this problem is to be found in the mystery revealed by the glorified Lord to and through Paul. As Pastor J. C. O'Hair has pointed out so beautifully in his book, *Daniel's Secret, Paul's Mystery, John's Revelation*, whenever it appears that God's prophetic program *cannot* be fulfilled, God reveals a secret that provides a glorious and satisfying answer.

Perhaps it will help at this point first to notice what the verse does *not* say. It does *not* say that God would *not* bless Abraham's multiplied seed, or through them the world. It does *not* say that God would bless *only* Christ, the single Seed, and make

Him *alone* a blessing to the world, though *in a sense* this is true, for all blessing flows from Him. The apostle simply states that in making the promises to Abraham and his progeny, God used the word "seed," which is singular in form, and that He did this because He had Christ in view. In other words, God specially avoided the use of plural words which might have been used, such as "in thy *children*," "in thy *descendants*," etc., for there was no generation of Abraham's offspring who, in themselves, could have proved a blessing to the world.

Perhaps the following diagram will help to explain the simple solution to the problem we have wrestled with.

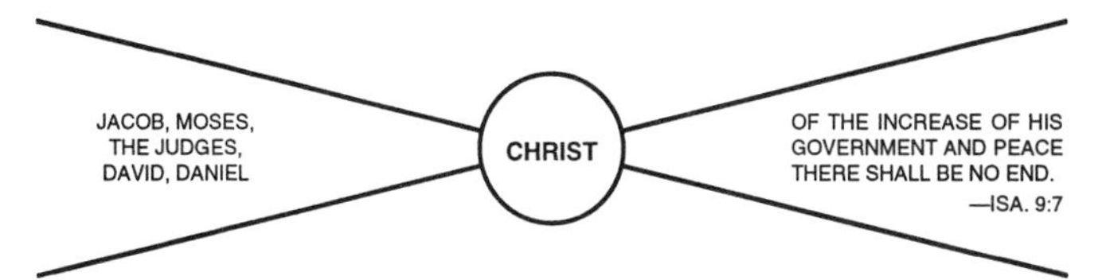

Considering the above diagram as representing the history of Abraham's physical seed, through which generation of that seed could the world possibly have been blessed? Through Jacob and his generation? Jacob himself swindled his own brother out of the birthright and his life from then on is a long story of human failure. Little wonder Psalm 146:5 declares: "Happy is he that hath the God of Jacob for his *help*, whose *hope* is in the Lord his God," for Jacob and his whole generation surely needed God's *help*.

Could the world have been blessed, then, through Moses' generation? Hardly, for under Moses Israel constantly murmured, complained, and rebelled. He called them "a stiff-necked people" (Ex. 33:3; *et al*), and indeed, Moses himself was not free from many human failures.

Could the world have been blessed through the generation of the Judges, then? Far from it, for Judges 17:6 says: *"Every man did that which was right in his own eyes."* This explains why the history of the Judges contains with wearying monotony the phrase: *"And Israel did evil again in the sight of the Lord."* How could they have been a blessing to the other nations?

Could David's generation have been the one to bring blessing to the world? How could they, when David himself, though a man after God's own heart, was guilty of adultery and murder, and when Israel had rejected God and had cried for a king to reign over them "like the other nations"?

Please glance now at the foregoing chart and note how the possibility of blessing to the world through Israel's multiplied seed diminishes steadily until we get to one Person—just *one* of the seed of Abraham: the *Lord Jesus Christ*.

Does it follow, then, that God's promises concerning the multiplied seed will not be fulfilled because they forfeited the blessing through failure and unbelief, and that therefore the nations will be blessed through Christ alone?

Not exactly. Are we hedging when we answer the question in this way? No, for God will indeed bless the world through the *multiplied* seed of Abraham. This has been proven, not only by the unconditional promises made to Abraham, Isaac, and Jacob, but also by repeated prophetic confirmations both before and after Pentecost. However, Israel will never become the world's blesser until she does so *through Christ* because the blessing of the world is wrapped up in Him alone.

Note that Christ is the focal point in the foregoing diagram. All blessing is centered in Him and must be found in Him. God has been demonstrating this for the past nineteen hundred years. Hear some of Paul's Spirit-inspired statements on this subject:

II Cor. 5:17: "Therefore if any man be *in Christ*, he is [or "there is"] a new creature...."

II Cor. 5:21: "For He [God] hath made Him to be sin for us, [Him] who knew no sin, that we might be made the righteousness of God *in Him*."

Gal. 2:20: "I am crucified *with Christ*: nevertheless I live; yet not I, but Christ liveth in me: and the life which I now live in the flesh, I live by the faith of the Son of God,[3] who loved me, and gave Himself for me."

Eph. 1:6,7: "To the praise of the glory of His grace, wherein He hath made us accepted in the Beloved: *In whom* we have redemption, through His blood, the forgiveness of sins, according to the riches of His grace."

Eph. 1:11: "*In whom* we also have obtained an inheritance, being predestinated according to the purpose of Him who worketh all things after the counsel of His own will."

Eph. 1:13: "*In whom* ye also trusted...*in whom*...ye were sealed...."

Eph. 3:6: "That the Gentiles should be fellow-heirs, and of the same Body, and partakers of His promise *in Christ* by the gospel."

3. Note carefully: "by *the faith of*," not my faith in. Faith is referred to here subjectively: our Lord's *worthiness to be believed*. See the author's booklet, *The Faith of Christ* and our comments on the Galatians 2:16 passage!

Phil. 3:8,9: "Yea, doubtless, and I count all things but loss for the excellency of the knowledge of Christ Jesus my Lord: for whom I have suffered the loss of all things, and do count them but dung, that I may win Christ,

"And be found *in Him*, not having mine own righteousness, which is of the law, but that which is through the faith of Christ,[4] the righteousness which is of God by faith."

Col. 2:6,7: "As ye have therefore received Christ Jesus the Lord, so walk ye *in Him*;

"Rooted and built up *in Him*...."

Col. 2:9,10: "For *in Him* dwelleth all the fulness of the Godhead bodily.

"And ye are complete *in Him*, who is the Head of all principality and power."

Col. 2:12: "Buried *with Him* in baptism, wherein also ye are risen *with Him*, through the faith of the operation of God, who hath raised Him from the dead."

Truly *"it pleased the Father that IN HIM should all fulness dwell"* (Col. 1:19). What do you want, unsaved friend, that is worth anything at all: forgiveness? peace? joy? assurance? They are to be found in Him and in Him alone. He is the Fount of every blessing, the Source of all supply. And what, dear Christian friend, do you have that is worthwhile that is of yourself? Nothing. All you have and are, you have and are *in Him*.

You have "redemption...the forgiveness of sins" *in Him*, because you were crucified *with Him*, and buried and raised *with Him*. You have been made "the righteousness of God" *in Him*, and God now "accepts" you *in Him*. You are "a new creation" *in Him* and have "obtained an inheritance," a most

4. See foregoing footnote.

glorious one, *in Him.* God now sees you *in Him* and has pronounced you "complete" *in Him.*

For nineteen hundred years God has been teaching this lesson, and not until Israel sees it and stops trying to "establish her own righteousness," humbly receiving Christ and the riches of His grace, will the blessing overflow to other nations. When Israel acknowledges Christ as her Messiah, then all nations will be blessed through Israel, *through Christ!*

Thus Paul, in Galatians 3:16, does not mean to imply that God will not fulfill the promises to Abraham's multiplied seed. He only points out that God used a *compound*, or *collective* noun in making these promises since He knew that the multiplied seed could not *in themselves* prove a blessing to the world. It is *redeemed Israel* that will bless the world (Zech. 8:13; Rom. 11:26).

Thus, even the *word* "seed," in Galatians 3:16, while singular in form ("Not many...but one"), is still plural in fact, for as we have said: we use the word "seed," whether of one single seed or of a bagfull. Moreover, one seed *contains* much seed, potentially. This agrees with our Lord's words in John 12:24:

> **"Verily, verily, I say unto you, Except a corn [kernel] of wheat fall into the ground and die, it abideth alone: but if it die, it bringeth forth much fruit."**

One more thing: As the possibility of world blessing through Abraham's multiplied seed diminished until Christ's appearance and redemptive work, so it will grow and expand once the favored nation is "saved" and finds her place *in Christ.* You say, "Christ is Israel's *Messiah*, her *King*; she does not belong to His Body." That is true. Yet morally and spiritually *every man* stands before God, either in Adam or in Christ. We can no more divorce ourselves from Adam than can the leaf from the twig, or the twig from the branch, or the branch from the bough, or the bough from the tree, *unless* we are *redeemed*—taken out of Adam, as it were, and given a position *in Christ*. This was so even of those who were saved before Paul was entrusted with "the revelation of the mystery," or was even converted to Christ, for in Romans 16:7 he refers to some who were *"in Christ before me."*

Unsaved friend, will you learn the lesson God is teaching today, as He forms "the Church which is His [Christ's] Body"? The lesson is simply that there is no true blessing to be found anywhere but *in Christ* and that *you* cannot possibly be a true blessing to anyone else, except *in Christ*.

Our generation is constantly emphasizing relevancy. Well then, this is the most relevant truth of all. Accept it and not only will your life be filled with meaning and purpose, but the blessing will overflow to others.

"Believe on the Lord Jesus Christ, and thou shalt be saved..." (Acts 16:31).

"Free from the law, O happy condition,
Jesus hath bled, and there is remission;
Cursed by the law and bruised by the fall,
Grace hath redeemed us once for all.

Now are we free—there's no condemnation,
Jesus provides a perfect salvation;
Come unto Me, O hear His sweet call,
Come, and He saves us once for all.

Children of God, O glorious calling,
Surely His grace will keep us from falling;

Passing from death to life at His call,
  Blessed salvation once for all.

Once for all, O sinner, receive it,
  Once for all, O brother, believe it;
Cling to the cross, the burden will fall,
  Christ hath redeemed us once for all.

—P. P. Bliss

Chapter 7 — Galatians 3:19-29

HEIRS ACCORDING TO THE PROMISE

WHY GOD GAVE THE LAW

"Wherefore then serveth the law? It was added because of transgressions, till the seed should come to whom the promise was made; and it was ordained by angels in the hand of a mediator.

"Now a mediator is not a mediator of one, but God is one.

"Is the law then against the promises of God? God forbid: for if there had been a law given which could have given life, verily righteousness should have been by the law" (Gal. 3:19-21).

My friend, you know that the law does not stop you from sinning, nor help you to be good. It rather stirs up in you that which is bad, so perverse is human nature. It makes you want to do the things that are forbidden.

Paul said this in Romans 7:7-8:

"...I had not known sin, but by the law: for I had not known lust, except the law had said, Thou shalt not covet. But sin, taking occasion by the commandment, wrought in me all manner of concupiscense. For without the law sin was dead."

Some people teach that Paul wrote Romans Chapter Seven at one time, and that later he came out of the struggle against sin and wrote the Eighth Chapter. But I tell you that he wrote both chapters right at the same sitting. The same man that said, "There is no condemnation to them which are in Christ Jesus" (Rom. 8:1), also said, "...the things that I do not want to do I find myself doing, and the things that I should do, I do not do. There is a law within me that when I would do good, sin worketh in me, O wretched man that I am!" (Rom. 7:15,16,17,24).

Paul did not blame the law; he blamed himself. Surely your own conscience and your own experience must bear the same witness. "The law was added because of transgression," to show you that by sinning you are transgressing the will of God, whether in thought or word or deed.

Just as when you have been given a ticket for speeding, an officer has brought the law into force to show that you have transgressed against "the powers that be," and you will have to pay for your offense.

"...till the seed should come to whom the promise was made" (Gal. 3:19).

As time passed there had been less and less possibility of Abraham's multiplied seed becoming a blessing to the Gentiles. Spiritually, Israel became worse instead of better, until we get to Christ, the Holy One, God manifested in the flesh. God's blessing was wrapped up in one individual, one Seed, the Lord Jesus Christ.

Does this mean that God will not fulfill His promises to and about Abraham's multiplied seed to the nation Israel? No, indeed. He will fulfill these promises when the children of Israel are saved and find their place in Christ. I quote to you again just one verse of many:

"And it shall come to pass, that as ye were a curse among the heathen, O house of Judah, and house of Israel; so will I save you, and ye shall be a blessing: fear not, but let your hands be strong" (Zech. 8:13).

Israel is going to be a blessing to the world when they are redeemed, i.e. when they find their position in Christ. They will be the first to admit that all the blessing that flows from them to the Gentiles comes from Christ.

The fact of blessing *in* Christ is relevant to every one of us. We can never find reconciliation to God outside of Christ. These are days when people want security, and you cannot find security outside of Christ.

"...and it was ordained by angels in the hand of a mediator" (Gal. 3:19).

Moses was the mediator. The law of Moses, or the covenant of the law, was a temporary institution; it was added until Christ came to take it out of the way (Col. 2:14). Paul's epistles have much to say about this.

The law is called *"the ministration of death,"* and *"the ministration of condemnation"* which the Apostle declares is *"done away"* and *"abolished"* by the cross of our Lord Jesus Christ (II Cor. 3:7,9,11,13).

"Having *abolished* in His flesh the enmity, even the law of commandments contained in ordinances; for to make in Himself of twain one new man, so making peace" (Eph. 2:15).

"Blotting out the handwriting of ordinances that was against us, which was contrary to us, and took it out of the way, nailing it to His cross" (Col. 2:14).

It is Paul who is first to state that the believer is *"dead to the law," "delivered from the law,"* and thus *"free from the law"* (Rom. 7:1-6). No wonder He declared exultantly:

"For sin shall not have dominion over you: *for ye are not under the law,* but under grace" (Rom. 6:14).

We have not quoted just a few verses to prove our point, as so many of the false cults do. I have given you a volume of Scripture on the purpose of the law and the meaning of grace. God's Word will stand forever, but as a covenant the law is a curse, for it can only condemn you. Christ bore that curse for us, and He stripped the law of all its claims against us, paying the price of the broken law Himself. Therefore the law was a temporary institution.

THE FAITH REVEALED IN DUE TIME

We have seen that Abraham's multiplied seed, through whom the world was and is to be blessed, are all incorporated into one seed, Christ. He is Abraham's single seed through whom alone Israel can become a blessing to the world.

A mediator is a go-between, and Moses was the mediator between God and Israel. He went up into the mountain to talk to God; he went down again to talk to Israel. This leads Paul to an important conclusion:

"Now a mediator is not a mediator of one, but God is one" (Gal. 3:20).

Notice the emphasis. God is *one*, and long before the law had been given He alone made unconditional promises to Abraham, Isaac, and Jacob. Those promises did not consist of a contract between two persons. The contract was on God's side:

"That in blessing I will bless thee, and in multiplying I will multiply thy seed as the stars of the heaven, and as the sand which is upon the sea shore; and thy seed shall possess the gate of his enemies; And in thy seed shall all the nations of the earth be blessed; because thou hast obeyed My voice" (Gen. 22:17,18).

There was no mediator needed for that.

The law was different. God said that *"if"* they obeyed His voice and kept His covenant which was the law, *"then"* they would be His special people (Ex. 19:5). This meant that two parties were involved in a contract—God and Israel. Moses was the mediator.

The Apostle Paul brought up the next question, "Is the law then against the promises of God?" He answers, "God forbid." The law is not against the promises, "for if there had been a law given which could have given life, verily righteousness should have been by the law" (Gal. 3:21).

In other words, if you could have saved yourself by fully obeying God's law, there would have been no problem at all. God would say, "Go ahead. You do not need Me; you can save yourself." Ah, but that is not so! No such situation could be possible. No such law could be given. Any righteous legal standard would have to condemn us because every one of us has sinned, not only ignorantly but in many cases willfully. We did what was wrong when we knew it was wrong.

This is why Paul argued in Galatians 3 that the law was a temporary institution or we should all perish.

"But the Scripture hath concluded all under sin, that the promise by faith of Jesus Christ might be given to them that believe" (Gal. 3:22).

Notice that we have the word *faith* twice in this verse. First, we have the word used subjectively, that is, His worthiness to be believed ("by faith of Jesus Christ"). The second usage is objective faith ("them that believe"). We believe in Christ. There is an object toward which our faith moves.

Galatians 3:23 shows the temporary character of the law and its inadequacy to save. It declares that "before" this principal of faith for salvation was made known, Israel was *"kept under the law, shut up unto the faith which should afterwards be revealed."*

Paul, was the first to say that faith provides escape from the law. When the Philippian jailer asked, "What must I do to be saved?" he replied: "Believe on the Lord Jesus Christ, and thou shalt be saved" (Acts 16:30,31). Paul answered this way because *Christ* is now manifested and therefore "the righteousness of God *without the law* is manifested" (Rom. 3:21).

"For there is one God, and one Mediator between God and men, the Man Christ Jesus; Who gave Himself a ransom for all, to be testified in due time. Whereunto I am ordained a preacher, and an apostle, (I speak the truth in Christ, and lie not;) a teacher of the Gentiles in faith and verity" (I Tim. 2:5-7).

God saved the chief of sinners, the one who was leading Israel in rebellion. He did not destroy him as an enemy, but saved him; by doing so, God showed what the cross had accomplished.

"For what the law could not do, in that it was weak through the flesh, God sending His own Son in the likeness of sinful flesh, and for sin, condemned sin in the flesh" (Rom. 8:3).

Paul exulted, "We have redemption through His blood, the forgiveness of sins according to the riches of His grace." God provided a Savior, and that Savior saved Paul, then Saul of Tarsus, the chief of sinners. After Paul's salvation, God sent him forth. How appropriate this was, for Paul was both the herald and living example of the riches of God's love, mercy, and grace.

THE LAW AS A SCHOOLMASTER

"Wherefore the law was our schoolmaster to bring us unto Christ, that we might be justified by faith.

"But after that faith is come, we are no longer under a schoolmaster" (Gal. 3:24-25).

The word "schoolmaster" in the original language does not refer to the schoolteacher which we have in our public and parochial schools, but rather to a sort of child-trainer. It was the individual who, in Bible times, was given strict supervision over little boys' conduct and morals. It is a rather stern word. If a boy did not obey, or if he misbehaved, he felt the schoolmaster's wrath. The trainer was expected to discipline the child as necessary with penalties imposed.

Note that in the King James Version the words "to bring us" are in italics. The italic means that the three words were not in the original text. The translator supplied them. In this case I truly feel that they should not have been supplied. While it is true that the law condemns us as sinners, and shows us that we need a Savior, the law does not actually bring us to Christ. No one in Old Testament times was brought to Christ. He had not yet come and was not known. Even the prophecies about Him were couched in veiled language.

The sense of verse 24 is that the law was our tutor until Christ, "that we might be justified by faith."

Verse 25 points out that after faith is come we are no longer under a tutor. It points out again that the law was only a temporary institution.

God is now dealing with men in pure grace. The apostle declared in II Corinthians 5:18-19:

"And all things are of God, who hath reconciled us to Himself by Jesus Christ, and hath given to us the ministry of reconciliation;

"To wit, that God was in Christ, reconciling the world unto Himself, not imputing their trespasses unto them; and hath committed unto us the word of reconciliation."

God's part has already been done! He has paid for your sins and says, "I hold nothing against you now." He pleads with you to put away your enmity and to be reconciled to Him.

A DISPENSATIONAL CHANGE

In this passage of Scripture in Galatians 3, glancing only at verses 17 through 25, I see at least nine words having to do with *Time* and God's changes in dispensation:

In verse 17—"before" and "after." The Abrahamic covenant was made about 2,000 years after Adam and we see that there had already been two changes in God's administration. Four hundred years *after* that God gave the law through Moses.

Verse 19—The law was a *temporary* addition to the promises made to Abraham. So far, we have five words counting those which are repeated: *"before," "after," "added," "until."* These are dispensational words—words that show that God (although He is Himself unchangeable), has changed His dealings with men from time to time through the centuries.

Verse 23: Here are the words *"before"* and *"after"* again. The Apostle said, "But *before* faith came, we were kept under the law, shut up unto the faith which should *afterwards* be revealed."

Verse 25: "But *after* that faith is come, we are *no longer* under a schoolmaster."

In these verses we find ten times that in the course of past generations and centuries several administrative changes have been made by God in His dealings with men.

About 2,000 years of human history had passed when God made His great covenant with Abraham. About 430 years later He gave the law to Moses. About 4,000 years had passed from Adam to when Christ died on Calvary. Then God raised up Paul, the chief of sinners, and saved him by His grace, to proclaim salvation and blessing by grace through faith in the finished, all-sufficient work of Christ at Calvary.

Paul uses another dispensational term in Romans 3:21: "*But now* the righteousness of God *without the law* is manifested."

As you study your Bible, do not forget to take the *time element* into consideration. Do not forget that God has dealt differently with men through the successive periods of history, teaching one lesson at a time.

There has been no change in dispensation since Paul. God has lingered long in mercy. He set Israel aside as a nation temporarily, and has since been dealing with the Gentiles. There are Gentile churches all over the world, companies of people rejoicing in Israel's Messiah as their Lord and Savior.

This present evil age is the age of grace. The dispensation of the law lasted for 1,500 years, and the dispensation of grace has already lasted for more than 1,900 years. When will it end? How will it end? When will the day of grace be brought to a close, and the day of God's wrath[1] ushered in? No one knows. Many trends of our time seem to indicate that the coming of our Lord for His own must be very near. He is *coming soon*, beloved, to recall His ambassadors.

Then, after letting the world bring its own troubles to a climax, He will declare war on the rebels and establish Christ as King of Kings and Lord of Lords. My dear friends, do not be among those who are judged in that *awful* day. We read that they will cry to the rocks and the mountains to fall on them and hide them from the wrath of God. The God who died on Calvary is not only kind and loving; He is also the righteous Judge and someday His wrath will be revealed.

"Why do the heathen [nations] rage, and the people [of Israel] imagine a vain thing? The kings of the earth set themselves, and the rulers take counsel together, against the Lord, and against His anointed, saying, Let us break their bands asunder, and cast away their cords from us" (Psa. 2:1-3).

How will the Lord answer their rebellion?

"He that sitteth in the heavens shall laugh: the Lord shall have them in derision. Then shall He speak unto them in His wrath, and vex them in His sore displeasure" (Psa. 2:4,5).

Both Daniel and the Lord Jesus say that it will be "a time of trouble" such as the world has never known (Dan. 12:1; Matt. 24:21).

---

1. A new dispensation.

CHILDREN OF GOD BY FAITH

"For ye are all the children of God by faith in Christ Jesus.

"For as many of you as have been baptized into Christ have put on Christ.

"There is neither Jew nor Greek, there is neither bond nor free, there is neither male nor female: for ye are all one in Christ Jesus.

"And if ye be Christ's, then are ye Abraham's seed, and heirs according to the promise" (Gal. 3:26-29).

Liberalism erases part of this verse and makes it read: *"For ye are all the children of God."* Bible-believing Christians know that this changes the truth into a lie and have rightly opposed this false teaching because it is not true that *all* are the children of God. What this passage says is that all who have placed their *faith* in Christ Jesus are the children of God: *"For ye are all the children of God BY FAITH IN CHRIST JESUS."*

But to add to the Word of God is no less serious than to take from it. Suppose someone should alter this verse to make it read: *"For ye are all the children of God by faith in Christ Jesus—and water baptism."* Surely we who believe the Pauline epistles to be the Word of God would reject this too as a *perversion* of the Scriptures. We would quote Ephesians 2:8,9 and other Scriptures to prove that water baptism has nothing to do with salvation in this dispensation of the grace of God.

Doubtless some reader will say that true believers do not add to the Scriptures in this way, but we must *insist* that the great majority of them do. Not only do many thousands actually teach that water baptism is necessary to salvation, but the great majority of the rest still make it a requirement for membership in their churches. One may join THE TRUE CHURCH by simple faith in Christ, but most churches will not receive him. God will accept him, but the brethren won't!

Thus Bible-believing, but mistaken, Christians have added to the Word of God by taking an ordinance from another dispensation and adding it to God's message for today. Water baptism has been added to faith in Christ as a requirement for membership in the Church on earth. Some merely "recommend" the ceremony, not knowing exactly why, but this is not in harmony with the Word, rightly divided either, for we are taught in the epistles of Paul that the sinner who trusts Christ as his Savior is *thereby* baptized into Christ through the operation of God (Col. 2:9-12).

This passage has been widely misunderstood and misinterpreted.

For that reason Paul declared here in Galatians 3:26:

"For ye are all the children of God by faith in Jesus Christ."

This is the great argument of Paul's letter to the Galatian churches. We shall see how this is confirmed by what follows in this passage.

"For as many of you as have been baptized into Christ have put on Christ" (Gal. 3:27).

The verse begins *"For"* rather than *"And."* It is *not an* additional thing which you must do. You are the children of God *by faith* in Christ, because "as many of you as have been baptized into Christ have put on Christ." When Paul said "as many of you," he realized that in the congregation there may have been individuals who had *not yet* received Christ. The point is that "as many as have been baptized into Christ have put on Christ."

This takes place when we trust the Lord Jesus, and accept Him as Savior by faith. Being baptized into Christ is so important. This is the glorious one baptism of which I have written in my booklet "Our Oneness with Christ—The Glory of the One Baptism."

With a tone of rebuke Paul wrote to the Romans—"Know ye not, that so many of us as were baptized into Jesus Christ were baptized into His death?" (Rom. 6:3). There he says again that we have put on Christ.

What does it mean to be *baptized* into Christ? The meaning is found in I Corinthians 12:13 where we read "For by one Spirit are we [believers] all baptized into one body." We know what that baptism means: when we trust Christ the Holy Spirit makes us one with the rest of the Body of Christ. We belong to the Church which is His Body, the true spiritual Church.

This makes sense because we cannot be baptized into Christ by a ritual ceremony. Please do not put a ritual ceremony into this passage or you will lose all the glory of it! We are grateful, dear Christian friends, that in this dispensation of the grace of God, we are all the children of God *by faith* in Jesus Christ.

Paul said, "I am [have been] crucified with Christ" (Gal. 2:20). He goes on to say that he is "buried with Him," "raised with Him" (Col. 2:12), "ascended with Him," and "glorified with Him" (Eph. 2:4-8).

Now do you see how we have been made one with Christ?

In this Body of believers, Christ Himself is the Head.

"There is neither Jew nor Greek, there is neither bond nor free, there is neither male nor female; for ye are all one in Christ Jesus" (Gal. 3:28).

This, of course, is our position before God in Christ. Differences should be maintained, especially those between male and female. The Bible shows that such differences are part of our daily lives. God told the wife to be subject to her husband, and the husband to love his wife. He told the slave to obey his master, and the master to be fair with his servant, giving him that which is just.

God certainly made a difference between the Jew and the Gentile, even those who are believers.

"I Paul, the prisoner of Jesus Christ, for you Gentiles" (Eph. 3:1).

The distinctions still remain, except that God now sees all believers *in Christ*. We are the beloved of God!

When Jesus came to John for baptism (a baptism of repentance for the remission of sins), John at first forbade Him. But Jesus said, "Suffer it to be so now: for thus it becometh us to fulfill all righteousness." He was baptized by John, and when He came away from that baptism, God broke through the heavens and said, "This is My beloved Son, in whom I am well pleased" (Matt. 3:13-17).

Ephesians 1:6 says that God "hath made *us* accepted in the Beloved," in the Lord Jesus Christ. How wonderful that God now sees us not in our poor sinful selves, but as believers in His own blessed Son. We now stand before God, complete in Christ!

"And if ye be Christ's, then are ye Abraham's seed, and heirs according to the promise" (Gal. 3:29).

This takes us back to the promise referred to in verses 6 to 22 where we saw that Abraham's offspring could be blessed and become a blessing to others only in Christ. By grace God has given us Gentiles a position in Christ, and He calls us Abraham's seed. We are not his physical seed, but we are his spiritual seed in Christ. A Gentile the seed of Abraham? Christ was Abraham's seed, and God has *baptized* us into Christ. We have a position *in Christ*. "And if ye be Christ's, then are ye Abraham's seed, *and heirs according to the promise*" (Gal. 3:29).

Compare this with Galatians 3:22 where we read that "the Scripture hath concluded *all* under sin," first the Gentiles before Abraham, then the Jew. The possibility of the multiplied seed of Abraham blessing the world then diminished and diminished, until finally God sold Israel into the hands of the Babylonian idolators. There seemed no hope, but then we come to Christ who was Abraham's seed. "The Scripture has concluded all under sin, that the promise by faith [the faithfulness] of Jesus Christ might be given to them that believe."

In I Corinthians 3:21-22 we read that "all [things] are yours." Is the promise about the land that God gave to Abraham for us too? Yes, and more. The Corinthian passage says, "All things are yours; Whether Paul, or Apollos, or Cephas, or the world, or life, or death, or things present, or things to come; all are yours."

How could this be? Because "For of Him, and through Him, and to Him, are all things: to whom be glory for ever. Amen" (Rom. 11:36). Every covenant has been fulfilled in Christ, even the covenant of the law. While the law condemns me as a sinner, it justifies me in Christ. Of Christ the law must say, "I find no fault in Him," and it says the same about me in Christ, and declares me righteous. May God help us to see this truth and to rejoice in it.

"For in Him dwelleth all the fulness of the Godhead bodily. And ye are complete in Him, which is the Head of all principality and power" (Col. 2:9-10).

Two days before the execution of Major John Andre (October 2, 1780) he was converted to Christ, and in that time composed this poem, which has long been one of my favorites:

MY HIDING PLACE

Hail, sovereign love, which first began,
The scheme to rescue fallen man!
Hail, matchless, free, eternal grace,
That gave my soul a Hiding Place!

Against the God who built the sky,
I fought with hands uplifted high,
Despised the mention of His grace,
Too proud to seek a Hiding Place.

Enwrapt in thick Egyptian night,
And fond of darkness more than light,
Madly I ran the sinful race,
Secure without a Hiding Place.

But thus the eternal counsel ran;
"Almighty love, arrest that man!"
I felt the arrows of distress,
And found I had no Hiding Place.

Indignant justice stood aview.
To Sinai's fiery mount I flew;
But justice cried, with frowning face:
"This mountain is no Hiding Place."

Ere long a heavenly voice I heard,
And Mercy's angel soon appeared;
He led me at a placid pace,
To Jesus, as a Hiding Place.

On Him almighty vengeance fell,
Which must have sunk a world to hell.
He bore it for a sinful race,
And thus became their Hiding Place.

Should sevenfold storms of thunder roll,
And shake this globe from pole to pole,
No thunderbolt shall daunt my face,
For Jesus is my Hiding Place.

A few more setting suns at most,
Shall land me on fair Canaan's coast,
Where I shall sing the song of grace,
And see my glorious Hiding Place.

What an understanding this author was given. Not only did he know Christ intellectually, but he knew Him *personally* as his glorious Hiding Place!

Chapter 8 — Galatians 4:1-31

THE BLESSEDNESS OF GRACE

SONSHIP

"Who are Israelites; to whom pertaineth the adoption, and the glory..." (Rom. 9:4).

"Having predestinated us unto the adoption of children..." (Eph. 1:5).

Both these statements were penned by the Apostle Paul who is the only New Testament writer to employ the word here translated *adoption*.

At first glance the apostle seems to contradict himself because after specifically stating in his letter to the Romans that the adoption and the glory pertain to Israel, he writes in his Ephesian letter that God has "predestinated *us* unto the adoption of children."

In order to arrive at a solution to this problem we must first determine the meaning of the New Testament word *adoption*.

a. Placing as Sons

In looking this word up in a Bible Dictionary some time ago, we were disappointed to find the following definition:

"Adoption is an act by which a person takes a stranger into his family, acknowledges him as his child, and constitutes him heir of his estate....In the New Testament, adoption denotes the act of God's free grace—by which, on being justified through

faith, we are received into the family of God, and made heirs of the inheritance of heaven."

That this is the present popular usage of our English word *adoption* no one will deny, but that it is NOT the meaning of the Greek word rendered "adoption" in the Authorized Version is clear from its usage in the New Testament.

Perhaps no passage of Scripture will shed so much light on the meaning of the original word as Galatians 4:1-7:

> ***"Now I say, That the heir, as long as he is a child, differeth nothing from a servant, though he be lord of all;***
>
> ***"But is under tutors and governors until the time appointed of the father.***
>
> ***"EVEN SO we, when we were children, were in bondage under the elements of the world:***
>
> ***"But when the fulness of the time was come, God sent forth His Son, made of a woman, made under the law,***
>
> ***"To redeem them that were under the law, that we might receive the adoption of sons.***
>
> ***"And because ye are sons, God hath sent forth the Spirit of His Son into your hearts, crying, Abba, Father.***
>
> ***"Wherefore thou art no more a servant, but a son; and if a son, then an heir of God through Christ."***

According to this passage, "adoption" is simply the "placing as a son"—that is, a grown-up son. This is the *definition of the word huiothesia* (adoption) as given by Young, Robinson, and others, while Thayer, referring to that adoption for which believers still wait, calls it, *"the consummate condition of the sons of God, which will render it evident that they are the sons of God."*

The adoption of children as we speak of it today generally refers to the taking in and bringing up of other people's children. This is not so of the Bible word *huiothesia*, for according to Galatians 4:1-7, this "placing as sons" affected those *already* children. This is not to imply, of course, that a stranger could not also be taken in and given a place as a full-grown son, but the point is that Bible "adoption" does not refer to mere acceptance into the family, but to a declaration of full sonship, with all its rights and privileges.

In the life of the Hebrew boy there came a time, appointed by the father, when "adoption" proceedings took place and the boy was *declared* to be the son and heir of the father.

Before that time he had been a son, indeed, but "under tutors and governors." He had been told what he must and must not do, as well as what he may and may not do. In this he differed nothing from a servant.

But finally the "time appointed" arrives. He is a grown son now. It is assumed that he will no longer need overseers to keep him in check. There will be natural understanding and cooperation between father and son. And so the "adoption" proceedings take place—a declaration that the son now enters into all the rights and privileges of full sonship.

Such is the meaning of the word *adoption* as it is used in the writings of Paul.

b. Israel and the Adoption

In Exodus 4:22 we find the striking statement:

"And thou shalt say unto Pharaoh, Thus saith the Lord, ISRAEL IS MY SON, EVEN MY FIRSTBORN."

But this does not signify that Israel was a full grown son while in Egypt. It was in Egypt that the nation had been born and by now it had scarcely begun to walk.

Hosea 11:1 says, "WHEN ISRAEL WAS A CHILD, THEN I LOVED HIM, AND CALLED MY SON OUT OF EGYPT," and Jeremiah 31:32 speaks of "THE DAY THAT I TOOK THEM BY THE HAND TO BRING THEM OUT OF THE LAND OF EGYPT."

So far were they from their time of "adoption" that it was only *after* God had taken them by the hand to bring them out of the land of Egypt that He first gave them the law. They had not by any means come to the place where God could make a declaration of full sonship. Instead He had to give them the Ten Commandments and a thousand other commandments beside. They had to be told "Thou shalt" and "Thou shalt not." Though "heir of the world," God's son, Israel, was placed "under tutors and governors until the time appointed of the Father."

Note carefully the phrase, *"the time appointed of the Father."*

Israel, left to herself, would never have reached the place of "adoption." She would never have attained to the place of full sonship, the place where she could be trusted to work in harmony with the Father. Often as we read about her in the Old Testament we find her described by such words as "rebellious," "perverse" and "stiff-necked."

By the time John the Baptist, the King's herald, had appeared, Israel had gotten farther from the place of adoption instead of nearer. He said, *"Now also the axe is laid unto the root of the trees: therefore every tree which bringeth not forth good fruit is hewn down and cast into the fire"* (Matt. 3:10). Yet all of John's warnings and pleadings had brought Israel morally no nearer to the place of "adoption," for the story ends with the reformer's head brought as a present to the daughter of a wicked woman with whom Herod, then king of the Jews, was living in adultery. The Lord Jesus had to take up where John had left off, crying to Israel to repent.

Thank God, however, that "adoption" does not depend primarily upon the son's attainments, but on the father's will. It takes place at *"the time appointed of the father,"* and it is heartening here, to see the Father take the first steps.

Israel would never have grown up or come to the place of adoption, "BUT WHEN THE FULNESS OF THE TIME WAS COME, GOD SENT FORTH HIS SON, MADE OF A WOMAN, MADE UNDER THE LAW, TO REDEEM THEM THAT WERE UNDER THE LAW, THAT WE MIGHT RECEIVE THE ADOPTION OF SONS" (Gal. 4:4,5).

The apostle speaks historically, of course, and it is not difficult to understand why "we," not "they," have received the adoption, when we consider what happened after the resurrection.

In the early chapters of the Book of Acts we find Peter offering to Israel the adoption and the glory. All the blessings of Israel's exaltation in the Millennium are bound up in the phrase *"the times of refreshing."*

"Repent ye therefore, and be converted, that your sins may be blotted out, when THE TIMES OF REFRESHING shall come from the presence of the Lord; And He shall

***send Jesus Christ, which before was preached unto you"* (Acts 3:19,20).**

As we know, the people of Israel refused both the Messiah and the glories He had purchased for them.

He had come to redeem them that were under the law that they might receive the adoption of sons, but they did not feel that they needed to be redeemed. He had come to "save His people from their sins," but they wanted to be saved from their troubles instead of from their sins. "Being ignorant of God's righteousness, and going about to establish their own righteousness," they refused to "submit themselves unto the righteousness of God" (Rom. 10:3).

"What then? ISRAEL HATH NOT OBTAINED THAT WHICH HE SEEKETH FOR" (Rom. 11:7).

Israel had become a rebellious son and even to this day remains out of God's favor.

As we see the nation groping about in darkness we recall the Word of God by Hosea the prophet:

"Then said God, Call his name Loammi; for YE ARE NOT MY PEOPLE, AND I WILL NOT BE YOUR GOD" (Hos. 1:9). This is what Paul calls the "fall," the "casting away," the "diminishing" of them. Thank God, this condition is only temporary! Israel will yet learn the lesson, for Hosea goes on to say:

***"Yet the number of the children of Israel shall be as the sand of the sea, which cannot be measured nor numbered; and it shall come to pass, that in the place where it was said unto them, Ye are not my people, there shall it be said unto them, YE ARE THE SONS OF THE LIVING GOD"* (Hos. 1:10).**

c. The Lord Jesus and the Adoption

When John the Baptist went to preach in the wilderness, we read:

***"Then went out to him Jerusalem, and all Judea, and all the region round about Jordan, AND WERE BAPTIZED OF HIM IN JORDAN, CONFESSING THEIR SINS"* (Matt. 3:5,6).**

John's baptism was a baptism of repentance for the remission of sins. Nothing could be clearer than that. There was nothing "non-essential" or "of secondary importance" about it. It lay at the very heart of his message and ministry. Those who doubt this should consider carefully and prayerfully Mark 1:4.

"JOHN DID BAPTIZE IN THE WILDERNESS, AND PREACH THE BAPTISM OF REPENTANCE FOR THE REMISSION OF SINS."

But what is this?

"THEN COMETH JESUS FROM GALILEE TO JORDAN UNTO JOHN, TO BE BAPTIZED OF HIM" (Matt. 3:13).

Little wonder that John "forbade Him." He had no sins to confess. Why should He be "numbered with the transgressors?"

And little wonder that God broke through the heavens, after that baptism, to say "THIS IS MY BELOVED SON, IN WHOM I AM WELL PLEASED" (Matt. 3:17).

Surely our blessed Lord need not wait for any adoption proceedings to be recognized as the Son of God! Surely He could be trusted to work in harmony with the Father! Surely it would be no risk on the part of the Father to exalt Him immediately to the position of full Sonship with its rights and privileges!

True, but our blessed Lord had come *to redeem others* from bondage so that *they*, by His merits, might be given the place of sonship. This is why Galatians 4:4 says, *"When the fulness of the time was come, God sent forth His Son, made of a woman, MADE UNDER THE LAW, TO REDEEM THEM THAT WERE UNDER THE LAW, THAT WE MIGHT RECEIVE THE ADOPTION OF SONS."*

Yes, He too—for the sake of others—was placed under tutors and governors until the time appointed of the Father.

He had to be placed in the position of a child, of a servant—in the position of *obedience—"MADE UNDER THE LAW."* Though equal with God, He had left the place of equality to go to the garden and cry, *"O my Father, if it be possible, let this cup pass from me! NEVERTHELESS NOT AS I WILL, BUT AS THOU WILT"* (Matt. 26:39).

"THOUGH HE WERE A SON, YET LEARNED HE OBEDIENCE BY THE THINGS WHICH HE SUFFERED" (Heb. 5:8).

Not that He had been *dis*obedient before. It simply had not been a question of obedience, for He was the eternal Son, equal with the Father, and in perfect agreement with Him. But now, for the sake of others, He assumed the place of subjection to learn obedience.

While on earth He was God's beloved Son, to be sure, but the declaration of full Sonship could not yet be made. The "adoption" proceedings could not yet take place.

It is in the second Psalm, however, that we read these significant words:

"I WILL DECLARE THE DECREE: THE LORD HATH SAID UNTO ME, THOU ARE MY SON; THIS DAY HAVE I BEGOTTEN THEE" (Psa. 2:7).

Should the reader ask *"What day?"* or *"When* was our Lord *declared* to be the Son of God?" he will find the answer in Acts 13:33.

"God hath fulfilled the same unto us their children, in that HE RAISED UP JESUS AGAIN; as it is also written in the second Psalm, Thou are my Son, THIS DAY have I begotten thee."

So it was at the resurrection that the "decree" was made and Christ was *"declared"* to be the Son of God,—"begotten" in the larger sense of the word.

This agrees with what we find in the first chapter of Romans, where Paul speaks of the good news of God,

***"Concerning His Son Jesus Christ our Lord, which was made of the seed of David according to the flesh; and DECLARED TO BE THE SON OF GOD WITH POWER, according to the spirit of holiness, BY THE RESURRECTION FROM THE DEAD"* (Rom. 1:4).**

The adoption proceedings over, He ascended *"far above all principality, and power, and might, and dominion"* to sit at the right hand of God—the place of favor and privilege and honor.

d. Our Adoption in Christ

"Blessed be the God and Father of our Lord Jesus Christ, who hath blessed us with all spiritual blessings in heavenly places in Christ:

"According as He hath chosen us in Him before the foundation of the world, that we should be holy and without blame before him in love:[1]

1. Perhaps the "in love" belongs with the next sentence, since there is no punctuation in the original.

"Having predestinated us unto the adoption of children by Jesus Christ to Himself, according to the good pleasure of His will,

***"To the praise of the glory of His grace, wherein He hath made us accepted in the beloved"* (Eph. 1:3-6).**

What a revelation!

Blessed *now* with all spiritual blessings in the heavenlies!

And let us not forget that the Ephesian letter was distinctly addressed to Gentiles in the flesh (3:1).

How is it that we, poor sinners, have thus been given free access to all the riches of the Father?

Was it according to our works, or character, or devotion? No, it was *"according to the good pleasure of His will,"—"According as He hath chosen us in Him before the foundation of the world."*

It was His own gracious plan to *make* us "holy and without blame before Him; IN LOVE HAVING PREDESTINATED US UNTO THE ADOPTION OF CHILDREN."

But *how* could He make us "holy and without blame before Him" and give us the place of "adoption?"

There is only one answer—*"BY JESUS CHRIST,"* and it is eternally "TO THE PRAISE OF THE GLORY OF HIS GRACE" that "HE HATH MADE US ACCEPTED IN THE BELOVED."

Now it is true that those referred to here as having been "adopted" were indeed strangers and aliens, graciously taken into the family of God; but a careful examination of the passage will clearly reveal that again more than present-day adoption is meant.

According to this passage we have not merely been saved, but we have also been accepted as grown sons in Christ, and given a place at the Father's right hand with free access to all the Father's riches in the heavenlies!

That we could not have *attained* to full sonship any more than Israel, is clear to any saved sinner. Indeed, it was when we came to a realization of our unworthiness, and put our trust in Christ, God's perfect Son, that He *gave* us this exalted position.

Thus, *as far as our position is concerned*, there is no period of preparation or discipline. God does not first place us "under tutors and governors," until we have shown that we are worthy of a position of full sonship.

Under the dispensation of law God demonstrated the insufficiency of man; Israel demonstrated how futile it is for the sons of Adam to *try*. Today, under the dispensation of grace He is demonstrating the all-sufficiency of Christ; now God is demonstrating His perfect satisfaction with those who take their place "in Christ."

But let us not proceed further with this thought until we have first seen that our "adoption," like Christ's, is bound up with His resurrection.

To see exactly what has taken place we need but turn to the second chapter of Ephesians, verses 3 and 4, where we are found to be *"children of disobedience"* and *"children of wrath."*

"BUT GOD, WHO IS RICH IN MERCY, FOR HIS GREAT LOVE WHEREWITH HE LOVED US,

"EVEN WHEN WE WERE DEAD IN SINS, HATH QUICKENED US TOGETHER WITH CHRIST (BY GRACE ARE YE SAVED).

"AND HATH RAISED US UP TOGETHER, AND MADE US SIT TOGETHER IN HEAVENLY PLACES IN CHRIST JESUS" (Eph. 2:4-6).

What infinite grace!

How far above the law He places us—and that immediately, without any period of probation!

But will this not produce careless living?

NO!

Such love will accomplish what the law never could. Those whose hearts have been won by His infinite grace will now *long* to serve their blessed Lord. God in love has drawn them close to Himself and brought about a mutual understanding.

This the law could never have done. Indeed, the apostle distinctly says in Romans 6:14: *"For sin shall not have dominion over you: FOR ye are not under law but under grace."*

"FOR YE HAVE NOT RECEIVED THE SPIRIT OF BONDAGE AGAIN TO FEAR; BUT YE HAVE RECEIVED THE SPIRIT OF ADOPTION, WHEREBY WE CRY, ABBA, FATHER" (Rom. 8:15).

As we have said, this is the *position* God has given us in Christ. But like salvation itself, the *realization* of it is progressive and also associated with resurrection.

How do we *enjoy* sonship now? By *resurrection,* for the 11th verse of this same chapter of Romans says:

"BUT IF THE SPIRIT OF HIM THAT RAISED UP JESUS FROM THE DEAD DWELL IN YOU, HE THAT RAISED UP CHRIST FROM THE DEAD SHALL ALSO QUICKEN YOUR MORTAL BODIES BY HIS SPIRIT THAT DWELLETH IN YOU" (Rom. 8:11).

This passage is often applied to the future resurrection of the body, but we believe it refers to experiencing the resurrection life now, for the next verse goes on to say,

"THEREFORE, BRETHREN, WE ARE DEBTORS, NOT TO THE FLESH, TO LIVE AFTER THE FLESH."

In other words, the Spirit of Him that raised up Christ from the dead will quicken our mortal bodies to help us to live the resurrection life—to walk in newness of life. This is what Paul meant when he exclaimed, "THAT I MIGHT KNOW HIM, AND THE POWER OF HIS RESURRECTION."

And some day we shall come into the *full* enjoyment of our position! Who knows how soon!

But until then we, *"which have the first-fruits of the Spirit, even we ourselves, groan within ourselves, waiting for the adoption, to wit, the redemption of our body"* (Rom. 8:23). But the blessed day will come! And *again* it will be a time of resurrection! "THE DEAD SHALL BE RAISED INCORRUPTIBLE, AND WE SHALL BE CHANGED. FOR THIS CORRUPTIBLE MUST PUT ON INCORRUPTION, AND THIS MORTAL MUST PUT ON IMMORTALITY" (I Cor. 15:52,53).

e. Back to Israel

"WHO ARE ISRAELITES; TO WHOM PERTAINETH THE ADOPTION, AND THE GLORY..." (Rom. 9:4).

"For I would not, brethren, that ye should be ignorant of this mystery, lest ye should be wise in your own conceits; that blindness in part is happened to Israel, until the fulness of the Gentiles be come in.

***"And so all Israel shall be saved; as it is written, There shall come out of Zion the Deliverer, and shall turn away ungodliness from Jacob:"* (Rom. 11:25,26).**

Finally Israel too, will come into the place of adoption. And once more it will be a resurrection.

"FOR IF THE CASTING AWAY OF THEM BE THE RECONCILING OF THE WORLD, WHAT SHALL THE RECEIVING OF THEM BE, BUT LIFE FROM THE DEAD!" (Rom. 11:15).

Then shall the world know that Israel, so long hated and despised, is God's son.

***"Thus saith the Lord of hosts; In those days it shall come to pass, that ten men shall take hold out of all languages of the nations, even shall take hold of the skirt of him that is a Jew, saying, We will go with you: for we have heard that God is with you"* (Zech. 8:23).**

Then shall Israel know that the position of sonship, with all its privilege and glory can only be obtained through the very One who was *"wounded in the house of His friends"—the house of Israel.*

And before the Millenium is over millions more will have learned that lesson, for God will yet keep His covenant with Abraham.

"That in blessing I will bless thee, and in multiplying I will multiply thy seed as the stars of heaven, and as the sand which is upon the sea shore; and thy seed shall possess the gate of his enemies;

***"AND IN THY SEED SHALL ALL THE NATIONS OF THE EARTH BE BLESSED; because thou hast obeyed my voice"* (Gen. 22:17,18).**

Even creation will feel the results: "BECAUSE THE CREATION ITSELF ALSO SHALL BE DELIVERED FROM THE BONDAGE OF CORRUPTION INTO THE GLORIOUS LIBERTY OF THE CHILDREN OF GOD" (Rom. 8:21).

f. The Mystery of His Will

Thank God that He has already *"made known unto us the mystery of His will...that in the dispen-*

sation of the fullness of times He might gather together in one all things in Christ, both which are in heaven, and which are on earth, even in Him" (Eph. 1:9,10).

Thus we, as His heavenly people, along with Israel and the Gentile nations on earth will come into the full enjoyment of "adoption." Our place, however, will be higher and closer than theirs, for we are the "members of His Body, of His flesh and of His bones" (Eph. 5:30).

TURNING BACK

"Howbeit then, when ye knew not God, ye did service [worship] unto them which by nature are no gods.

"But now, after that ye have known God, or rather are known of God, how turn ye again to the weak and beggarly elements, whereunto ye desire again to be in bondage?

"Ye observe days, and months, and times, and years.

"I am afraid of you, lest I have bestowed upon you labor in vain" (Gal. 4:8-11).

This described the past of the Gentiles. They were not the children of Abraham physically; the law had not been given to them. They had been idolatrous Gentiles. They had not known God, and they had worshipped false gods of wood, silver, gold, and stone. But Paul had preached Christ to these Galatian Gentiles and they had found salvation in trusting the redemptive work of the Lord Jesus Christ.

Paul was asking them, "Why do you want to go back to kindergarten again, where the teacher must tell you, 'Do this; do not do that'? You did not know God; you were strangers to God; you worshipped things that by nature were not gods. Why go back to that when through Christ you have come to actually know God?"

What a precious privilege it is for any individual to know God—to know Him personally and to be able to say to Him, "Father." Years ago I went with a young man to his church and everyone knelt to pray very frequently during the service: "Our Father which art in heaven, hallowed be Thy name..." and so on. It sounded irreverent to me. After the service we went out together and he asked, "How did you like the service?" "What was that prayer you were repeating?" I inquired. He said, "Do you not know that? It was the 'Our Father.'" I answered him, "Yes, I know the prayer, but Jesus specifically instructed in regard to it that we are not to pray with "vain repetitions, as the heathen do." This is stated in Matthew 6:7,8. He said that they repeat their prayers many times "for they think that they shall be heard for their much speaking."

After an interval I said to my friend, "Tell me, do you know God personally and intimately?" "Oh no," he answered. "I cannot claim to know God personally." "In that case then what did you mean when you prayed 'Our Father Which art in heaven?' If He is your Father, you surely ought to know Him very personally and intimately."

The young man confessed, "No, I acknowledge that I do not know God. I have said that prayer thousands of times, and I do not know God."

Beloved, there are many people like that. They say their prayers regularly and often, but they do not know God. What good does their praying do? The apostle wanted the Galatians, and God wants us, to know the joy of sonship.

Paul said that because we are accepted as sons, full-grown sons, by believing in Christ, "God hath sent forth the Spirit of His Son into your [our] hearts, crying, *Abba, Father*" (Gal. 4:6). We have the same loving, personal relationship to God as His Own begotten Son has.

"Wherefore remember, that ye being in time past Gentiles in the flesh, who are called Uncircumcision by that which is called the Circumcision in the flesh made by hands;

"That at that time ye were without Christ, being aliens from the commonwealth of Israel, and strangers from the covenants of promise, having no hope, and without God in the world:

"But now in Christ Jesus ye who sometimes were far off are made nigh by the blood of Christ" (Eph. 2:11-13).

Paul wrote to the Galatian Gentiles that in time past they did not know God but "after that, ye have known God, or rather you are known of God..." (Ver. 9).

It is so wonderful to know God personally and intimately, and be able to address Him and talk to Him. But it is far more wonderful to know that He recognizes me, hears my every cry, and talks to me in His Word. His ear is open and attentive to my call and my interests.

ACCESS TO GOD

"By whom also [Christ] we have access by faith into this grace wherein we stand..." (Rom. 5:2).

The believer's access to God is one of the most precious truths of the Bible.

When the Law was given the people "stood afar off" and were warned repeatedly that they should not come near to Mt. Sinai, where God spoke to Moses, "lest they die." Later, when the tabernacle was built, a thick veil separated the people, even the priests, from God's presence: *"The Holy Ghost this signifying, that the way into the holiest of all* [God's actual presence] *was not yet made manifest..."* (Heb. 9:8).

But now, under grace, the believer is given *free access* into God's presence. Indeed, in Hebrews 4:16, we are urged to come confidently to *the throne of grace*, not when it is convenient for God, but in *our* "time of need." Furthermore, the "mercy seat" of the Old Testament tabernacle has now become a *"throne of grace."* And as a throne surpasses a seat or chair in glory, so does grace far surpass mercy.

Some, failing to distinguish between standing and state, affirm that access to the throne of grace has nothing to do with the members of the Body of Christ since they are already seated in the heavenlies in Christ (Eph. 2:6).

This is a mistake, for the very epistle that has the *most* to say about our position in the heavenlies *also* says:

"For through Him [the Lord Jesus Christ] we both have access by one Spirit unto the Father" (Eph. 2:18).

Indeed, Romans 5:2 thus distinguishes between our position and our privilege, for it says that "we have *access by faith* into *this grace wherein we stand.*"

Every believer falls short of *occupying* his position in the heavenlies in Christ and of *appropriating* all his spiritual blessings, but we have free access to enter into these blessings "by faith" at any time.

It would take some doing for this writer to obtain even one fifteen-minute audience with the President of the United States, a finite human being who will soon pass away. Indeed *no one* has free access to him *at all times*—not his wife or children, not the Secretary of State, not his most intimate adviser. *No one* has free access at *all* times. But *we* are bidden, as we have seen, to approach *God* and *talk with Him while He listens*—at *our* convenience. Moreover, *we* are soon confused when two or more people talk to us at once, but He who manages the universe, from the mightiest heavenly body to the tiniest part of an atom, who rules over men and angels, is *infinite* and *omniscient*. He can give *individual attention* to a million supplicants at the same time!

So God, the God of the universe, says to the humblest believer: "Come. Come with your sorrow and grief, your questions and problems, your anxiety and fear, your troubles and woes, and I will help you."

He does not necessarily give us all we ask for; He does better than this. He gives us what is *best* for us (Rom. 8:26-28), and we may *rest* in this fact.

"Be careful [anxious] for nothing; but in every thing by prayer and supplication, with thanksgiving, let your requests be made known unto God.

"And the peace of God, which passeth all understanding, shall keep your hearts and minds through Christ Jesus" (Phil. 4:6,7).

"Now unto Him that is able to do exceeding abundantly above all that we ask or think, according to the power that worketh in us,

"Unto Him be glory in the Church by Christ Jesus, throughout all ages, world without end. Amen" (Eph. 3:20,21).

ENTERING INTO BONDAGE

"You observe days, and months, and times, and years. I am afraid of you, lest I have bestowed upon you labour in vain" (Gal. 4:10-11).

At least twice in this context, Paul said, "You desire to be under the law."

"Tell me, ye that desire to be under the law, do you not hear the law?" (Gal. 4:21).

Never be among those who *desire* to be in bondage. It is strange that where civil matters are concerned, people are always crying, "Liberty, give me liberty or give me death! I want freedom now." But when it comes to the things of God many seem to want to put themselves under the law. They say, "We must do our part," not realizing that the law was given only to show that we need Christ to find deliverance in salvation and liberty.

"Now we know that what things soever the law saith, it saith to them who are under the law: that every mouth may be stopped, and all the world may become guilty before God.

"Therefore by the deeds of the law there shall no flesh be justified in His sight: for by the law is the knowledge of sin" (Rom. 3:19,20).

The Galatians, sad to say, had come to the place where they desired to be under the law. Paul had to say to them:

"You observe days, and months, and times, and years. I am afraid of you, lest I have bestowed upon you labour in vain" (Gal. 4:10-11).

The observing of *days* and *months* and *times* and *years* must not be confused with what we might call celebrations. The apostle found no fault with any glad and legitimate celebration. In fact he gave a glad celebration—*the Lord's Supper.*[2] He certainly found no fault with our going to Church on Sundays, regularly meeting with God's people, singing hymns together, and joining our hearts in prayer.

There is no fault to be found, for example, with our Thanksgiving Day. We ought to give thanks every day, but I think it is a wonderful thing that one day in the year we have a grand celebration of the goodness of God in temporal and spiritual gifts to us.

The times and days and months and years which the Galatian believers were observing had to be observed for acceptance with God under the Mosaic law. It was legalism and bondage. Once these things had been in order, and had been the rule of the day. But grace had appeared, and the antitype of all the types had come—the Lord Jesus Christ.

He had died on Calvary and had settled the sin question once for all.

"For Christ is the end of the law for righteousness to every one that believeth" (Rom. 10:4).

The Gentile believers wanted to go back under the law that had held sway in a previous dispensation. They wanted to go back under a legal system that had never been given to Gentiles. No wonder the apostle was concerned about them.

He begged them in verse twelve:

"Brethren, I beseech you, be as I am; for I am as ye are: ye have not injured me at all."

Paul was saying to them, "I have been through this just like you. I had to learn that the law could

2. See the author's book, *The Lord's Supper and the Bible.*

not save me. I had to put away my own righteousness which is of the law. I had to find the righteousness that is provided by the Lord Jesus Christ."

"But what things were gain to me, those I counted loss for Christ.

"Yea doubtless, and I count all things but loss for the excellency of the knowledge of Christ Jesus my Lord: for whom I have suffered the loss of all things, and do count them but dung, that I may win Christ,

"And be found in Him, not having mine own righteousness, which is of the law, but that which is through the faith of Christ, the righteousness which is of God by faith" (Phil. 3:7-9).

SHOULD CHRISTIANS OBSERVE LENT?

Lent is a forty-day period of fasting, self-examination, and penitence observed by vast numbers of religious people prior to and in preparation for Easter. Denominational and other factors determine what foods and pleasures the observers of Lent may and may not enjoy during this period, but in general it is a time of abstinence from such things as may gratify and please.

Under the law God set aside one annual holy day when, above all other days, the children of Israel were to contemplate the sins they had committed during the past year and were to "afflict their souls" in penitence before God. This was the great *Day of Atonement*, observed annually on October 10th.

On that day, after the offering of certain sacrifices, the tabernacle was cleared of all personnel except the high priest, and he, alone and stripped of his priestly garments of "glory" and "beauty," entered—"not without blood"—into the Holy of holies before God to make atonement for himself and for the people of Israel (Lev. 16:14-17). In addition, both he and they afflicted their souls, i.e., condemned and reproached themselves for sins committed during the past year (Lev. 16:29,31; 23:27,29,32). The observance of this time of self-reproach and sorrow for sin was not optional; it was required of every man who would not be "cut off from among his people" (Lev. 23:29).

Referring specifically to this annual Day of Atonement, the Apostle Paul later declared by divine inspiration: *"...the law...can never...with those sacrifices which they offered year by year continually make the comers thereunto perfect,"* for had they availed to take away sins, he argues, repeated sacrifices would no longer have been necessary, since *"the worshippers once purged should have had no more conscience of sins"* (Heb. 10:2). *"But,"* he adds: *"in those sacrifices"* there was actually *"a REMEMBRANCE again made of sins every year"* (Heb. 10:3).

Thus, the apostle of grace demonstrates the insufficiency of the sacrifices of the law as compared with the all-sufficiency of the redemptive work of Christ. The blood of Christ purges the believer's conscience (Heb. 9:14); while we are still *conscious* of our sins, we have "no more *conscience* of sins," i.e., we are no longer plagued with a guilty conscience before God. We now have *"boldness to enter into the holiest by the blood of Jesus...our hearts [having been] sprinkled [cleansed] from an evil conscience"* (Heb. 10:19-22).

It is on this basis that believers are *not* now to give themselves over to periods of introspection and self-reproach but, leaving the past with God, are to go forward with His help. Thus, the apostle writes to the Philippian believers:

"Not as though I had already attained, either were already perfect....Brethren, I count not my self to have apprehended; but THIS ONE THING I DO: FORGETTING THOSE THINGS WHICH ARE BEHIND, AND REACHING FORTH UNTO THOSE THINGS WHICH ARE BEFORE,

"I PRESS TOWARD THE MARK [Lit., STRAIN TOWARD THE GOAL] FOR THE PRIZE OF THE HIGH CALLING OF GOD IN CHRIST JESUS" (Phil. 3:12-14).

And to the Hebrew believers he says:

"...Let us lay aside every weight, and the sin which doth so easily beset us, and let us run with patience the race that is set before us, LOOKING UNTO JESUS THE AUTHOR AND FINISHER OF OUR FAITH..." (Heb. 12:1,2).

But organized religion has always opposed the most precious truths of God. Organized religion killed the prophets, nailed Christ to the cross, and sent Paul to prison and death. Organized religion, turning from God's grace and "improving" on His Law, has prescribed not one, but forty days, in each year in which its devotees are to afflict their souls and deny themselves wholesome foods and pleasures which they otherwise might enjoy.

There is no indication in the Scriptures that any of the apostles or disciples ever observed, much less were instructed to observe, Lent, or any comparable period of fasting and penitence, after the dispensation of grace was ushered in. Indeed, the Apostle Paul severely condemns this lack of appreciation of Christ's all-sufficient redemptive work, whether by the observance of "holy" days or by religious acts of self-denial. To the Galatian and Colossian believers, respectively, he wrote as follows:

"But now, after that ye have known God, or rather are known of God, HOW TURN YE AGAIN TO THE WEAK AND BEGGARLY ELEMENTS WHEREUNTO YE DESIRE AGAIN TO BE IN BONDAGE?

"YE OBSERVE DAYS, AND MONTHS, AND TIMES, AND YEARS.

"I AM AFRAID OF [ABOUT] YOU, LEST I HAVE BESTOWED UPON YOU LABOR IN VAIN."

"I DESIRE TO BE PRESENT WITH YOU NOW, AND TO CHANGE MY VOICE [TONE]; FOR I STAND IN DOUBT OF YOU" (Gal. 4:9-11,20).

"Wherefore, if ye be dead with Christ...WHY...ARE YE SUBJECT TO ORDINANCES

"(Touch not; taste not; handle not...) after the commandments and doctrines of men?" (Col. 2:20-22).

These things, he says in the following verse, have indeed "a show of wisdom" in "will worship," i.e., worship according to *man's* will, but "they do not really honor God, but only satisfy the flesh (i.e., by creating a reputation for superior sanctity)." (*Scofield Reference Bible,* margin).

THE BELIEVER'S SINS AND THE CROSS OF CHRIST

We do not for a moment mean that believers should not recognize their sins and seek divine grace to overcome them, but this should always be done in the light of Calvary. It is at the cross that we find deliverance, not only from the penalty of sins, but also from sin's power in our lives. It is not the believer's willpower, but the cross of Christ that ultimately stands between him and his *sins*, his *sin*, and his *sinning*.

1. *The cross stands between the believer and his SINS*. Where human effort and religious works

have always failed, the cross availed to remove the penalty of our sins. "We have redemption through His blood, *the forgiveness of SINS*, according to the riches of His grace" (Eph. 1:7). "Christ died for our SINS" (I Cor. 15:3) is the heart of our message to the lost, and we ourselves rejoice in Paul's inspired declaration:

"And you, that were sometime alienated and enemies in your mind by WICKED WORKS, yet now hath He reconciled in the body of His flesh through death, to present you holy and unblameable and unreproveable in His sight" (Col. 1:21,22).

2. *The cross stands between the believer and his SIN*. It has judged and dealt with the *sin nature* itself.

Unsaved people sometimes forget that it is not only their sins, but their *sin* that keeps them out of heaven. It is not only what they have done, but what they *are* and *would do* if tempted, that makes them unacceptable to God. It is not merely their wicked works, but their fallen and depraved *nature* that condemns them before a holy God.

"...by one man sin entered into the world, and death by sin; and so death passed upon all men for that all have sinned" (Rom. 5:12).

Mark well, death passed upon all men, not because *one* sinned, but because they *all* sinned—i.e., *in Adam*, "the one" from whom all descended. We can no more disassociate ourselves from Adam than the branch can repudiate the tree. We have all come out of Adam and were "in Adam" when he sinned; thus we are guilty, not only by practice, but *by nature* as well. Let us thank God, however, that the redemption wrought by Christ at Calvary dealt not only with our individual sins (the fruit) but with our *sin*, or sinful nature (the root).

"For He [God] hath made Him to be sin for us, [Christ] who knew no sin, that we might be made the righteousness of God in Him" (II Cor. 5:21).

3. *The cross stands between the believer and his SINNING.*

Here the reader would do well to read the whole of Romans 6, a few passages of which we quote below:

"Knowing this, that our old man is crucified with Him, that the body of sin might be destroyed, that henceforth we should not serve sin."

"Likewise reckon ye also yourselves to be dead indeed unto sin, but alive unto God through Jesus Christ our Lord.

"Let not sin therefore reign in your mortal body, that ye should obey it in the lusts thereof.

"Neither yield ye your members as instruments of unrighteousness unto sin; but yield yourselves unto God, as those that are alive from the dead, and your members as instruments of righteousness unto God.

"FOR SIN SHALL NOT HAVE DOMINION OVER YOU: FOR YE ARE NOT UNDER LAW, BUT UNDER GRACE" (Rom. 6:6,11-14).

What joy and blessing come to the heart of the believer who realizes that *he has already been put to death for sin in Christ!* What power can the law have over such a one? How can it condemn him? What *greater* joy and blessing than to realize that since he died *in Christ*, he is now also raised from the dead and already seated in the heavenlies in Christ at the right hand of God, the place of honor and privilege and blessing (Eph. 2:4-6). Is it not perfectly clear that such a person will seek to serve God acceptably, not from a spirit of fear or concern about his future, but out of *sheer gratitude*—out of a sense of deep obligation to the One who has done so much for him? Did I say "serve God *acceptably*"? Such an one will give himself and all he is and has to God; he will burn out his little life as a blazing torch of love for the One who paid so great a price to save and justify and glorify him.

What instructed and appreciative Christian would wish to go back to "the weak and beggarly elements" of the Mosaic law with its religious restrictions? What instructed and appreciative Christian would wish to cast reflections on Christ's finished work in this way? What instructed and appreciative Christian would suppose that Christ could be more pleased with the observance of days and months and times and years, or a period of regulated self-denial, than with loving, grateful *service for Him?*

The unrestrained celebration of *Mardi Gras*, just before Lent, may be the extreme demonstration of the inconsistency of millions who observe Lent, but certainly whatever is wrong or unbecoming for the Christian during the Lenten period is just as wrong and unbecoming at any other season of the year.

Those who truly trust Christ as Savior should long be past the observance of religious rites which only *dis*honor God and cast reflections on the glorious redemptive work of our Lord and Savior Jesus Christ.

"Let no man therefore judge you in meat, or in drink, or in respect of an holy day, or of the new moon, or of the sabbath days:

"Which are a shadow of things to come; but the body [substance] is of Christ" (Col. 2:16,17).

CHRIST, PAUL, AND THE GALATIAN BELIEVERS

"Brethren, I beseech you, be as I am; for I am as ye are: ye have not injured me at all.

"Ye know how through infirmity of the flesh I preached the gospel unto you at the first.

"And my temptation [testing] which was in my flesh ye despised not, nor rejected; but received me as an angel of God, even as Christ Jesus.

"Where is then the blessedness ye spake of? for I bear you record, that, if it had been possible, ye would have plucked out your own eyes, and have given them to me.

"Am I therefore become your enemy, because I tell you the truth?

"They zealously affect you, but not well: yea, they would exclude you, that ye might affect them.

"But it is good to be zealously affected always in a good thing, and not only when I am present with you" (Gal. 4:12-18).

FAILURE OF THE GALATIAN CHURCHES

Once the Galatian believers had been charmed with Christ. All they could talk about was Christ. He had revolutionized their lives and homes and captivated their hearts.

As a result they had a deep affection for the Apostle Paul, through whose ministry Jesus Christ had been so plainly set forth among them. So blessed were these Galatian believers by Paul's ministry that they received him as Christ Himself—the Christ whom he so faithfully represented.

What *had* happened to the blessedness which the Galatian believers once experienced? What happened to their ardent love for Paul and their joy in fellowship and service?

The answer is found in the same chapter, Verses 17 and 18. The legalizers were, with some measure of success, seeking to bring them back under the law of Moses. In these verses the apostle describes the tactics the legalizers had used to accomplish this:

"They zealously affect you, but not well: yea, they would exclude you,[3] that ye might affect them.

"But it is good to be zealously affected always in a good thing, and not only when I am present with you" (Gal. 4:17,18).

This passage seems obscure until we take into account the fact that the word "affect" here means to affect *the emotions*. It is used by Paul in II Corinthians 11:2, where he writes to the Corinthians: "I am *jealous* over you."

Thus, the idea is that the legalizers were courting the Galatians, as it were, to win them *away from Paul* and his message of grace. Indeed, they were seeking to "exclude" the Galatians—*from him*; to "cut him out," as we say, so that the Galatians might court *them*.

To this the apostle responds that it is always good to be "affected," to have deep feelings, about any good thing—as they had previously had about Paul's God-given message of grace. And then, as a rebuke: *"and not only when I am present with you."*

How happy in grace, how thoroughly blessed, had the Galatian Christians been—*when Paul was with them!* But let the apostle turn his back, as it

3. I.e., "from me."

were; let the legalizers come courting on the morrow and suddenly they are about to go back under the law. *"So soon"* had they fallen from grace! The apostle was dumbfounded! *"I marvel that ye are so soon removed from him that called you into the grace of Christ unto another gospel"* (Gal. 1:6).

The Judaizers had been largely successful in courting the Galatians, so that the Galatians were now charmed with the personalities of these legalizers rather than with Christ. Paul had drawn their hearts to *Christ*; the Judaizers drew their affections to *themselves* and charmed them as true "holy" people.

The Galatians had received him *"as an angel of God, even as Christ Jesus."* They had sympathized so deeply with his infirmity that if it had been possible, they would have plucked out their own eyes and given them to him. Illness had detained him among them, and still he preached. What a man of God!

He had preached and they had come to the services. They were so eager to hear Paul that they sat in the front seats and listened attentively as he spoke.

But all that had changed. They were cursed with fighting and bickering until Paul had to say, "Take heed that ye be not devoured one of another" (5:15). Why this sad change? Had they denied the Scriptures? No, the legalists had come to them with Scriptures from the Old Testament. They had done what nine-tenths of the professing church is doing today. They took rites and ceremonies and forms and decrees from a former dispensation and added them *to* and mixed them *with* God's pure message of grace.

The result: The apostle now had to ask the Galatians: *"Where is then the blessedness ye spake of?"* (Gal. 4:15). And not only did they lose their blessedness, but they also lost their love for Paul, the one who had introduced them to Christ and His grace and glory. Indeed, the apostle now had to ask these Galatians, who had once sympathized with his infirmities and would gladly have given him their own eyes: *"Am I therefore become your enemy, because I tell you the truth?"* (Ver. 16).

These Galatian believers did not lose their blessedness and become Paul's enemy through falling into sins of the flesh or through worldliness, but rather through that which *seemed good.* They "desired" to be under the law again, to do *more* than God required. They sought to give to God that which he does not ask for and even refuses to accept, since *He* has provided all the sinner needs *in Christ.*

How unspeakably sad! And how natural that, hearing the news, the apostle should arise immediately to write them this urgent epistle, in large letters.[4]

We today should heed this lesson and learn what happens to the believer who becomes enamored of *anything* but *Christ.*

The temptations to "fall from grace," are as great today as they ever were. It would be well, therefore, to read this letter to the Galatians often so that we might be among those who "stand fast."

To paraphrase, Paul is saying, "Do not tamper with grace. Do not change it in any way; do not

4. The phrase "how large a letter" evidently refers to the *size of letter* he used to make up his words, for this *epistle* is certainly *not* large. This harmonizes with Galatians 4:15, where he refers to the eye problem with which he was afflicted.

confuse it with the law or the Sermon on the Mount, or with Peter's message at Pentecost. This is a further revelation; if you corrupt it you will bring a curse upon yourselves and upon those to whom you minister."

APPEASING GOD?

"My little children, of whom I travail in birth again until Christ be formed in you,

"I desire to be present with you now, and to change my voice [that is, my tone]; for I stand in doubt of you.

"Tell me, ye that desire to be under the law, do you not hear the law?" (Gal. 4:19-21).

This is the second time that the apostle has said in this epistle that they "desired to be under the law." In the same chapter (chapter 4), verse 9, he said, "Ye desire again to be in bondage." Think of that! They desired to put themselves under the bondage, the yoke of the law. Peter had called the law of Moses "a yoke...which neither our fathers nor we were able to bear" (Acts 15:10). The Galatians certainly have their counterpart in many believers today, true believers in Christ, who nevertheless think that they will please and honor God more by putting themselves under the law of Moses, even though God has abolished it and revealed His grace.

Perhaps I should explain here that God has not abolished the law as the written standard of righteousness or of His moral principles, but He has abolished the law as a covenant. Now that it has been done away, God calls it the *old covenant*.

To those who desired to be under the law Paul said "Do ye not hear the law?"

ABRAHAM, GOD'S EXAMPLE

"For it is written, that Abraham had two sons, the one by a bondmaid, the other by a freewoman.

"But he who was of the bondwoman was born after the flesh; but he of the free woman was by promise.

"Which things are an allegory: for these are the two covenants; the one from the mount Sinai, which gendereth to bondage, which is Agar.

"For this Agar is mount Sinai in Arabia, and answereth to Jerusalem which now is, and is in bondage with her children.

"But Jerusalem which is above is free, which is the mother of us all.

"For it is written, Rejoice, thou barren that bearest not; break forth and cry, thou that travailest not: for the desolate hath many more children than she which hath an husband.

"Now we, brethren, as Isaac was, are the children of promise.

"But as then he that was born after the flesh persecuted him that was born after the Spirit, even so it is now.

"Nevertheless what saith the Scripture? Cast out the bondwoman and her son: for the son of the bondwoman shall not be heir with the son of the freewoman.

"So then, brethren, we are not children of the bondwoman, but of the free" (Gal. 4:22-31).

THE MOTHER OF US ALL

Paul recalled the story of Abraham and Sarah, and her maid, in Genesis 16. Has the reader ever asked himself, "Who is *the mother of us all*"? One woman in Scripture is so called, and who but Abraham's wife, *Sarah* (Gal. 4:26-31)! The Bible narrative is an absorbing one.

Abraham is promised a son. His wife is barren, however, and both are getting older. They begin to get anxious—at least Sarah does, so in effect she says to Abraham, "I must not stand in your way. Take Hagar, my slave girl, to wife and it may be that I can still have a son—*through her*" (See Gen. 16:1,2). Abraham did as Sarah suggested and Hagar did bear a son, Ishmael. But God said, as it were: "No, this is not the son I promised. You do not need to help Me fulfill My promise" (See Gen. 17:18-21).

It was not until Abraham was one hundred years old, and Sarah ninety, that she bore Abraham a son as God had promised. The Scriptures portray them laughing together with pure delight; thus, Abraham called his son Isaac (Heb., *laughter*) according to the Word of God. Sarah said:

"God hath made me to laugh, so that all that hear will laugh with me.

"And Sarah said, Who would have said unto Abraham, that Sarah should have given children suck? for I have born him a son in his old age" (Gen. 21:6,7).

In Galatians 4 Paul uses this example, declaring that Hagar, the slave girl, speaks to us of the Law and its bondage and represents Jerusalem of that day, "in bondage with her children" (Ver. 25). Sarah on the other hand, speaks of *grace*, and represents *"Jerusalem which is above, [which] is free, which is the mother of us all"* (Ver. 26).

Ah, many people, religious people, think that the Law produces greater results than grace. *How wrong they are!*

"For it is written, Rejoice thou barren, that bearest not; break forth and cry, thou that travailest not: for the desolate hath many more children than she which hath an husband!" (Gal. 4:27).

So here Abraham's wife, Sarah, represents *grace*, as Abraham represents *faith* in Scripture. Hagar, the slave girl, could only bring forth the son of a slave, but Sarah, the free woman, brought forth *the son of promise!*

"So then, brethren, we are not children of the bondwoman, but of the free" (Gal. 4:31).

Chapter 9 — Galatians 5:1-26

THE BELIEVER'S LIBERTY IN CHRIST

IS CHRIST SUFFICIENT?

"Stand fast therefore in the liberty wherewith Christ hath made us free, and be not entangled again with the yoke of bondage.

"Behold, I Paul say unto you, that if ye be circumcised, Christ shall profit you nothing.

"For I testify again to every man that is circumcised, that he is a debtor to do the whole law.

"Christ is become of no effect unto you, whosoever of you are justified by the law; ye are fallen from grace.

"For we through the Spirit wait for the hope of righteousness by faith.

"For in Jesus Christ neither circumcision availeth any thing, nor uncircumcision; but faith which worketh by love" (Gal. 5:1-6).

Please understand that Paul was not some anarchist inciting the Galatians to rebellion and disobedience. This was an apostle of Christ urging believers to enjoy the liberty that Christ had bought for them at infinite price. Paul not only wrote by divine *inspiration*, he wrote by divine *revelation*. It was the glorified Lord who reached down and saved His great enemy on earth, Saul of Tarsus, and He sent him forth to proclaim the wonderful good news of God's grace to a dying, cursed world and the wonderful liberty that goes with that gospel.

Christ died to set us free from sin, the law, religious tradition, and every form of bondage. He wants us to serve Him as the Galatians had once freely served Him—from glad, thankful, grateful hearts. To deny by our actions that Christ died to set us free is ingratitude indeed. This is why the apostle wrote that the Galatians were disobedient to the truth.

You see, you can make yourself subject to the law and be obedient to the law, but disobey the truth. You may have all sorts of reasons for wanting to put yourself under the Mosaic law or the Ten Commandments, but God's Word says that Christ died to set you free.

"Christ hath redeemed us from the curse of the law, being made a curse for us: for it is written, Cursed is everyone that hangeth on a tree" (Gal. 3:13).

In Galatians 4:4-5 the apostle said:

"But when the fulness of the time was come, God sent forth His Son, made of a woman, made under the law, to redeem them that were under the law, that we might receive the adoption of sons."

We must remember that in John 8:36 the Lord said, with regard to bondage to sin,

"If the Son therefore shall make you free, ye shall be free indeed."

Glorious liberty!

All of this is just as true concerning bondage to the law. Christ has made us free, and we should rejoice that in Him we are free indeed. Since Christ has died, since He has bought our liberty *at the price of His own blood*, surely it is base ingratitude to bind ourselves again with the law, from which Christ died to set us free.

With the Galatians the rite of circumcision was an issue. It was circumcision that had separated Israel from the immoral pagans around them. The legalizers from Jerusalem had persuaded the Gentile believers that they ought to submit to circumcision, thus making sure that they were the people of God. To this Paul's answer was twofold:

> **"Behold, I Paul say unto you, that if you be circumcised, Christ shall profit you nothing. For I testify again to every man that is circumcised, that he is a debtor to do the whole law" (Gal. 5:2-3).**

They were choosing which part of the law to keep, but the law is a unit. Quoting from the words of Moses in Deuteronomy 27:26—Paul said:

> **"Cursed is everyone that continueth not in all [the] things which are written in the book of the law to do them" (Gal. 3:10).**

And again from the words of Moses, Paul showed that those who subject themselves to the law must live by the law. If you want to obey the law you cannot choose a part that you might like to obey.

I have heard people say, "I have never killed anybody; I have never stolen anything." They are just choosing one or two items of which they feel they are not guilty, but can they say that they have loved God with all of their hearts, with all of their souls, and all of their minds and all of their strengths, and their neighbor as themselves? That is the very essence of the Ten Commandments as given by both Moses and Christ. You cannot choose what you want to obey; if you are going to be under the law, you must obey the whole law. Remember that curse—Cursed is everyone who does not continue to do *all* the law.

James, writing to the twelve tribes of Israel scattered away from Jerusalem, said that if a man "keep the whole law, and yet offend in one point, he is guilty of all" (Jas. 2:10). That is, he is a lawbreaker. You might stand before a judge charged with arson, and say to the judge, "But I have never murdered anyone." It would make no difference. If you have committed arson you have broken the law, and you must be judged for it.

FALLEN FROM GRACE

This is why Paul said in Galatians 5:4:

"Christ is become of no effect unto you, whosoever of you are justified by the law; ye are fallen from grace."

Paul is arguing from logic here. He is not saying that if you, as a Christian, put yourself back under law that you are now lost again. Of course not! Of those who have trusted Christ, God says, "He that believeth on the Son hath everlasting life." That is life forever. Paul's point is that logically, if you are saved partly by the law, then you are not saved wholly by Christ's all-sufficient work. Notice the strong emphasis Paul placed on this in the Galatians 5:2,3, and 4. Notice the word *"nothing."* If you want to submit to the rite of circumcision, then, logically, Christ profits you nothing. And if you want to submit to this rite you are a debtor to do the whole law. Christ has become of no effect unto you if you are justified by the law. You are fallen from grace.

Christ's work was a finished work and it was all-sufficient for the payment of sin. If you are going to do something yourself for salvation, that indicates that Christ's death at Calvary was not sufficient.

Then how do you know that any of His works satisfy for any of your sins? My friends, Christ is either everything or He is nothing! It is not partly His work and partly your work that saves you; it is *all His work*, as we saw in the strong argument about Hagar and Sarah. Paul asked, "Do you not see that what was born of the slave girl could only produce bondage? The son of a slave girl could be only a slave boy, and there would always be that relationship. It must be a free son, a legitimate son, the son of Sarah.

So it is with law and grace. The law can only produce bondage, and trying to keep the law can only produce slavery. Paul said that salvation is not bondage, but grace. It is not partly the result of your keeping the law and partly the result of Christ's work. You do not have to help God as Sarah and Abraham tried to do, to their own confusion and frustration. Christ paid the whole price for sin—just as we sing in the wonderful hymn "Jesus paid it all, All to Him I owe; Sin had left a crimson stain, He washed it white as snow." You cannot be saved, even partially, by your own good works and law-keeping. You cannot help God save you.

"But to him that worketh not, but believeth on Him that justifieth the ungodly, his faith is counted for righteousness" (Rom. 4:5).

Some sincere believer may ask, "But can I be trusted with such liberty? I know my own tendencies to do what is wrong. Can I be trusted with the liberty of full sonship?" Let me reply by asking, "For what did you come to Christ? Did you come to be free to sin or to be free *from* sin?"

Every true believer surely came to the Lord Jesus Christ to find *deliverance* and *freedom* from sin—free from its dreadful power, its awful results, and its crushing penalty. If you came to Christ to be free from sin, you surely long to do what is right. What did bondage produce for you in the first place? Before you accepted Christ as your Savior, you tried and tried to be good. You tried to discipline yourself, but all your efforts were vain. If you could not find salvation by trying, do you think that you can be kept saved by trying? *No*, dear friend. Listen again to the words of Paul:

"Stand fast therefore in the liberty where with Christ hath made us free, and be not entangled again with the yoke of bondage" (Gal. 5:1).

"As ye have therefore received Christ Jesus the Lord, so walk ye in Him" (Col. 2:6).

You received Him by grace, now go on in grace. You came to Him just as you were, at the end of yourself. You said, "I give up; I believe Christ died for my sins, and I accept Him as my Lord and Savior." All right, now continue the same way. You are no better in yourself now than you were when you were first saved. The old nature has never improved, so Paul said in Romans 6:11:

"...Reckon ye also yourselves to be dead indeed unto sin...."

The old man, the old nature, has died in Christ. Consider the old man dead, for this is how God views him. Put him out of your mind. Ignore the old nature and live unto God. Be all wrapped up in Christ, praising Him for His grace and the spiritual blessings He gives you in the heavenlies.

Help God?

"Behold, I Paul say unto you, that if ye be circumcised, Christ shall profit you nothing" (Gal. 5:2).

You may want to go back to that ceremony, Paul explained, but if you do, you will be witnessing that you do not believe that Christ is sufficient. This applies with equal force to those who, after they had been saved by the finished work of Christ, want to go back to the rite of water baptism. Under the Great Commission given to the eleven, who were preaching the gospel of the Kingdom, water baptism *was* necessary to salvation (Mark 16:15-16).

That is why Peter preached the baptism of repentance at Pentecost.

Notice that he did not say, "Christ died for your sins; believe on Him and you have everlasting life; and if you think it a good testimony, be baptized." No! No, he said:

"Repent, and be baptized every one of you in the name of Jesus Christ for the remission of sins, and ye shall receive the gift of the Holy Ghost" (Acts 2:38).

How different that is from the further revelation given by the rejected but glorified Christ in heaven through the Apostle Paul:

"For Christ sent me *not* to baptize, but to preach the gospel [of grace]: not with wisdom of words, lest the cross of Christ should be made of none effect. For the preaching of the cross is to them that perish foolishness; but unto us which are saved it is the power of God" (I Cor. 1:17-18).

That was not what Peter preached at Pentecost. God has raised up another apostle, Paul, and sent him forth with *"the good news of the grace of God"*

(Acts 20:24). That is why *Paul* argued with tremendous force again and again that salvation is no longer by works of any kind, but by grace alone (Gal. 1:6,7; Rom. 4:4,5; Eph. 2:8,9).

He said in Galatians not to add works after salvation either. The Galatians were already saved, but they wanted to submit to the rite of circumcision, and Paul said that if they did so, they would be saying that Christ profited them nothing. That is simple logic. My friend, if you append anything that was once necessary to salvation to the present gospel of the grace of God, you are testifying that Christ is not sufficient. You are casting reflections upon His finished work.

We are told that water baptism is just meant as a testimony. Yes, I am afraid it is a testimony, but a very bad one as practiced today by a confused Church. It is a testimony that you do not really believe that the finished work of Christ is enough.

"For in Him dwelleth all the fulness of the Godhead bodily.

"And ye are complete in Him, which is the head of all principality and power:

"In Whom also ye are circumcised with the circumcision made without hands, in putting off the body of the sins of the flesh by the circumcision of Christ.

"Buried with Him in baptism, wherein also ye are risen with Him through the faith of the operation of God, who hath raised Him from the dead" (Col. 2:9-12).

Do we "get it"? Paul told the Colossians that they were complete in Him. He said that they have put off that body of fleshly passion and sin by the circumcision of Christ—a circumcision made without hands.

Paul also dealt with baptism. "Buried with Him in baptism"—no, do not put any water in here. "Buried *with* Him," not *like* Him, not *as* Him. The burial with Christ was done in the baptism of *Christ*. (Lk. 12:50). "Buried with Him in baptism, wherein also ye are risen with Him through the faith of the operation of God [not the operation of a minister as a baptizer], Who hath raised Him from the dead" (Col. 2:12).

Paul had said of himself in Galatians 2:20 that he was "crucified with Christ." In Colossians 2:10 he said, "Ye are complete in Him." Our crucifixion, the putting off of the old man, the old body of sin, was done in the circumcision not made with hands when our blessed Lord and Savior was "cut off" out of the land of the living. It is therefore through the operation of God, *through the death of the Lord Jesus Christ* and the work of the Holy Spirit, that we are *saved* and *sanctified* and *accepted* in the Beloved One, and pronounced *complete in Him*. Everything we need has been given to us in Christ.

PERFECT PERSONAL RIGHTEOUSNESS

"For we through the Spirit wait for the hope of righteousness by faith" (Gal. 5:5).

Here Paul is speaking of our desire for perfect personal righteousness. We all wish we were more righteous. Thank God that we are perfectly righteous in Christ, and now God wants us to live for Him out of gratitude. We live for Him because we love Him. "Stand fast in the liberty wherewith Christ hath made us free, and be not entangled again with the yoke of bondage."

Never let anyone, be he ever so godly and sweet a Christian, or ever so authoritative a student of

Scripture, tell you that you are complete in Christ, BUT that you ought to do this or that, submit to this rite or that rite, to be *really* complete. "It would be a good testimony," some say, or "an outward sign of an inward work of grace," or "it is following Christ's example." But God says, "YE ARE COMPLETE IN CHRIST."

So, stand fast in that liberty, dear Christian friend.

"For in Jesus Christ neither circumcision availeth any thing, nor uncircumcision; but faith which worketh by love" (Gal. 5:6).

I have had so many people ask me questions about water baptism that I have written a booklet entitled: *"Water Baptism, Is It Included in God's Program for This Age?"* The Church today is so confused; there are so many kinds of baptism, and the division is so great, that to me it is an evidence that there is something basically wrong in the teaching about baptism. The Church has forgotten to ask the first question, "*Should* we be baptized in water?" Instead they ask, "How should we be baptized in water?" I have tried to answer this in my booklet.

In our study of Paul's letter to the Galatians we have tried to show that the cure for sin is not the law of Moses but the grace of God. True, we need civil laws to curb crime, punish evil doers, and protect the innocent, but such laws cannot save men's souls. The law that frightens man and keeps him from committing crime will not change his heart or make him a good man; only the grace of God can do that.

Go to the hardened sinner and say, "You must not do this; you must not do that." Argue with him, reason with him, add threats, explain the dire results of law-breaking. None of this will change him. It will not make him a different man. But go and tell the hardened criminal that God loves him and that Christ died on Calvary's cross to pay for all of his sins, and you'll have his attention. Explain how Christ will justify him fully and freely. If that sinner believes in Christ, his whole life will be revolutionized.

The Spirit of God has thus touched the hearts of millions of men who otherwise would have gone farther down the road to perdition. This principle also holds true for the believer. Nothing will make a man want to live a life pleasing to God like a sense of His wonderful, infinite love. That is why Paul was so disappointed when the Galatians wanted to go back under law, the law of a previous dispensation. When he had come to them they were pagans, worshiping other gods. He had come to them preaching Christ and His grace, and they had rejoiced in God and Christ their Savior.

They had marveled at the love of Christ which caused Him to die for their sins, that they might stand with no condemnation in the presence of God. Then they decided to go back under the law, and we saw that Paul was disappointed in them. He was so disturbed to learn about it that he wrote them this strong letter. He wanted to save them from ruining their lives as Christians, not by immorality or heresy, but by *legalism*. He showed them that God had accepted them as full-grown sons in Christ, no longer under tutors and governors, no longer under a schoolmaster.

You see, God deals with us in grace. That is why the apostle wrote in Galatians 5:1, "Stand fast therefore in the liberty wherewith Christ hath made us free, and be not entangled again with the yoke of bondage."

Spurgeon called the desire to approach God with good works a hydra-headed monster. He said that you cut off what you think is the last head, the last good argument for your good work, and you think that now it is dead and gone. But another head pops up. He was right. People want to *do* things; they want to become accepted in the sight of God by doing *their* part, and the motive behind this is pure pride. They want to have the credit themselves. In their subconscious minds is the thought of being self-made men.

Pride is the condition of the unsaved and it is always a temptation to man—even to the saved man.

After men have been saved, after they have been justified completely and fully by the grace of God and the finished work of Christ, how often, like the Galatians to whom Paul wrote, believers desire to go back under law again and to be in bondage. Listen to what Paul wrote about this in regard to his own kinsmen:

"Brethren, my heart's desire and prayer to God for Israel is, that they might be saved.

"For I bear them record that they have a zeal of God, but not according to knowledge.

"For they being ignorant of God's righteousness, and going about to establish their own righteousness, have not submitted themselves unto the righteousness of God.

"For *Christ* is the end of the law for righteousness to everyone that believeth" (Rom. 10:1-4).

LITTLE FOXES AND A LITTLE LEAVEN

"Ye did run well; who did hinder you that ye should not obey the truth?

"This persuasion cometh not of Him that calleth you.

"A little leaven leaveneth the whole lump.

"I have confidence in you through the Lord, that ye will be none otherwise minded: but he that troubleth you shall bear his judgment, whosoever he be" (Gal. 5:7-10).

Many Christian people entertain the notion that apostasy from the truth begins with a denial of one or more of the fundamentals of the faith (such as the infallibility of the Bible, the deity of Christ, or the efficacy of His redemptive work). The moral aspect of apostasy, they suppose, comes about in much the same way.

This view is not wholly correct, for apostasy generally *begins* not with believing spiritual or moral error, but with *condoning* it.

Eve fell into sin, not by denying what God had said, but by *listening* to Satan.

a. The Little Foxes that Spoil the Vines

In the Song of Solomon, the Shulamite damsel, quoting the words of Solomon, her beloved bridegroom, notes that the vineyards are in full blossom. Soon the grapes will be ripe for the marriage feast. But a danger threatens the harvest: *"the foxes, the little foxes, that spoil the vines."* These must without fail be "taken," or *caught* (Song of Solomon 2:15).

What a beautiful lesson we have here! How often God's people have stood at the threshold of great blessing, the refreshing odor of an abundant spiritual harvest in the air when, alas, all has been lost—not through a frontal attack by the adversary, but by those wily little foxes that had been permitted to spoil the vines. Some doctrine or practice, clearly unscriptural and subversive of spiritual blessing, had been condoned when, like the little foxes of Solomon's song, they should have been caught and disposed of.

b. A Little Leaven and Lost Blessing

It is difficult, if not impossible, to determine from Paul's Epistle to the Galatians just what the Galatian believers thought the rite of circumcision would accomplish for them spiritually. We doubt that they knew themselves, but the Judaizers had come in among them and had captured their attention so that they now "desired to be under the law" (Gal. 4:21). They did not deny the efficacy of the finished work of Christ, but they were interested—just interested—in submitting to a religious ceremony which would in itself be a denial of the all-sufficiency of His redemptive work (3:1; 5:2-4). Result: the blessing was already vanishing (4:15) and the apostle had to warn them: *"A little leaven leaveneth the whole lump"* (5:9).

c. The Path to Restoration

In these days when both spiritual error and moral wrong are made so palatable, when apostate unbelief and worldliness are presented so appetizingly, we do well to take heed to the Spirit's warning to quickly purge out the leaven that threatens to permeate the whole loaf.

Many Bible-believing churches and organizations that once knew the power and joy of the Spirit have condoned too much doctrinal error. The apostle's question could appropriately be asked of them: "Where is then the blessedness ye spake of?"

This blessedness cannot be restored by any amount of mere praying or planning. Resolute action must be taken. Those little foxes must be caught and dispatched. The "little leaven" must be purged out.

GRACE IN ACTION!

"And I, brethren, if I yet preach circumcision, why do I yet suffer persecution? then is the offence of the cross ceased.

"I would they were even cut off which trouble you.

"For, brethren, ye have been called unto liberty; only use not liberty for an occasion to the flesh, but by love serve one another.

"For all the law is fulfilled in one word, even in this; Thou shalt love thy neighbour as thyself.

"But if ye bite and devour one another, take heed that ye be not consumed one of another" (Gal. 5:11-15).

If we can preach something for man to do in addition to all that Christ has done, then the offense of the cross will cease. The cross is an offense to the world. The unbeliever asks, "Am I so bad that someone had to die for me?" Paul said that was why he was suffering persecution—because of "the offense of the cross." He was preaching the truth that the cross is the only thing that God will accept for salvation.

"I would they were even cut off which trouble you" (Gal. 5:12).

The Jerusalem leaders in Acts 15 had agreed that the Judaizers had caused trouble among the Gentile believers by saying that they were to be under the law of Moses. That law was given to Israel alone, and in Galatians 1:7, Paul said "...there be some that trouble you, and would pervert the gospel of Christ." He wished that they were out of the way and were not always agitating (5:12).

"For, brethren, ye have been called unto liberty; only use not liberty for an occasion to the flesh, but by love serve one another" (Gal. 5:13).

Perhaps you have noticed how naturally this verse falls into three parts. The first, "brethren, ye have been called unto liberty." The second, "use not liberty for an occasion unto the flesh." The third, "by love serve one another." Let us look at them separately.

BELIEVERS CALLED UNTO LIBERTY

In light of the Word of God, we have no right to forego our liberty in Christ. We would be disobeying the truth as well as being foolish if we left our standing in grace to go back under law. God tells us that Christ died to deliver us from the curse of the law so that we no longer need to be under that curse. Therefore, it is a sin to put ourselves back under it. We may forego our rights for the welfare of others, but we have no right to forego our liberty and allow men or theologians or religious leaders to entangle us with a yoke of bondage. God tells us to "Stand fast in the liberty wherewith Christ hath made us free, and be not entangled again with the yoke of bondage."

If we were to forego our liberty and put ourselves under the law again we would be poor representatives of Christ who died to save us *from the law*. We would be in a poor position to preach the gospel of the grace of God. That is why the apostle, all through this epistle, emphasized so strongly that we are *not* under the Mosaic law with its Ten Commandments.

Galatians 3:13 says very clearly that "Christ hath redeemed us from the curse of the law." *Galatians 3:25* says that "after faith is come, we are no longer under the schoolmaster." *Galatians 4:4,5* says that "when the fullness of time was come, God sent forth His Son...to redeem them that were under the law, that we might receive the adoption [placing as full-grown] of sons."

"Christ is become of no effect unto you, whosoever of you are justified by the law; *ye are fallen from grace*" (Gal. 5:4).

Did you get that? It does not mean that after you are saved you can be lost again. But Christ profits you *nothing* if He does not profit *everything*. He must be all or nothing, and as we just read in verse 13, "Brethren, we have been called unto liberty."

I wish believers would let this great truth sink deep into their hearts: *"Brethren, ye have been called unto liberty."* God wants you to go to work in the morning, to go about during the day, to come home in the evening, to go to bed at night, and to get up again with the knowledge that you are not a slave under law, but a son *under grace*.

DO NOT USE LIBERTY TO INDULGE THE FLESH

However, Paul went on to say in the next portion of the passage, "Use not liberty as an occasion to the flesh." Some people have said that Paul taught that you can do anything you desire as a believer;

it does not matter. Of course, Paul said nothing of the kind, and neither have I. I have said that grace is the only key to right living. It provides the only motivation that God can accept, the only motivation that brings results.

Paul wrote in his letter to the Romans:

"And not rather, (as we be slanderously reported, and as some affirm that we say,) Let us do evil, that good may come? whose damnation is just" (Rom. 3:8).

It is true that there are people who say that if we are under grace we can do anything we desire. Theoretically this may be true. It is true that when the Lord gave the blind man his sight again, He said, "Go thy way; thy faith hath made thee whole" (Mark 10:52). But you know what the man did; the very next phrase tells us that he *"followed Jesus in the way."* There you have it exactly. God has redeemed us from the condemnation of sin, redeemed us "by His grace through the redemption that is in Christ Jesus," and there are no strings attached. He says, "Your faith has made you whole, go your way." "Whomsoever the Son shall make free shall be free indeed."

Our liberty is real. Ah, but the result of this grace is that the recipient wants to live for the Lord Jesus Christ, and he offers *himself* as a bondslave to Christ, as Paul did. Paul wrote of himself again and again as the servant, the bondslave, of Christ. The believer wants to follow Christ in the way and *obey* Him. I know that there are always ungodly men who want to "turn the grace of God into lasciviousness," (Jude 4). But we are not following them; they know nothing about grace. If they have come to Christ at all, perhaps in some intellectual sense, they did not come to be freed *from* sin; they came to be freed *to* sin. They accepted God's grace intellectually, in order to have a license to sin. I Peter 2:15-16, puts it beautifully:

> **"For so is the will of God, that with well doing ye may put to silence the ignorance of foolish men: As free, and not using your liberty for a cloak of maliciousness, but as the servants of God."**

Is that not beautiful? Free, but not using our liberty for a cloak. If we do that, we are all hypocrites, and we show clearly that we do not understand the grace of God. So the apostle said: "Ye have been called unto liberty; only use not liberty for an occasion to the flesh...."

BY LOVE SERVE ONE ANOTHER

"But by love serve one another." My dear friend, this clause certainly needs our attention too.

> **"All things are lawful for me, but all things are not expedient: all things are lawful for me, but all things edify not. Let no man seek his own, but every man another's wealth [good]" (I Cor. 10:23-24).**

Now there you have the true use of *liberty*. It is not license to do wrong, but liberty to enjoy all that is right.

> **"But take heed lest by any means this liberty of yours become a stumbling block to them that are weak" (I Cor. 8:9).**

Sometimes we may be tempted to do something gratifying to the flesh, but because it does not edify or help build up others, we may decide that under grace it is the wrong thing to do. Paul says to be careful that grace, that liberty, does not become a stumbling block to one of your brethren.

"So then every one of us shall give account of himself to God" (Rom. 14:12). Often people who have been careless in their Christian lives forget their responsibilities to God and to others. When someone suggests that their conduct may be a stumbling block to another, they answer, "But I am not responsible for him." But are you not? We remember the great mistake that Cain made when he said to God, "Am I my brother's keeper?" (Gen. 4:9).

Look at the application Paul made of this fact. "So then, every one of us shall give account of himself to God."

"Let us not therefore judge one another any more: but judge this rather, that no man put a stumbling block or an occasion to fall in his brother's way" (Rom. 14:13).

There indeed is grace in action. Those who think that grace is only God's kindness to man so that he can now continue in sin do not have a very good understanding of God or of His grace. Grace is not only bestowed upon us, it works in us.

Let me try to describe this and make it as plain as I can. Is it not true that the poor sinner who sees that the Lord Jesus Christ has died to pay for all of his sins will normally marvel at the infinite love and grace of God in providing salvation for him? And should not this make a difference in his life?

"For the grace of God that bringeth salvation hath appeared to all men,

"Teaching us that, denying ungodliness and worldly lusts, we should live soberly, righteously, and godly, in this present world;

"Looking for that blessed hope, and the glorious appearing of the great God and our Savior Jesus Christ;

"Who gave Himself for us, that He might redeem us from all iniquity, and purify unto Himself a peculiar people, zealous of good works" (Titus 2:11-14).

I desire that the unsaved may learn to trust in the Lord Jesus Christ and be gloriously saved from sin and the curse of the law; but I also desire that those who have believed may be very careful to fully appreciate the infinite grace of God and to live the lives they should for His glory and the welfare of other men.

At least twice in Paul's epistles we find pairs of verses which bear this out.

"For by grace are ye saved through faith; and that not of yourselves: it is the gift of God:

"Not of works, lest any man should boast" (Eph. 2:8-9).

With verse 10:

"For we are His workmanship, created in Christ Jesus unto good works, which God hath before ordained that we should walk in them."

So, we are not saved *by* works, but we are saved *unto* good works.

Another pair of verses is found in Titus 3:5 and verse 8:

"Not by works of righteousness which we have done, but according to His mercy He saved us...."

"This a faithful saying, and these things I will that thou affirm constantly, that they which have believed in God might be careful to maintain good works. These things are good and profitable unto men."

I tell you that the best Christian will be the best citizen too. The one who has come to know and appreciate the grace of God will be the best neighbor, the best friend, the best partner in business.

"For, brethren, ye have been called unto liberty; only use not liberty for an occasion to the flesh, but by love serve one another."

A FULFILLED LAW

"For all the law is fulfilled in the one word, even in this; Thou shalt love thy neighbour as thyself" (Gal. 5:14).

The normal mother does not need laws to make her take care of her child. She loves that child; she nurses it, washes it, dresses it, cares for it, protects it, feeds it. Why? Because the law says that she must? No, because she *loves* the child. In just the same way love will motivate us to right living far more than the requirements of the law could ever do. Yes, my unsaved friend, you may try until Doom's Day to keep the law, but you will go out of this world lost in your sins if you reject God's grace. "For the wages of sin is death; but the gift of God is eternal life through Jesus Christ our Lord" (Rom. 6:23). May all of us who know Him as Savior seek *by His grace* to live in ways that will please and honor Him.

THE SPIRIT-LED CHRISTIAN

"This I say then, Walk in the Spirit, and ye shall not fulfill the lusts of the flesh.

"For the flesh lusteth against the Spirit, and the Spirit against the flesh: and these are contrary the one to the other; so that ye cannot do the things that ye would.

"But if ye be led of the Spirit, ye are not under the law.

"Now the works of the flesh are manifest, which are these; Adultery, fornication, uncleanness, lasciviousness,

"Idolatry, witchcraft, hatred, variance, emulations, wrath, strife, seditions, heresies,

"Envyings, murders, drunkenness, revellings, and such like: of the which I tell you before, as I have also told

you in time past, that they which do such things shall not inherit the kingdom of God.

"But the fruit of the Spirit is love, joy, peace, longsuffering, gentleness, goodness, faith,

"Meekness, temperance: against such there is no law.

"And they that are Christ's have crucified the flesh with the affections and lusts.

"If we live in the Spirit, let us also walk in the Spirit.

"Let us not be desirous of vainglory, provoking one another, envying one another" (Gal. 5:16-26).

In the latter part of Galatians the Apostle Paul concluded his great argument for Christian liberty, that is, the liberty of believers in Christ. Only believers in Christ have *true* liberty. The unsaved are in bondage to their own sinful natures and to the Devil, who the Scriptures say leads them captive at his will (II Tim. 2:26). Their bondage might take on different forms. They may indulge in gross sin, depraved drunkenness, and debauchery. Or their bondage may take the form of proud self-righteousness, which can be even worse. It could also include hypocrisy, trying to be what one really is not.

In any case, the unsaved are in bondage. They have nothing with which to overcome either their own sinful natures or the Devil, the adversary of their souls. I do not mean to say for a moment that believers never sin or fall; they do so, of course, but the point is that they need not do so. God has given us the Holy Spirit with whom we may overcome every single temptation. He dwells within and is always ready to help.

"For sin shall not have dominion over you: for ye are not under the law, but under grace" (Rom. 6:14).

No longer in bondage to the law, to self, or to the Devil. We are truly free! It is wonderful to know the liberty of believers in Christ.

"This I say then, Walk in the Spirit, and ye shall not fulfil the lust of the flesh" (Gal. 5:16).

Here the apostle gives us the great secret of victorious Christian living, and again it is on the side of liberty, not bondage. Perhaps we should first define these terms. What is the flesh? And what is the Spirit in this passage? The flesh is surely more than the body, that is clear from the way Paul uses the word in his writings. He has a great deal to say about the flesh. Not merely the body, it is the Adamic nature, the old nature within the believer, of which he speaks.

The Spirit here is not man's own spirit, but the Spirit of God dwelling within the believer. This is evident from the whole passage and even from this verse. If man's spirit were referred to here, the conclusion of the passage would not be true. For Paul said, "Walk in the Spirit, and ye shall not fulfill the lusts of the flesh" (Gal. 5:16). Most men walk largely according to their own spirits, and that is no protection against falling into the sins of the flesh. So this reference to the spirit has to do with the *Spirit* of God, as indicated in our Authorized Version with a capital "S".

Romans 8:11 confirms this:

"But if the Spirit of Him that raised up Jesus from the dead dwell in you, He that raised up Christ from the dead shall also quicken your mortal bodies by His Spirit that dwelleth in you."

Do you understand the importance of this verse? If the Spirit of God could raise Christ from the dead,

He can certainly *quicken* your mortal body and give you the strength to overcome sin.

"Therefore, brethren, we are debtors, not to the flesh, to live after the flesh" (Rom. 8:12).

We are *not* debtors to the flesh. We have no cause to say, "I had to do it; the old nature is so powerful in me that I could not help myself." We are no longer debtors to the flesh because the Spirit of God dwells within us.

"What? know ye not that your body is the temple of the Holy Ghost which is in you, which ye have of God, and ye are not your own?

"For ye are bought with a price: therefore glorify God in your body, and in your spirit, which are God's" (I Cor. 6:19,20).

How many people have tried in vain to overcome fleshly desires by other methods! They have repented in tears and promised never to fall again. They have made new resolutions. They have tried to exert more will-power. They have become very religious. They have spent more time praying and going to church. They have put themselves under the law. They have subjected themselves to deprivation and pain. How many methods have been tried!

Man must have the Spirit of God within him in order to live a godly life. As Christ said to the people of His day:

"It is the Spirit that quickeneth [giveth life]; the flesh profiteth nothing..." (John 6:63).

The apostle said to the believers, "Walk in the Spirit." You have the Spirit within you. When you believed in Christ, the Spirit came to dwell in you. Now let Him lead; let Him be the master in your life. Walk in the Spirit. Be all wrapped up in the things of the Spirit, of the Word of God, of prayer, and of the throne of grace. Give time to the study of the Word and prayer and you will find that the old nature will be overcome. It is only in the measure that we walk in the Spirit, that we shall not fulfill the desires of the flesh.

I would like to call your attention to the word *"walk,"* and emphasize it. Paul said, "WALK in the Spirit." Having the Spirit is not enough. There are many believers who have the Spirit dwelling within, yet they are worldly and carnal in their behavior. There is no final, complete victory over sin in this life. Just because the Spirit has taken up His residence in the believer does not mean that the believer will automatically overcome all sin. We must *walk* in the Spirit; we must seek His help step by step, for we are not sinless yet! The old nature in the believer is just as bad as the old nature in the unbeliever. It is Adam's old fallen nature. That is why Galatians 5:5 says,

"We through the Spirit wait for the hope of righteousness [personal righteousness] by faith."

There is no cure-all, beloved. You cannot touch a button or click a switch and have all temptations cease.

Look what Paul said:

"For the flesh lusteth against the Spirit, and the Spirit against the flesh: and these are contrary the one to the other: so that ye cannot do the things that ye would" (Gal. 5:17).

Experientially we are not yet free from sin!

What can that last phrase mean? "Ye cannot do the things that ye would." For one thing, it refutes the doctrine of the annihilation of the old nature in the believer. The believer is no better in himself than the unbeliever. As Paul remarked, "In me dwelleth no good thing" (Rom. 7:18). The believer has the same temptations to sin and the same evil depraved heart as before; but because the Spirit of God has come to dwell within, and the believer belongs to Him, there is now a battle which did not exist before. A man may have struggled against temptations, but now it is different.

There is within the believer a distinct warfare between two natures: the new nature, the nature of the Spirit of God, and the old nature, the nature of fallen Adam. There is a constant battle, and therefore Paul said, "Ye cannot do the things that ye would."

I can almost hear someone say, "That does not sound like victory to me; that sounds like defeat. It sounds like the believer cannot do what he wants to do to please God. He will constantly fail and fall into sin."

This last phrase, "Ye cannot do the things that ye would" is not meant to show our weakness or our helplessness. It does not offer excuse for sin, as though we could say, "I could not help it." There are Christian people who constantly argue for the weakness of the flesh. They never seem to argue for the power of the Spirit within them. I say that this phrase, "Ye cannot do the things that ye would," is not given to show how weak we are, but how *depraved* we are by nature. Thank God, Christ died for our sins and He has perfected forever those who are sanctified. We stand before Him perfect, "accepted in the Beloved One," and "complete in Christ."

"Who shall lay anything to the charge of God's elect?" (Rom. 8:33). That is our standing in Christ. But as to our experience in ourselves, we are still inherently sinful, as bad as we ever were. We can never relax and say that sin is gone and that we will never be troubled again with temptation to sin.

This is what the apostle meant when he said, "These are contrary the one to the other: so that ye cannot do the things that ye would." You cannot take a vacation from sin and say that you have no problem with it any more. The old nature, and our adversary the Devil will see to that. So Galatians 5:17 is just simply saying that the Spirit of God and the old nature within us are constantly at enmity with each other, so that we cannot do what we would like to do. We must be constantly on our toes, constantly alert against temptation.

This is a simple statement of facts. If any man would deny it, let him ask himself, "Have I found complete personal victory over myself?" Let him ask himself, "Do I have no more trouble with temptation?" Of course he does. Therefore we all must "walk in the Spirit." Paul did not say, "*If* you have the Spirit within you"—But "If you *walk* in the Spirit."

"If ye be led of the Spirit, ye are not under the law" (Gal. 5:18).

This is where the believer's liberty in Christ comes in. God no longer treats us like little children. He tells us that we are now grown-up sons in Christ and He puts us under grace, not law. What good would the law do to one who walks in the Spirit? If you are led of the Spirit, your one great desire will be to please Him, and there is the secret of victory. "For as many as are led by the Spirit of God, they are the sons of God" (Rom. 8:14). The word for "son" is "huios"—full-grown son, no longer under tutorage. The son is grown up, "Wherefore thou are no more a servant, but a son; and if a son, then an heir of God through Christ" (Gal. 4:7).

Beloved, all believers are full-grown sons *by position* in Christ, but all believers are not full grown sons *in experience*. The Corinthians, you remember, were babes. That is why Romans 8:14 says, "As many as are *led* by the Spirit, they are the [full-grown] sons of God." That is, experientially they live as grownups and not as babes who have to be told what to do and what not to do.

"Now the works of the flesh are manifest, which are these; Adultery, fornication, uncleanness, lasciviousness, Idolatry, witchcraft, hatred, variance, emulations, wrath, strife, seditions, heresies, Envyings, murders, drunkenness, revellings, and such like: of the which I tell you before, as I have also told you in time past, that they which do such things shall not inherit the kingdom of God" (Gal. 5:19-21).

These are all things that fallen Adam does. These things are manifest; just read the newspaper. As far as the works of the flesh are concerned, Paul was certainly right when he said, "These are manifest." You cannot hide them.

"But the fruit of the Spirit is love, joy, peace, longsuffering, gentleness, goodness, faith, meekness, temperance: against such there is no law" (Gal. 5:22-23).

This list, the fruit of the Spirit, is entirely different. Blessed virtues are listed. The world likes aggressiveness and self-confidence and self-assurance. But there is nothing of that kind in this list.

Notice, please, that over against the works of the flesh we have the fruit of the Spirit. Do you see, beloved, that it is not by struggling and trying that we overcome sin? That is just putting ourselves under another kind of bondage. Men who have not taken Christ as personal Savior have certainly proved that they break their best resolves. The fruit of the Spirit cannot be works. If only we would be more occupied with the things of the Spirit!

What does it mean to walk in the Spirit? The Word of God was written by the Spirit. Get more interested in it. It is *in* the Spirit and *through* the Spirit that we approach God in prayer. Spend more time in prayer. That is what it is to walk in the Spirit, and to be led by the Spirit. It does not mean that you hear voices or have strange compunctions or hunches. It means to spend more time in the Word of God and prayer, and in that measure, beloved, you will not fulfill the lusts of the flesh.

If you will be like a tree taking in the sunshine and rain that God graciously gives, you will bear the precious fruit of the Spirit. Do not struggle to try to overcome the old nature, but become *occupied* more and more with *the things of God*. That is the secret.

"And they that are Christ's have crucified the flesh with the affections and lusts.

"If we live in the Spirit, let us also *walk* in the Spirit.

"Let us not be desirous of vainglory, provoking one another, envying one another" (Gal. 5:24-26).

Chapter 10 — Galatians 6:1-18

CHRISTIAN FELLOWSHIP

RESTORING THE FALLEN

"Brethren, if a man be overtaken in a fault, ye which are spiritual, restore such an one in the spirit of meekness; considering thyself, lest thou also be tempted.

"Bear ye one another's burdens, and so fulfill the law of Christ.

"For if a man think himself to be something, when he is nothing, he deceiveth himself.

"But let every man prove his own work, and then shall he have rejoicing in himself alone, and not in another.

"For every man shall bear his own burden.

"Let him that is taught in the word communicate unto him that teacheth in all good things" (Gal. 6:1-6).

I have said that there is no part of the Bible where we read so much about grace as in Paul's epistles, and there is no place in Paul's epistles where we read so much about grace as in this epistle to the Galatians. The lash of the law never caused anyone to serve God more acceptably. In Galatians 6 we again see grace in action in our relationship with each other as Christians.

The wonderful fact that our sins have been paid for is why God can now proclaim salvation, and that is why the Christian life also must be lived under grace, not law. In Chapter 6 the apostle deals with *Christian fellowship*.

It would be strange if the Apostle Paul, of all men a supreme logician, should contradict himself in verses so very close to each other and dealing with the same subject. In fact, there is *no* contradiction. Verses two and five are not contradictory; they are *complimentary*. Certainly God, the Author behind the human writer, could not contradict Himself. Therefore it will help us understand this seeming contradiction if we remember that in both these verses Paul is writing to believers. Let us put ourselves in the places of the Galatians. Paul is writing to us, not to our neighbor. If you, my dear Christian friend, will just remember that he speaks to you in both cases you will have no problem.

Each of us should say to himself, "I must courageously bear my own burden, and yet sympathetically help to bear the burdens of others also." What a full and blessed fellowship the Church would enjoy today if every believer listened to both of these verses and sought by God's grace to carry them out. If we did this, it would already be proved that they are not contradictory, but complimentary.

It was Dan Crawford, that great missionary in the Belgian Congo, who wrote,

"In this world of froth and bubble,
Two things stand like stone:
Kindness in another's trouble;
Courage in one's own."

That is exactly what the Apostle Paul, by the Spirit, is teaching believers in this passage.

There is an even further and fuller explanation. The words for "burden" in Galatians 6:2 and Galatians 6:5 are not the same in the Greek. In verse two the word which in English would be spelled "baros" gives us our English word "barology," the study of weights and gravity, the downward pull to the earth. We also have the word "barometer," an instrument by which we determine the atmospheric pressure, the weight of the atmosphere. The apostle used this word also in his second letter to the Corinthians.

"For we would not, brethren, have you ignorant of our trouble which came to us in Asia, that we *were pressed* out of measure, above strength, insomuch that we despaired even of life" (II Cor. 1:8).

The word "pressed" is the same derivation translated "burden" in Galatians 6:2.

And again in II Corinthians 5:4 Paul used the same word in reference to just living here when he said:

"We that are in this tabernacle do groan, *being burdened....*"

It is the same word, so the word "burdened," in Galatians 6:2, where he told the believers to bear one another's burdens, has to do with those weights that oppress and bear down upon us. Sometimes they are seemingly too heavy to bear, are they not?

But the other word "burden" in Galatians 6:5 is different entirely. It is the Greek word "phortion" and it means a designated load or cargo. "Every man shall bear his own burden." This word is used for example of the soldier's knapsack. That is his load; heavy or light, he is expected to carry it. It has to do with personal responsibility before God. Each one has his own designated load or burden and must be ready to bear it.

Using this explanation and seeming contradiction in the first part of Galatians 6, let us deal with the passage as a whole. "Brethren," Paul said, "If a man be overtaken in a fault...."

I must stop there. Notice the first word "if." *If* a man be overtaken—first, be very sure that the brother is in fact taken in a fault. Do not get your mental exercise by jumping to conclusions, as many people seem to do.

I Corinthians 13 fits well here, for there we read that love believeth all things for the good. Love is very thoughtful; it is not suspicious.

"Brethren, *if* a man be overtaken...." Has someone come to you with gossip? Has someone said to you, "Oh, did you hear what so-and-so did?" Be very slow to believe it. Be slow even to listen to it. But suppose it is true? Suppose the accusation is proved to be completely true? Then what?

Paul went on "...ye which are spiritual, restore such an one in the spirit of meekness; considering thyself, lest thou also be tempted." Restore him. Do not rake him over the coals. Do not try to make things worse for him. Do not condemn him; that will not help him. Seek by God's grace to restore him to fellowship; that is where something deeper than mere brotherhood comes in. Paul called us "Brethren" in this verse, and elsewhere he had said that we are all members of one Body, all one in Christ.

"So we, being many, are one Body in Christ, and every one members one of another" (Rom. 12:5).

In I Corinthians Chapter 12, he taught that when one member suffers, all the members suffer with him. He used the analogy of the human body. When a part of the body is injured the whole body suffers.

It is no compliment to us when a Christian brother falls into sin. It does not do us any good to keep him down. Paul said that we are the Body of Christ and members in particular. For that reason, in I Corinthians 12:25, he stated that all members "should have the same care one for the other."

Suppose that in my physical body I have a wound. Would it do it any good to agitate it, to cause it to fester, and perhaps make amputation necessary? What do you want to do to your fallen brother? Do you want him to go deeper into sin? Do you want to discourage him and cause him to give up? Do you want it to become necessary for the church to excommunicate, shun, and avoid him? "No," said Paul. "If a man be overtaken in a fault, ye which are spiritual, restore such an one."

It is taken for granted, of course, that the brother in question has actually been overtaken in a fault. There have been those who have lived openly in sin and apostasy and continued so, and have been disgracefully unconcerned. The apostle gave very different instructions for such, even instructing excommunication from the local congregation. And in such cases he said to reprove them before all, that others may learn not to go on in sin.

However, this statement in Galatians 6:1 has to do with cases such as we often find—a real brother in Christ has been tempted and has fallen, overtaken in a fault. God's Word says to restore such an one. Indeed, God put a little test before us here. He said, "...ye *which are spiritual* restore such an one...." This is a true test of spirituality.

"And be ye kind one to another, tenderhearted, forgiving one another, even as God for Christ's sake hath forgiven you" (Eph. 4:32).

There is the test of true spirituality. You claim to be spiritual, but you are not very spiritual if you act holier-than-thou and say in a haughty tone, "How could he do that? I will not associate with him any more." That is pure pride and selfishness. It is very different from true spirituality. The truly spiritual person realizes the pit from which he has been dug. The truly spiritual person realizes that it took the death of Christ to save him, and he is going to be tenderhearted, forgiving, and sympathetic toward his brother, knowing that God has forgiven him for Christ's sake.

The apostle went even farther in this passage. He said, "...restore such an one *in the spirit of meekness*." Do not be condescending when you help another. Do not look down upon your brother who has fallen. Do not gaze down from your dizzy heights of spiritual pride and self-satisfaction; do not look down upon him and tell him what he should have done and how he should live from now on. No, restore him out of love, considering yourself. What if it had been you? It can be you who will some day stand in the same position as your brother does now. It is only by faith that we stand today, and every step we take must be as we lean on the arm of our gracious Savior, or we too may fall.

In Galatians 6:2, Paul brings in the law of Christ: "Bear ye one another's burdens, and so fulfill the law of Christ." Do you recall what the law of Christ was? Jesus said: "A new commandment I give unto you, That ye love one another..." (John 13:34). If we want to practice the words of Christ, there is one law that is perfectly compatible with the dispensation of grace:

"For all the law is fulfilled in one word, even in this; Thou shalt love thy neighbour as thyself" (Gal. 5:14).

This is the rule as far as our contacts with each other are concerned. Do not say, "I would not have denied Christ if I had been Peter." Do not say, "If I had been Jacob, I would not have been so dishonest." Do not say, "If I had been in this brother's place, I would not have fallen into his temptation." You do not know all of the circumstances. You cannot say that you would not have stumbled over the same stone. Let us fulfill the law of Christ then and truly love each other.

Indeed, my Christian friend, there is one reason why God allows testings, why He sometimes gives us burdens that seem greater than we can carry. He tells us, for example, in Hebrews 2:18, that as Christ "hath suffered being tempted, He is able to succour [help] them that are tempted."

The apostle had the same idea in II Corinthians 7:5-6, where he spoke of his own testing.

"For, when we were come into Macedonia, our flesh had no rest, but we were troubled on every side; without were fightings, within were fears.

"Nevertheless God, that comforteth those that are cast down, comforted us by the coming of Titus."

This is why God allows us to be tested, beloved, so that we in turn may be able to help others who are tested, or in distress, or have fallen into temptation.

Paul drew the argument to a conclusion. He hit the nail on the head when he said in Galatians 6:3:

"For if a man think himself to be something, when he is nothing, he deceiveth himself."

Do you think that you would not have sinned like your fallen brother? "Be careful," Paul admonished. "You are only deceiving yourself."

I remember the incident of a young man who came to old William R. Newell one time, and said, very solemnly: "Mr. Newell, I wish you would pray for me that I may be nothing." But the old man snapped back at the young man and said, "You *are* nothing; take it by faith!"

That is exactly the truth Paul was trying to convey in our text. If a man thinks himself to be something when in fact he is nothing, he only deceives himself. "But let every man prove his own work."

Do not condemn your brother. Prove your own work and then you will have rejoicing in yourself, for every man at the final day will "bear his own burden" as he stands before God.

SOWING AND REAPING

"Let him that is taught in the Word communicate unto him that teacheth in all good things.

"Be not deceived; God is not mocked: for whatsoever a man soweth, that shall he also reap.

"For he that soweth to his flesh shall of the flesh reap corruption; but he that soweth to the Spirit shall of the Spirit reap life everlasting.

"And let us not be weary in well doing: for in due season we shall reap, if we faint not.

"As we have therefore opportunity, let us do good unto all men, especially unto them who are of the household of faith" (Gal. 6:6-10).

It is strange that the apostle should have had to remind believers that God is not mocked, but he knew that there would be some believers who would so misunderstand grace that they would consider it a license to do whatever they wished. Tell me, why did you come to Christ in the first place? Did you come to be free *from* sin, or to be free *to* sin? If you came to be free from sin, then you have some understanding of grace, for that is exactly what God wants to do—free you from the *penalty* and the *power*, and some day from the very *presence* of sin. But if you came to Christ to get a license to sin, or if after being saved you have come to look upon grace as a license to sin, you do not understand grace. Galatians 6:7 must come to you with great force: "Be not deceived. God is not mocked." You cannot make a fool out of God.

You cannot live as you please, for "whatsoever a man [believer] soweth, that shall he also reap." Mr. Moody had a great sermon on this passage. He had three main points. The first was that when a farmer sows, he expects to reap. Second, he expects to reap what he sowed. And third, he expects to reap more than he sowed.

That is why the prophet Hosea spoke about "sowing the wind" and "reaping the whirlwind" (Hos. 8:7)! My Christian friend, if you ever entertain the thought that because you are under grace you can do as you please, that you can partake of the worldliness which is displeasing to God, do not be deceived. God is not mocked.

This was even so in the life of the Apostle Paul, God's great example of *grace*. You will recall that just after Paul's conversion, God spoke to a godly man by the name of Ananias, and said to him:

"Arise, and go into the street which is called Straight, and inquire in the house of Judas for one called Saul, of Tarsus: for, behold, he prayeth....

"Then Ananias answered, Lord, I have heard by many of this man, how much evil he hath done to thy saints at Jerusalem:

"And here he hath authority from the chief priests to bind all that call on thy name.

"But the Lord said unto him, Go thy way: for he is a chosen vessel unto Me, to bear my name before the Gentiles, and kings, and the children of Israel:

"For I will show him how great things he must suffer for My name's sake" (Acts 9:11,13-16).

Paul was to become a great sufferer, the persecuted one. From his very first steps into Damascus until the last steps into that jail at Rome, Paul suffered the very persecutions that he had previously caused others to suffer. This has always been true; that balancing process always seems to hold. Thus the apostle spoke especially to believers, for he himself was a believer when he had to bear all that suffering.

Read the long list of things that Paul went through in II Corinthians, Chapters 11 and 12. He had suffered *cold* and *hunger* and *nakedness*; he had been *beaten* and *robbed* and *stoned*; he had suffered *shipwreck* and *imprisonment*, and much more. He knew what it was to suffer as he had caused others to suffer, and he accepted it gladly. Thus he said, "Do not be deceived. God is not mocked." You cannot make a fool out of God, doing only what you want to do, and still think you can bear His name.

"Nevertheless the foundation of God standeth sure, having this seal, The Lord knoweth them that are His. And, let every one that nameth the name of Christ depart from iniquity" (II Tim. 2:19).

"For they that are after the flesh do mind the things of the flesh; but they that are after the Spirit the things of the Spirit" (Rom. 8:5).

In what are you most interested? Are you interested in the things of this life, the things of the flesh, the common existence down here, the few thrills and joys you can get out of life? Paul said to be interested in the things of the Spirit, the Word of God and prayer.

"For to be carnally minded is death; but to be spiritually minded is life and peace" (Rom. 8:6).

Put that away in your mind; let it sink down into your heart; "to be spiritually minded is life and peace."

"For if ye live after the flesh, ye shall die: but if ye through the Spirit do mortify [put to death] the deeds of the body, ye shall live" (Rom. 8:13).

Let me first explain what this does not mean. It has nothing to do with salvation. It does not mean that if a Christian does not live the life he should, he will be lost again and die the second death. The context here in Galatians 6 shows that Paul considered the people to whom he wrote, although they were failing Christians, to be children of God. He called them saints and brethren. No, he did not mean that if you live after the flesh, you will die, in the sense that you will be lost again.

This is what Paul meant: As far as your Christian life, your testimony, and your Christian experience are concerned, you may flourish like a blooming plant that is showing its beauty, or you may wither and die, as far as your *spiritual experience* is concerned. Paul wrote to the believers at Rome, at Corinth, and at Ephesus:

"Awake thou that sleepest, and arise from the dead, and Christ shall give thee light" (Eph. 5:14).

He was not talking to the unsaved; he was speaking to *believers* who were asleep and dead as far as their spiritual experiences were concerned. How many Christians are like that today! They fill our churches. Hundreds of born-again people have come to Christ in tears for forgiveness and have been justified freely by His once-for-all sacrifice. The Devil cannot keep them from eternal life. But he will make them miserable Christians and poor testimonies if he can. This is what the apostle was speaking of when he said that if you are going to sow to your flesh, not thinking of the things of God, you are going to die as far as your Christian experience is concerned.

How blessedly true it is that "to be spiritually minded is life and peace." That is what God wants us to experience and enjoy. We know that the happiest Christians are the ones who set their minds on the things of God. When we are happy as Christians, we are the most powerful and influential in our testimony. We are most at peace and most greatly used when we sow to the Spirit, that is, when we do those things that will naturally bring forth the *fruit* that only the Spirit can produce.

"And let us not be weary in well doing: for in due season we shall reap, if we faint not" (Gal. 6:9).

In due season, God knows the time, we shall reap if we do not faint. Do you remember what Paul wrote in I Corinthians 15:58?

"Therefore, my beloved brethren, be ye steadfast, unmoveable, always abounding in the work of the Lord, forasmuch as ye know that your labour is not in vain in the Lord."

This admonition implies that there is a tendency on the part of believers to want to give up and quit, as far as Christian living and testimony are concerned. It is true that sometimes through discouragement and disappointment, sometimes through testing, sometimes for other reasons, there is a tendency in the believer to say, "Well, I give up." You recall that Jeremiah had something of that temptation and his words might be paraphrased: "Lord, everyone is making fun of me, everyone mocks me daily, I am in derision. I am not going to speak in your name any more; I am not going to mention the message you have given me." But he could not give up. He could not keep quiet. He wrote:

> **"But His Word was in mine heart as a burning fire shut up in my bones, and I was weary with forbearing, and I could not stay" (Jer. 20:9).**

Good for Jeremiah! But I wonder if all of us who are believers have been like him at times. Have we been able to give up and keep quiet? Sad to say, the apostle had to exhort us for our failures and weaknesses and tell us not to be moved but to be *steadfast* no matter what the disappointments. "Always abounding in the work of the Lord, for you know that your labor is not in vain in the Lord" (I Cor. 15:58). Here in Galatians 6, Paul gave us an even greater promise. Not only is our labor not in vain in the Lord, but we may anticipate fruit from our labor if we faint not. Verse 9 contains a very particular and precious promise: "Let us not be weary in well doing; for in due season we shall reap, if we faint not."

Let me ask you, are you sowing to the flesh or sowing to the Spirit? Are you living for yourself or living for God?

God speaks indirectly to unbelievers here as well. Believers shall reap what they sow, and of course, unbelievers will do so also. Whoever you are, you cannot live a carnal, careless life without reaping the consequences.

Believers will appear before the Judgment Seat of Christ. Not only that, a poor testimony is going to be evident in this life. You are going to have a guilty conscience; you are going to find your spiritual power waning, and you will have little influence upon others. You will reap what you sow in this life.

In contrast, you will also reap the fruit of living after the Spirit. Being occupied with the things of God, speaking to others of the things of God, and living a life that pleases God, will bring a harvest of spiritual fruit—if you faint not. It may be hard going at times, but it will be thrilling to fight the good fight of faith.

Do you notice how Paul always put an emphasis on Christian brotherhood, on members of the Body of Christ being one in Christ?

"As we have therefore opportunity, let us do good unto all men, especially unto them who are of the household of faith" (Gal. 6:10).

RELIGIOUS TNT

"Ye see how large a letter I have written unto you with mine own hand.

"As many as desire to make a fair show in the flesh, they constrain you to be circumcised; only lest they should suffer persecution for the cross of Christ.

"For neither they themselves who are circumcised keep the law; but desire to have you circumcised, that they may glory in your flesh" (Gal. 6:11-13).

Pastor J. C. O'Hair used to call the subject of water baptism "religious TNT." He was right, for there appears to be no subject on which our denominational brethren, especially the immersionists among them, are so sensitive.

It is now more than 30 years ago that we published a small item titled: *"Is It Wrong to Baptize?"* dealing with the subject only from a Scriptural standpoint. Nothing ungracious or unkind was said about those who do practice water baptism. We simply sought to show *from the Scriptures* that water baptism does not belong in God's program for today.

This was years ago, yet at this writing we are still receiving angry letters about that brief item. And this has consistently been our experience. There is nothing that so riles many sincere Christians as simple proof from the Scriptures that water baptism, like circumcision and the sacrifices, is not included in *our* Great Commission—this even though the professing Church is so hopelessly divided over the subject that *there is no majority* for any one view.

This last fact should surely indicate to the thoughtful believer that there may be something *basically* wrong with the practice itself. Else why this Babel of confusion? *God* is not the author of confusion. The answer to this question must be *in the Bible*.

The trouble is that while many believers sincerely wish there could be unity in the Church as to the mode and meaning of baptism, they have no thought of giving up the physical rite. They have not come to the place where they are willing to consider that the Church must find its unity in that divine baptism by which we all *have been* baptized into Christ and His Body.

"For by ONE SPIRIT are we ALL BAPTIZED into ONE BODY..." (I Cor. 12:13).

"There is ONE BODY, and ONE SPIRIT...ONE BAPTISM..." (Eph. 4:4,5).

It is not strange that Paul had a spiritual battle on his hands over the subject of circumcision. For 1900 years this rite had been practiced by God's people, and long-established customs are not easily shaken.

Paul had proclaimed the *finished* work of Christ and with it the abolition of physical circumcision. Yet even believers in Christ kept reverting from the substance to the shadows, from the reality to the rituals. They even sought to persuade each other that circumcision was "necessary," though they did not always make clear what they thought it was necessary *for*.

The Judaizers had persuaded some of the Galatian believers that they should submit to circumcision, even though they were already saved. As a result we have Paul's stern letter of rebuke, in which he points out to them how much is involved in adding the rite of circumcision to the finished work of Christ; he said that *logically* this would make Christ's work of none effect (Gal. 5:2) and make them debtors "to do the whole law" (5:3).

Today we have a similar battle on our hands where the rite of water baptism is concerned. Many sincere believers cling to this rite, and it is difficult to make them see how this logically affects the truth of the finished work of Christ. We can show how water baptism, when commanded, was required for the remission of sins (Mark 1:4; 16:16; Acts 2:38; etc.) and that to add it now is to cast reflections on our Lord's *finished* work and to involve us (logically) in legalism to the same extent as circumcision once did. It is often hard to get others to see this because water baptism today, like circumcision in Paul's day, has a 1900-year background of tradition which is difficult to overcome.

We are convinced that Paul, knowing full well that water baptism was associated with our Lord's Messiahship (John 1:31) expected it soon to pass off the scene. Certainly *he* was not sent to baptize (I Cor. 1:17). But in his own lifetime there was already a large-scale return by believers to legalism and ritualism which culminated in the dark ages, and from which the Church is still but slowly recovering.

In Paul's early epistles he put both circumcision and water baptism where they belong in the light of the cross:

PAUL

on

THE CROSS OF CHRIST

VERSUS

CIRCUMCISION

"...If I yet preach circumcision, why do I yet suffer persecution? then is the offence of the cross ceased."

"But God forbid that I should glory, save in the cross of our Lord Jesus Christ, by whom the world is crucified unto me and I unto the world" (Gal. 5:11; 6:14).

WATER BAPTISM

"For Christ sent me not to baptize, but to preach the gospel; not with wisdom of words, lest the cross of Christ should be made of none effect.

"For the preaching of the cross is to them that perish foolishness; but unto us which are saved it is the power of God" (I Cor. 1:17,18).

ONE REASON FOR BOASTING

"But God forbid that I should glory, save in the cross of our Lord Jesus Christ, by whom the world is crucified unto me, and I unto the world.

"For in Christ Jesus neither circumcision availeth any thing, nor uncircumcision, but a new creature.

"And as many as walk according to this rule, peace be on them, and mercy, and upon the Israel of God.

"From henceforth let no man trouble me: for I bear in my body the marks of the Lord Jesus.

"Brethren, the grace of our Lord Jesus Christ be with your spirit. Amen" (Gal. 6:14-18).

The whole letter to the Galatians is filled with strong words, and these words are fully warranted. The Galatians were desperately ill spiritually and needed strong medicine. Only drastic action could possibly help them. Before we consider the last words of this epistle, let us consider the opening words, and briefly look at the epistle as a whole.

In the first verse of Galatians 1, the apostle declared that he was "an apostle, (not of men, neither by man, but by Jesus Christ, and God the Father, who raised Him from the dead)." The rejected Father and the rejected Son had appointed Paul as their apostle to bring in a new dispensation. In Galatians 1:3, Paul proclaimed the great key to his message. This was the core of his gospel: "Grace be to you and peace from God the Father, and from our Lord Jesus Christ." (The Father and the Son a second time.) In the fourth verse Paul said that the Son "gave Himself for our sins, that He might deliver us from this present evil world [age], according to the will of God and of our Father," (The Father and the Son a third time.)

The Galatian people were heathen, pagan idolators, and Paul had come among them, not with religion or human works, but with the message of the finished work of the Lord Jesus Christ. He had come preaching to them the wonderful cross of Christ by which He had paid for the sins of all mankind. The Galatians had been satisfied with Christ. Oh, how glad they were, how thankful for all that the Lord Jesus Christ had done for them!

But it was not long before legalistic Jewish teachers had come from Jerusalem, and they had come to trouble the believers among the Galatians. In Galatians 1:6-7, Paul said that he "marvelled that ye [they] are so soon removed from Him that called you into the grace of Christ unto another gospel."

The twelve apostles and the elders at Jerusalem, gathered at the great Council there, had agreed with Paul's estimate of those men. They had written letters to the believers at Antioch and Syria about the legalizers who had tried to get Gentiles under the law of Moses. The Galatians had listened to the troublemakers, but the irony of it was that the law had never been given to the Gentiles in the first place. The law of Moses was distinctly a covenant between God and His nation Israel and had been given to demonstrate to all the world, through Israel, that all men are guilty and must stand condemned before God, unless God Himself provides some way of salvation.

The legalizers came trying to get the Galatian Gentiles to submit themselves to the law of circumcision for acceptance with God. They were Scriptural; they could point to the Scriptures and show that God had indeed given circumcision as an ordinance of the law. Of course, they could show too that the whole law had been given by God through Moses. But the trouble was that they did not recognize the further revelation given by the glorified Lord in heaven through Paul. They did not recognize the distinctive ministry of the apostle for men today, and of course they did not recognize that the law had not been given to anyone but to the people of Israel.

That is why Paul used such strong language: "...though we, or an angel from heaven, preach any other gospel to you than that which we have preached unto you, let him be accursed." Paul knew that this was strong language, and he repeated it. Many believers and many ministers of the gospel today ought to read those two statements and thoughtfully consider them.

These verses do not mean that if people fail to understand the gospel of the grace of God, and perhaps mix it with law or with human works, they are not saved. Christians can reap curses as well as blessings. The Galatians were believers; they were Christians, but they were suffering under God's curse. They were confused and divided, biting and devouring one another. God's ancient people in Old Testament times often reaped curses instead of blessings when they departed from His Word. In the same way the Church has reaped the curse of Galatians 1:8-9.

The Church today is *confused*. The poor man on the street does not know what to believe. One denomination teaches one thing, and another denomination teaches another. How can he know what is correct? We ought to read these verses and listen to them carefully. What was the gospel that Paul preached? Read it in Acts 20:24—*the gospel of the grace of God.*

From Galatians 1:11 through the second chapter, Paul threw down the certificate of his apostleship, as it were. He showed by detail after detail, evidence upon evidence, that he was indeed the apostle of the glorified Lord to the Gentiles, and to the members of the Body of Christ. He showed the Galatians the folly of their retreat into law. They were actually obeying more laws, taking them from God's requirements of a past age, but they were not obeying the truth. Christ had been plainly set before them as their crucified Savior, but they were charmed with people and things to do on their own. Paul said that they were not obeying the truth, and he repeated it several times in this epistle.

The Apostle Paul recounted how he had been commissioned and given a further revelation, not about the law, but about the grace of God. He asked the Galatians, "How were you saved?" And he answered, "Not by the works of the law but by the hearing of faith."

Do you not see that now that Paul has been raised up to show the grace and glory of the finished work of Christ, these other things must vanish away? They can only be barnacles; they can only be things that will retard us in our spiritual growth. They keep us from rejoicing in the wonders of the finished work of the Lord Jesus Christ, because we have contributed something to our salvation by *doing*, in this case by being baptized in water.

Paul closed his epistle in Galatians 6:14, by saying:

"But God forbid that I should glory [boast], save in the cross of our Lord Jesus Christ, by whom the world is crucified unto me, and I unto the world."

OUR BOAST

"Having made peace through the blood of His cross" (Col. 1:20).

"Having slain the enmity thereby" (Eph. 2:16).

Is this not strange and wonderful! One would suppose that the cross would have *broken* the peace and *made* the enmity between God and man. (Prophetically and nationally speaking it *did*; see in Jeremiah 25:31, Hosea 4:1, 12:2 and Micah 6:2, how God has a controversy with the nations and especially with His own nation—a controversy that will not be settled until they repent.) It was only in God's secret purpose and grace toward a world of individual sinners that the cross was to slay the enmity and seal our peace.

At Pentecost the crucifixion was considered a matter of shame and Peter called upon his nation to repent of the horrible crime. Because Israel would not repent the nation has now been set aside dispensationally (Rom. 9-11).

By contrast, Paul boasted in the cross and proclaimed it as the glorious remedy for man's dreadful malady. Hear him cry:

"For the preaching of the cross is to them that perish foolishness; but unto us which are saved it is the power of God."

"Where is the wise? Where is the scribe? Where is the disputer of this world? Hath not God made foolish the wisdom of this world?"

"For the Jews require a sign, and the Greeks seek after wisdom.

"But WE PREACH CHRIST CRUCIFIED, unto the Jews a stumbling block and unto the Greeks foolishness;

"But unto them which are called, both Jews and Greeks, Christ the power of God, and the wisdom of God" (I Cor. 1:18,20,22-24).

Indeed, this revelation of the cross has eliminated all human works for salvation and with this, all human boasting.

Now salvation is "TO HIM THAT WORKETH NOT, BUT BELIEVETH" (Rom. 4:5). "WHERE IS BOASTING THEN? IT IS EXCLUDED" (Rom. 3:27).

All we can now boast in is the cross! And that is worth boasting in! What perfect righteousness was there manifested, yet what infinite love! What unfathomable wisdom! What unlimited power!

Little wonder the apostle cries, "Let others glory in the flesh,"

"BUT GOD FORBID THAT I SHOULD GLORY, SAVE IN THE CROSS OF OUR LORD JESUS CHRIST, BY WHOM THE WORLD IS CRUCIFIED UNTO ME, AND I UNTO THE WORLD" (Gal. 6:14).

My Christian friend, can we make this our motto? Can we who trust Christ as Lord and Savior make it our motto and say, "God forbid that I should boast, except in the cross of our Lord Jesus Christ?" That is what we ought to boast about. To think that in infinite grace and love the Lord Jesus left the glory of heaven, and died in shame and agony, in order that we might be "justified from all things, from which ye [we] could not be justified by the law of Moses" (Acts 13:38-39). We ought to be boasting in Christ alone, and in His glorious finished work.

No wonder Paul said in Galatians 6:17:

"From henceforth let no man trouble me: for I bear in my body the marks of the Lord Jesus."

I Corinthians 1:17-18:

"For Christ sent me not to baptize, but to preach the gospel: not with wisdom of words, lest the cross of Christ should be made of none effect. For the preaching of the cross is to them that perish foolishness; but unto us which are saved it is the power of God."

As in Paul's day, many today are neutralizing the great work that Christ has done in our behalf, so that the cross is obscure. Paul said to the Galatians that it is not circumcision that counts. He could just as well say, and he did say, as he wrote to the Corinthians that it is not baptism, but Christ that counts.

Little wonder that Paul said in verse 17: "Henceforth let no man trouble me." (Don't bother me any more.) Paul's words could be paraphrased as, "If all I have said fails to persuade, you do not want to be persuaded. No matter what you say, you are retreating from grace and losing the spiritual victory. If you do not want to go on, at least do not hinder me. Get out of the way; there are battles to be fought, victories to be won. Trouble me no more. I am battlescarred. I have been branded for Christ; I bear in my body the marks of the Lord Jesus Christ."

Yet Paul closed his letter to the Galatians very tenderly, and I want to close this commentary with this message to you, "Brethren, the grace of our Lord Jesus Christ be with your spirit. Amen."

Let me say to the saved as well as the unsaved, "Grace be to you, and peace."

There is only one way to find peace, either peace *with* God or the peace *of* God, and that is by grace. The more one grows in grace the more one appreciates and enjoys the finished work of the Lord Jesus Christ, the all-sufficiency of His redemption at Calvary.

IF PAUL WERE ALIVE TODAY, WOULD HE BE A BAPTIST, A PRESBYTERIAN, A METHODIST, A LUTHERAN? WOULD HE BELONG TO ANY DENOMINATION?

Appendix

DID THE TWELVE APOSTLES BECOME MEMBERS OF THE BODY OF CHRIST?

By CORNELIUS R. STAM

For many years we have discussed whether or not the kingdom believers who lived until after the raising up of Paul became members of the Body of Christ, the Church of the heavenly calling. Usually this question has been asked particularly with regard to the twelve apostles, since our Lord specifically promised them that they would occupy twelve thrones with Him in His reign *on earth*.

For more than twenty years the writer has refrained from making an issue of the subject, feeling that it is always easy to cause division over matters which neither affect our basic doctrines nor our practices, but it is not so easy to restore unity once it has been broken.

Therefore, we trust that this treatise will be accepted in the spirit of Christian love in which it is written.

WHAT WE BELIEVE

We believe that when God ushered in the dispensation of grace and began to form the Body of Christ *all* believers were included in it, just as *all* the children of Israel came under the dispensation of law when the law was given at Sinai, even though they had previously lived under another dispensation.

God's dispensations are not dependent upon degrees of human understanding, but upon His own sovereign will.

Nevertheless, the truth of "the mystery" was gradually revealed to and through the Apostle Paul (Acts 26:16; II Cor. 12:1) so that there was a gradual transition from the old *program* to the new. The old program did not immediately disappear, to be replaced by the new, thus:

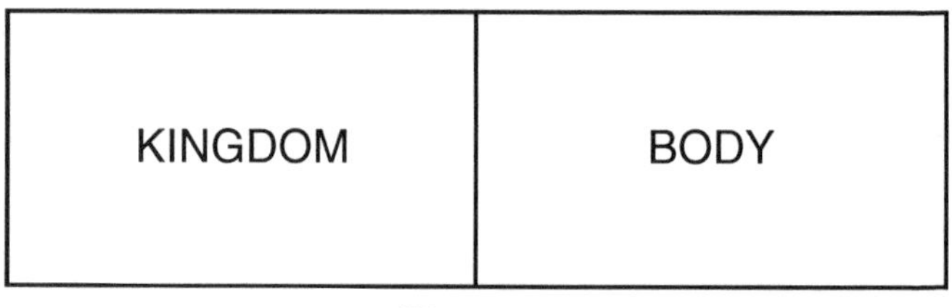

Figure 1

Rather, the kingdom program *gradually* disappeared, as the program for the one Body emerged, thus:

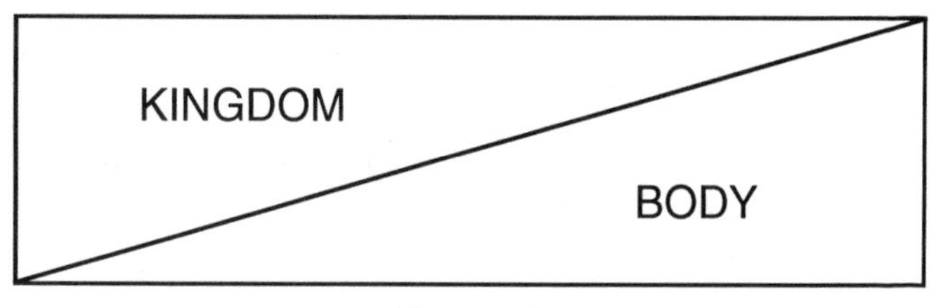

Figure 2

We do not mean to say that there were not those among the Judean believers who tenaciously held on to the old program. There were, in fact, many such believers. There were even some who sought to bring the *Gentile* believers under the old program. But in spite of them, we note in the book of

Acts as well as in the Epistles, a gradual breaking down of the "middle wall of partition"—Jewish believers gradually leaving Judaism behind and coming more and more fully to enjoy their oneness with the Gentile believers in Christ.

This is why we *reject* the argument that the kingdom believers living after the raising up of Paul did *not* become members of the Body of Christ, but that it was God's will for them to continue in their kingdom calling indefinitely, while the members of the Body continued in theirs, the two economies running parallel, thus:

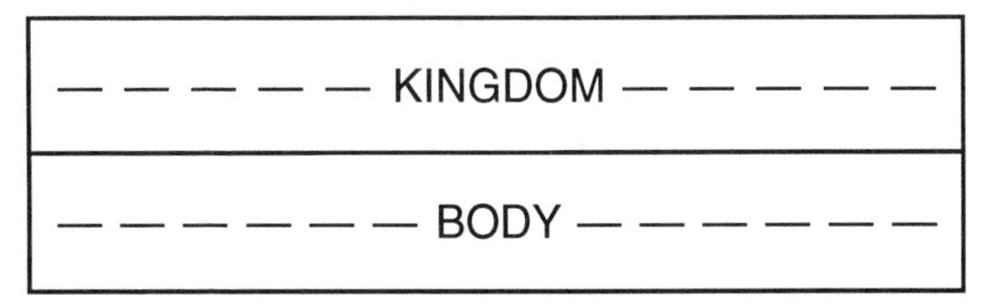

Figure 3

Our object in this article, then, will be to defend by Scripture the position represented by figure 2 against that represented by figure 3, and to show how these kingdom saints, having now become members of the one Body, were brought into an enlarged[1] position and hope.

AN OBJECTION ANSWERED

It is sometimes objected that if the twelve apostles are to occupy twelve thrones in the kingdom on

1. In years gone by the twelve were sometimes spoken of as having been "transferred" into the Body, but this, we believe, is an unfortunate choice of terminology. It gives the impression that they were taken permanently *from* one position and hope and placed into another. We all agree that this is not so; that the twelve, for example, *will* reign with Christ in His kingdom, as He promised they would.

earth, then how can they be members of the Body of Christ, with its position in heaven? This question seems to bear some weight. Many, indeed, accept this argument as conclusive, but the subject is not as simple as that.

Our Lord Himself will reign with the twelve on earth and *He* is the *Head* of the Body. We believe there are many more evidences too that the twelve and the kingdom believers living after the raising up of Paul *did in fact* become members of the Body of Christ.

TOO MANY EXCEPTIONS

It is certain that *some* of the kingdom saints became members of the Body of Christ. Among these were:

Barnabas, the Levite, who sold his land for the common good just after Pentecost (Acts 4:36,37) but later was called by God to become Paul's co-worker (Acts 13:2).

Silas, a leading member of the Jerusalem church (Acts 15:22) who also later became Paul's co-worker (Acts 15:39,40).

John Mark, Barnabas' nephew, who became Paul's helper, and is referred to in Paul's latest epistles as a co-worker (Acts 12:25; 13:5; Col. 4:10; II Tim. 4:11).

Luke, the "beloved physician," who wrote one of the synoptic "gospels," but became Paul's constant companion, even after his imprisonment at Rome (See Acts and II Tim. 4:11).

Apollos, a Jew who knew only "the baptism of John," until shown "the way of God more perfectly" by Aquilla and Priscilla (Acts 18:24-26). Later we find him "watering" what Paul had "planted," as "one" with Paul (I Cor. 3:6-8).

Andronicus and Junia, who were "in Christ" before Paul, but later became his "fellow prisoners" (Rom. 16:7).

In addition to these there are *many* more who are not specifically *named*. These evidently became, and recognized themselves to be, members of the one Body, for they could hardly have been Paul's fellow workers and fellow prisoners had they continued preaching the kingdom message.

It is not enough to say that these mentioned were exceptions. Rather they are examples which prove at the very least that it *is* possible that kingdom saints could become members of the Body of Christ.

What about the Pentecostal believers who travelled, for example, to Rome, and to whom Paul writes, telling them that they are members of the "one Body" (Rom. 12:5)? It is evident that these individuals did not become members of the Body of Christ by merely seeing and accepting the truths concerning the Body. Otherwise it would follow that millions of believers today are *not* members of the Body because they do not understand "Body truth." Evidently the dispensation of the mystery had united all believers into one Body—which truth some gradually came to understand and others never came to understand, even as many believers today do not understand it.

ALL MEN EVERYWHERE

There are other evidences that the kingdom saints of Paul's day became members of the Body of Christ.

In I Corinthians 1:2, Paul addresses his letter to the Corinthian church, "*with all* that in *every place* call upon the name of Jesus Christ our Lord, both theirs [those in every place] and ours [those with Paul]." And he says to "all" these believers "in every place": "For by one Spirit are we *all* baptized into one Body, *whether we be Jews or Gentiles*" (I Cor. 12:13). How can this be made to exclude the Judean believers?

Further, in II Corinthians 5:16, the apostle says: "Wherefore *henceforth know we NO MAN after the flesh.*" Can this sweeping declaration be made to exclude the Judean believers? And does Paul not emphasize the fact that he is including *kingdom* saints when he goes on to say: "Yea, though we have known *Christ* after the flesh, [as had the kingdom believers] yet now, henceforth know we Him [so] no more."?

But our apostle has still more to say about this matter, for continuing in Verse 17 he says: "Therefore if ANY MAN be in Christ, he is a *new creation....*" Does not this phrase "any *man*" include the Judean saints? Were they not men? Were they not "in Christ"? Like Paul's kinsmen of Romans 16:7, they were in Christ before him, and Paul now declares that *all* in Christ are "henceforth" members of the "new creation" (Cf. Eph. 2:14-16; 3:1-6).

Again, in Galatians 3:27,28, the apostle declares that in Christ *"there is neither Jew nor Greek...for ye are all one in Christ Jesus."* Some people make this passage to read that there is neither Jew nor Greek in the *Body* of Christ. This, of course, we all know, but it is not what Paul says in Galatians 3:28. In this passage he says that *in Christ* there is neither Jew nor Greek, and as we have shown from Scripture, these believers were in Christ even before Paul, therefore they were "henceforth" one with the Gentile believers in the joint Body.

THE EPISTLE TO THE HEBREWS

Did not Paul, or certainly some Pauline person, write to the *Hebrews* (not just the Jews of the dispersion) to *leave Judaism* and take their stand with the rejected Christ (Heb. 13:13)? Did he not bid them to go *"without the camp"* and *"within the veil,"* to take their places with Christ at God's right hand (Heb. 6:19,20; 10:19,20)? Did he not bid them *enter into God's rest* and to sit down with Christ in the heavenlies (Heb. 4:9,10)? Did he not call them *"partakers of the heavenly calling"* (Heb. 3:1) and bring them into a *"better hope"* (Heb. 7:19)?

Is it objected that the terminology of Hebrews is different from that of Paul's epistles to the Gentiles? *Of course! He is writing to Hebrews!*

In light of these facts it is difficult to understand how some can say that there is not any scriptural support for the argument that the twelve apostles became members of the Body of Christ.

THE TRANSITION

Some brethren do not even deal with the *transition* so evident in the Acts and the Epistles of *both* Paul and Peter. Some do not even believe there *was* a transition, contending that even Peter's epistles are no advance upon his message at Pentecost. They hold the view illustrated in figure 3, while we believe that there *was* such a transition (see figure 2) and that the gradual breaking down of "the middle wall of partition" affected those on *both sides*. Let us see what the Scriptures say about this.

Paul, himself having been baptized under the kingdom program, had the truths of the mystery revealed to him gradually (Acts 26:16; II Cor. 12:1). In his early epistles he still recognizes water baptism and the Pentecostal signs, but these are "done away" by the time we reach his prison epistles. Similarly, we come more and more fully into the glorious truths of the mystery as we proceed from his earlier to his later epistles. Thus there is a fading out of the old program and gradual unfolding of the new.

Peter, too, began dealing with Israel only (Acts 2), then later was shown by God that he could and should eat with uncircumcised Gentiles (Acts 10).[2] Still later at the Jerusalem Council his testimony induced the Judean saints to recognize the Gentile believers as one with them in Christ, Peter declaring that God had made "no difference between us and them" (Acts 15:9) and that *"through the grace of the Lord Jesus Christ"* the Jewish believers would be saved *"even as they"* (the Gentile believers). In this connection we should also compare Acts 2:38, where, in obedience to the "Great Commission," Peter demands repentance and baptism "for the remission of sins," with his epistles where, later, he proclaims the finished work of Christ for salvation (I Pet. 1:18,19; 2:24; 3:18). Also Acts 3:19-21, where he offers the return of Christ to reign, with II Peter 3:3,4,8,9,15,16,18, where he explains the *delay* in

2. Later he enjoyed more of this fellowship with the Gentiles at Antioch and was rebuked when he let some from James' party frighten him out of it (Gal. 2:11-14).

Christ's return and refers his readers to "our beloved brother Paul," whose epistles speak of "these things."

We must confine this section to these examples for there are so many evidences of transition from the old program to the new, that one finds it difficult to understand how anyone could question that it exists.

ANSWERS TO OBJECTIONS

We now proceed from our own arguments for the affirmative, to deal with those arguments of some for the negative.

1. If the twelve are to reign on earth with Christ, how can they belong to the Body of Christ, with its position in the heavenlies?

The answer to this, the over-all argument, is simply that like Christ they will have a dual position during the kingdom reign. Their reign on twelve thrones with Christ surely does not imply that each one will sit on one seat in Jerusalem for a thousand years! The twelve and those associated with them will have a position in the kingdom, but will not be *confined to earth* as will those who survive the "great tribulation" to enter the kingdom.

This writer believes that we ourselves will reign with Christ, *not on*, but *over* the earth, much as the "principalities and powers in the heavenlies" reign over it now, behind the scenes. Why, then, cannot the twelve reign with Christ, *both* over and on the earth?

Surely the members of the Body will not be separated from their Head for 1,000 years but will reign with Him (Col. 1:13 cf. I Thes. 2:12; II Tim. 2:12; 4:18). Indeed I Thessalonians 4:17 *states* that after our Rapture to heaven we will be *with Christ forever*. Thus our Lord will occupy a *dual* position, with us in the heavenlies and with Israel on earth.

2. Some say that to believe that the twelve apostles have a *dual* calling destroys the foundation of our distinctive message.

The promise to the twelve to reign on earth was not made to them as members of the Body, but as heirs of the kingdom; however, it does not follow from this that they could not have later also been baptized into one Body with the Gentile believers. If it did, this would necessarily also be true with regard to Barnabas and the others we have listed above; it would mean that the Holy Spirit "called" at least one person to help gather members into the Body who was not himself a member of the Body! (Acts 13:2).

Let us not forget that Christ, the Head of that Body to which no earthly promises are made, will nevertheless sit on David's throne in fulfillment of Old Testament promises.

3. Others say that we are confused as to the basic salvation message—all one in Christ as the Head of the new race, as compared with our dispensational position. They say that this basic salvation, through Christ's work is a matter of one's faith and is true of all believers regardless of calling.

We should like to ask who, before Paul, proclaimed the finished work of Christ for salvation. Did Peter preach this at Pentecost? (See Acts 2:38 and cf. Rom. 3:21; Gal. 3:23; I Tim. 2:5-7). And who before Paul presented Christ as the Head of a new race? Did Peter at Pentecost? Did he not rather present Him as the King of Israel? (See Acts 2 and 3). Christ as Head of a new race was revealed through Paul with the ushering in of the dispensation of grace and the mystery (Rom. 5:12-19; cf. Eph. 2:15; 3:1-3). Does this sound as if "basic salvation" was presented for the faith of "*all* believers, regardless of calling"?

4. Some brethren read more into Galatians 2:7-9, than the passage states. Galatians 2:7 does not say that "the gospel of the circumcision" was committed to Peter at that time, nor does Verse 9 indicate that he was *then* sent to the circumcision to proclaim this gospel to them. Rather Verse 7 states that the Jerusalem believers "*saw* that the gospel of the uncircumcision *was* [i.e., *had been*] committed unto [Paul] as the gospel of the circumcision *was* [*had been*] committed unto Peter." Verse 9 then adds that Peter agreed to confine his ministry to "the circumcision," but it does not say what he should preach.

Thus Galatians 2:2-9 does not indicate that the *two* groups were henceforth to continue with their present programs, but rather indicates a recognition by the Judean believers of the further revelation given to Paul. Certainly, if Peter agreed to continue preaching "the gospel of the circumcision," he broke his word, for he does not proclaim this gospel in his Epistles.

We should compare Galatians 2 with Acts 15, where the great Jerusalem Council agreed only that the *Gentiles* should not be subject to circumcision or the law but made no decision as to the

Jews, nor did they even discuss how the new turn of events might affect the Jews.

Then note Acts 15:9 where Peter declares that God had shown him that He had henceforth put "no difference" between Jew and Gentile and goes so far as to acknowledge:

> **"But we believe that THROUGH THE GRACE OF OUR LORD JESUS CHRIST, WE [JEWS] SHALL BE SAVED EVEN AS THEY" (Ver. 11).**

Certainly Peter returned to his people with a greater knowledge of what God was doing. Surely he could hardly have kept still, in his ministry at Jerusalem, about the all-sufficiency of Christ's finished work, or about the grace that had made Jewish and Gentile believers one in Christ.

5. Some also read far more into Acts 21:20 than it says. This passage simply records the statement of James and the Judean elders that many thousands of Jews which believed were "all zealous of the law." This does not at all prove that they *ought to have been* zealous of the law (See Heb. 5:11). Many of the Galatians also were zealous of the law. Does this mean they were not members of the Body of Christ?

Here we must remember what the Scriptures say about James, the legalist, and his influence over the Judean Church. James, "the Lord's brother," was not even one of the twelve and certainly not Christ's appointed *head* over the twelve. Our Lord had clearly appointed *Peter* to this position (Matt. 16:19) but somehow James had gained the leadership, probably because of his physical relationship to the Lord. In Acts 15 we even find him presiding over the Jerusalem council and closing it with the words: *"Wherefore, my sentence is..."* (Lit., *"Wherefore I decide."*)

Providentially the Holy Spirit had used the testimonies of Paul, Barnabas, and Peter to persuade the council to recognize officially the liberty of the believing Gentiles, but this was clearly *not* due to James' influence.[3]

Peter, not James, should have presided over the council and the church at Jerusalem. This is doubtless why, in Galatians 2, Paul so strongly emphasizes Peter's call to the apostleship of the circumcision (Vers. 7,8) and refers to the *present* leadership as "those who *seemed* to be somewhat," adding: *"Whatsoever they were, it maketh no matter to me"* (Ver. 6).

Three times in this passage Paul, by the Spirit, refers to these leaders as those who *seemed* to be somewhat, and this shows how remarkably God overruled in this troubled convention so that even James, the legalist, joined with Cephas and John in giving to Paul and Barnabas "the right hands of fellowship," officially recognizing Paul's message and his ministry among the Gentiles (Ver. 9).

6. It is said that Peter wrote to the circumcision believers, *not* in order to lead them on into further and new truth, but to stir up their memories in the things they had already received by the Old Testament prophets and our Lord after the flesh and their apostles. They say that the message Peter proclaimed at Pentecost was the present truth in

3. The Editor's *Acts, Dispensationally Considered, Vol. IV* contains a whole chapter on the role James played at the Jerusalem church.

which they were established by his epistles. See II Pet. 1:10-12).

Just think: In I Peter 1:18,19; 2:24; 3:18, Peter tells his readers how they were redeemed by *"the precious blood of Christ,"* how Christ Himself *"bore our sins in His own body on the tree"* and how He *"suffered, the Just for the unjust, to bring us to God."* Does this sound like his Pentecostal message, where he referred to the cross only to blame his hearers for it and then, in response to their "What shall we do?" demanded that they "repent and be baptized...for the remission of sins" (Acts 2:37,38)? Surely Peter did not preach the finished work of Christ at Pentecost.

As to II Peter, it is true that here the apostle reminds his readers of their stake in the kingdom and declares that he had not been telling them fables when he made known to them the power and coming of Christ, but he does this to prepare them for his *further declaration* that God, in longsuffering, is now to *delay* Christ's return to judge and reign (II Pet. 3:3,4, 8,9) and *then* he commends them to "our beloved brother Paul," who "in all his epistles," writes of "these things" (II Pet. 3:15,16).

It should be noted here too that Peter states that Paul had already written to them about these things (Ver. 15). If these Jews were to "retain their fleshly standing" and were not to be members of the one Body, what business did Paul have writing them?

In the light of the above it is significant that Peter opens his second epistle with the words: "Grace and peace be *multiplied* unto you *through the knowledge of God, and of our Lord Jesus Christ.*"

It is true that Peter does not deal with "Body truth," *as such*, in his epistles. Here the selective principle in divine inspiration is in operation because God would keep Paul as the distinctive apostle of this great truth. But who can deny that Peter, in his epistles, taught his readers more—and wished that they might know still more, about our glorified Lord than they had known in the Pentecostal era? How, then, can we agree that Peter's epistles contain no new or further truth from that which he had proclaimed at Pentecost?

7. It is objected that although Peter heard something of the heavenly calling of the one Body from Paul, he was not called to it, but he retained his fleshly standing (Gal. 2:9-11).

If this is true, why does Galatians 2 go on to tell how Paul rebuked Peter when he *stopped* eating with the Gentiles at Antioch (Gal. 2:11-14)? If Peter "retained his fleshly standing," he should have been rebuked for *eating* with Gentiles. Had not Peter himself indicated that his fleshly standing no longer counted when he said that God had put *"no difference between us and them, purifying their hearts by faith"* (Acts 15:9)? And is it not true that those who had come "from James" had intimidated Peter, so that in withdrawing from the Gentiles he went back on light which *all* of them had received (Acts 15:9; Gal. 2:2,9-16)? Had he not previously relinquished his fleshly standing to rejoice in his oneness with Gentile believers in Christ?

Again, if Peter only "*heard* something of the heavenly calling," but himself retained his *fleshly* standing, as it is contended, why was he called, in Hebrews 3:1, a "partaker of the *heavenly* calling," along with the other Hebrew believers of his time? Surely this argument breaks down completely here.

8. Some say that to believe that the twelve apostles have a dual calling renders Paul's statement in Ephesians 4:4 ["one hope of your calling"] false.

We have never subscribed to the idea that the "hope" here refers only to the Rapture of the Church, as compared with our Lord's return to earth. We rather connect this passage with Ephesians 1:18, where Paul expresses his desire that believers may know, or understand, "what is the hope of His calling [of us]" i.e., *"the hope which His call to you inspires"* (Weymouth Translation). This "calling" is, of course, the "holy calling" referred to in II Timothy 1:9, with its "all spiritual blessings in heavenly places." It is a *present* matter rather than merely a future one. And this was the "heavenly calling" into which these Jewish believers now came and which, as they came to understand it more fully, would inspire them with "hope" despite the postponement of the kingdom. As to the future aspect of this hope and calling, we must not forget that even today the instructed and spiritual believer longs not only to go and be with Christ at the Rapture, he also longs to reign with Christ.

9. Based on Ephesians 4:4-6, some say that there is only one hope and calling for members of Christ's Body and that to say that the twelve came into a heavenly calling renders Paul's statement in Ephesians 4:4 false.

We agree that "there is only one hope and calling *for members of Christ's Body*," but this is not what Ephesians 4:4 teaches. Read Ephesians 4:4-6 carefully. It does not say that *in the Body* there is one

Spirit, one hope, one Lord, one faith, one baptism, one God and Father (though this would be true). It rather lists the one Body *along with* all the other unities, indicating that *God recognized* but one Body, one hope, one baptism, etc. This means that the Jewish believers then living *were* recognized as one Body with the Gentile believers, that they should now be enjoying the *present* "holy calling" which inspired the Gentile believers with hope. It also means that water baptism was now a thing of the past and that both should rejoice together in the one baptism by which they had been united. Thus it is they, not we, who violate Ephesians 4:4-6, for by leaving the Judean believers of Paul's day *out* of the one Body, to continue with their Pentecostal program, they must also recognize two separate hopes, two callings and two baptisms.

10. Some say that because there is neither Jew nor Gentile, circumcision nor uncircumcision before God in Christ's Body, the twelve circumcision apostles could not be members of the Body of Christ with its ONE spiritual heavenly calling.

If this is so, what about all the Jews among the Gentiles saved under Paul's ministry? Were these not members of "the circumcision"? Yet our objectors agree that *they* became members of the one Body. This is the whole tenor of I Corinthians 12:13.

Further, they have overlooked the fact that according to Paul's own statement, in Christ's Body there is "*neither* circumcision *nor uncircumcision.*" Therefore if the circumcision of the twelve would keep them out of the Body, our *un*circumcision would keep *us* out! The fact is that believers from *both* the circumcision and the uncircumcision have been made one in Christ, where these distinctions disappear.

CONCLUSION

With this we must close, though there is *much* more to say. We rejoice that in the "Grace Movement" we may freely discuss these matters, and we ask only that the above arguments be considered prayerfully in the light of the Word, for any one truth misunderstood can affect our understanding of other truths and bring us into confusion in our study and proclamation of the Word.

Together, thank God, we stand for the distinctive character of the revelation committed to Paul. The question is simply whether or not the Judean "kingdom" believers living after the raising up of Paul became members of the one Body with which his message was concerned. Therefore let us not make this issue a larger one than it is, lest we cause division among those who, above all people, should be united in making known the riches of God's grace.

Daniel

Hosea

Joel

Micah

Zechariah

Matthew

Matthew (Cont'd)

Mark

Luke

John

Acts

Acts (Cont'd)

Acts (Cont'd)

Romans

Romans (Cont'd)

Romans (Cont'd)

I Corinthians

II Corinthians

Galatians

Galatians (Cont'd)

Galatians (Cont'd)

Ephesians

Colossians (Cont'd)

I Thessalonians

II Thessalonians

I Timothy

II Timothy

Titus

Hebrews

James

I Peter

II Peter

Jude

Revelation

Classic Grace Works

The Twofold Purpose of God

By C. R. Stam

We recommend this work for those who are new to the Grace message. Pastor Stam effectively contrasts the two programs of God in relation to Christ's incarnation, death, burial and resurrection.

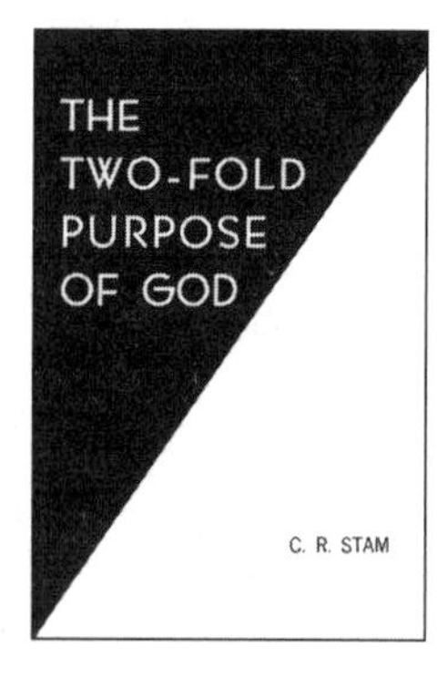

HARDCOVER

85 PAGES

Moses and Paul

By C. R. Stam

Those who struggle with rightly dividing the Word of truth will find this work most helpful. Here Pastor Stam contrasts Law and Grace and the two revelators, Moses and Paul, who were used of God to dispense these truths.

PAPERBACK **78 PAGES**

Orders:

BEREAN BIBLE SOCIETY
PO Box 756
Germantown, WI 53022

www.bereanbiblesociety.org

OTHER BOOKS BY THE SAME AUTHOR

Things That Differ (w/Bible Index)
Rightly Dividing the Word of Truth

The Twofold Purpose of God
Prophecy and Mystery

True Spirituality
The Secret of a Blessed Christian Life

Moses and Paul
The Dispensers of Law and Grace

The Author's Choice
Of His Own Writings

Two Minutes with the Bible
A Daily Bible Study Devotional

Our Great Commission, What Is It?

Divine Election and Human Responsibility

Man, His Nature and Destiny

Baptism and the Bible

The Lord's Supper and the Bible

Holding Fast the Faithful Word

Satan In Derision

The Sermon on the Mount

Acts, Dispensationally Considered (4 Volumes)

Commentary on Romans

Commentary on I Corinthians

Commentary on II Corinthians

Commentary on Colossians

Commentary on the Pastoral Epistles

Commentary on I and II Thessalonians

Hebrews, Who Wrote It and Why?

The Present Peril

No Other Doctrine

Suggestions For Young Pastors

Paul, His Apostleship and Message

Write for a Free Price List of All Our Literature

Berean Bible Society, PO Box 756,
Germantown, WI 53022

www.bereanbiblesociety.org

NOTES